WIRELESS PRIEST

ARCHIBALD SHAW
AND THE
MARITIME WIRELESS TELEGRAPH COMPANY

Matthew Ryan completed post-graduate studies in physics and theology and has a graduate certificate in documentary filmmaking. He is a Churchill Fellow and was the inaugural Science Teacher Fellow at the University of Sydney in the School of Physics. He is a licensed radio amateur and has conducted several contacts between students and astronauts aboard the International Space Station. He has built equipment powerful enough to bounce radio signals off the moon.

Of all the gifts of science that have enriched mankind, none is of more vital importance than Wireless communication.

Communication constitutes the nervous system of a country and is an indispensable factor in commercial and social progress.

Rapid and efficient means for the dissemination of information, both within Australia and between Australia and other countries, are essential for the development of Australia's vast resources and the progress of her people.

Amalgamated Wireless (Australasia)
Advertising copy, 1924

For there is nothing hidden that will not be disclosed, and nothing concealed that will not be known or brought out into the open.

Luke 8:17

WIRELESS PRIEST

ARCHIBALD SHAW AND THE MARITIME WIRELESS TELEGRAPH COMPANY

MATTHEW RYAN

WIRELESS PRIEST
First published in Australia in 2024 by
Studio20
PO Box 243, Coogee NSW 2034

© Matthew Ryan 2024

Every effort has been made to obtain permission with reference to copyright material, both illustrative and quoted. Should there be any omission in this respect the appropriate acknowledgement will be made in any future edition of this book.

National Library of Australia
Catalogue data:

> Ryan, Matthew, 1961-
> Wireless Priest: Archibald Shaw and the Maritime Wireless Telegraph Company
>
> Includes endnotes.
> ISBN 978-1-7636375-0-4
>
> 1. Biography 2. Archibald Shaw (1870-1916). 3. Radio - Wireless. 4. Science.
> 5. History - Australian, Industrial, social, religious. 6. Pacific Missions.
> 7. Government Procurement Practices.

Set in Times New Roman 12/15
Printed in Australia

In memory of my father

Contents

I	Prologue: Between Two Worlds	1
II	Boyhood in Adelong	18
III	From Messenger Boy to Religious Novice	29
IV	Missionary on Yule Island	36
V	Priest and Procurator	47
VI	Difficult Years	55
VII	Inspiration from an Island Massacre	70
VIII	Fr Shaw's Road	81
IX	The First Workshop	94
X	Company Business	106
XI	An Extraordinary Year	120
XII	Adventure on King Island	138
XIII	Prosperous Years	150
XIV	Hubert Linckens Comes to Town	171
XV	Crossroads: Meeting Evie	184
XVI	Missing Money & Mysterious Death	202
XVII	Blackmail, Fraud and a Royal Commission	222
XVIII	Settling Matters	238
IXX	Epilogue	249
	Author's Note	261
	Notes & References	265
	Index	295

Pictures

Archibald's parents   20

Charles Shaw   21

Archie Shaw   22

Shaw children   24

Louis-André Navarre   40

Archibald on Thursday Island   44

St Cecilia, painting   45

Jesus in the Temple, painting   46

Archibald the priest   52

Road building in New Britain   78

Gayundah wreck and plaque   82

Steam tractors, Bulga Saw Mill Co.   89-90

Fernand Arnoult & timber cutters   91

Peter Tréand painting   96

Joseph Slattery postage stamp   97

Edward Hope Kirkby   100

Kirkby's workshop   104

Location of Maritime Wireless   108

Walter Hannam, Cape Denison   111

Wireless Works antenna tower   114

Archibald, Guis, Kirkby & staff   124

Staniforth Smith's New Guinea Map   125

The steamship, *Mataram*   126

Antenna assembly, Thursday Island   128

Thursday Island antenna masts   129

Archibald's car   137

King Island Wireless Station   140

King Island mast assembly   141

Maritime Wireless Heads of department   149

Archibald Shaw   152

Positions vacant   158-159

Wireless Works 1913 photographs   166-170

Hubert Linckens   172

Evie Providence Hoad   182

Fernand Arnoult   198

The Melbourne Coffee Palace   204

London Bank, Melbourne   205

Cheque butt of missing money   206

Blanche Monday   214

Navy Wireless Works picnic, 1917   221

Melbourne Law Courts   228

AWA building & tower, Sydney   237

Archibald's headstone   248

Charles William Fraser Shaw   254

Wackett Widgeon flying boat   258

I

Prologue: Between Two Worlds

St Paul Mission near Baining, New Britain
German Protectorate of New Guinea
August 13, 1904

In the early morning, long before dawn, a feint crescent moon hung in the sky. It was occasionally obscured by clouds that were always present in the humid mountain country away from the coast. Tomari, a Baining tribesman, could not sleep. He lay awake on a bunk in the hut which had been his home on the St. Paul mission for the past fourteen years. The moon shone through a glassless window-opening and he heard the nighttime sounds of the nearby sleeping jungle. Adrenaline coursed through his veins as he thought through his plans for the day. He was convinced nothing had been overlooked; after all he had been preparing this assault for many weeks. Tomari was head-native on the mission which was one of the largest in New Britain. It offered a refuge for the Baining people who were often taken advantage of by the more powerful Tolai tribes living on the coast.

The St. Paul mission had been kind to Tomari and offered him sanctuary. In fact, being the head-native made him one of the most trusted laymen on the mission, but recent events brought him anguish and distress. A week ago, his attempt at starting a revolution against German imperialism and the accompanying European white missionaries was postponed because a neighbouring plantation manager, from the *New Guinea Company,* had just visited St. Paul

Mission with a large well-armed bodyguard. Today he would make another attempt at insurgency, or at least take some personal retribution by targeting the missionaries and their native supporters. This time he was determined to succeed.

In the mind of Tomari, the missionaries who ran St. Paul confusingly represented all that the European occupiers in the country stood for and they were easy targets because, unlike the plantation owners, the businessmen and the German administrator's police force, they were unarmed and somewhat dismissive of the increasing hostility that was developing on the peninsula between indigenous and colonialists. There was also another more personal reason for Tomari's anger. He wanted to divorce his current wife and take another woman who was already married as his new partner. This conflicted with the Catholic model of marriage taught by the missioners. Some weeks ago the mission leader, a German Catholic priest called Fr Matthäus Rascher, dispensed an embarrassing and humiliating punishment to both Tomari and his intended wife: a very painful 'lesson' about the consequences of flouting Catholic morality. With the passage of time Tomari's anger had not subsided and he was determined to seek violent revenge. But he was waiting for the right time and, in the interim, he had recruited a large force of supporters through a deception:

> *He would often go to outlying villages and buy pigs, saying that they were for the use of the mission, telling the villagers that Fr Rascher would eventually pay for them. He would take the pigs to his friends and they would feast. After many pigs had been secured this way, he told the natives to go to Fr Rascher for their pay. Naturally the priest was surprised, as he had never seen one of the pigs; he told the natives this, and refused to pay for what he had not received.[1]*

The natives then turned on Tomari and accused him of trickery but he remained indignant, telling them that Rascher had lied and that the missionaries themselves had eaten all the pigs. He said,

> *'That is what your missionary does for you. He is no true missionary, and we will kill him.' Exasperated at the idea that the missionaries had cheated them, they agreed, and the*

massacre was arranged to take place...[2]

Now with sufficient accomplices and having an intimate familiarity with blood-feuds, he instructed them to act out their vengeance on the allocated targets once the signal was given; the targets being specific priests, brothers and sisters of the mission and any natives who supported them.

There had been disquiet and widespread talk of murderous revenge in the district for some time. This was ignored by Rascher who had even refused an offer from the New Britain German Governor, Albert Hahl, for a police detachment to be temporarily stationed at the mission until things quietened down.

Immediately before dawn Tomari met secretly with his co-conspirators and confirmed they were armed and ready with their tomahawks and clubs. One of the accomplices quietly made his way to a mission outstation a few kilometres to the west that was manned by a lone Trappist monk. Armed with an axe, the conspirator listened intently for the signal to attack.

Before the sun crept over the horizon, clouds began to lift and rise toward the peaks of the surrounding mountains. The sleeping mission came to life. The missionaries, made up of European priests, brothers and sisters from the *Missionaries of the Sacred Heart* (MSC)[3] order and the native Baining families who lived at St. Paul, started to assemble in the little timber church for morning mass. Tomari thought the church was the ideal place to exact his revenge because everyone would be together and contained within the building.

> *The priest turned toward his congregation saying the words: 'Dominus vobiscum,' and his eye fell by accident on Tomari, who hurried from the church thinking he had been discovered.*[4]

Tomari quickly ran outside thinking that his plot had been uncovered by Rascher but he soon regained confidence and returned when it became obvious this was not the case. After Mass the missionaries ate breakfast and began their chores for the day. Smoke rose from huts scattered across the fields as fires were started to boil water and cook breakfast. It appeared to be an otherwise normal

Saturday. Despite his recent conflict with Rascher, Tomari, one of the longest serving native residents on the mission, continued to act as mission warden, a position of significant trust and responsibility. One of his tasks was to shoot animals for food using Rascher's shotgun.

Around mid-morning, he went to the priest's hut and asked Rascher if he could borrow his gun and ammunition on the pretext of shooting wood-pigeons for the mission kitchen. The unusual gun had three barrels; two for shot and one for ball-cartridges. The unsuspecting Rascher gave the weapon to Tomari and then, feeling sick from the effects of chronic tropical disease, went to lay down on his bunk in the priests' house.

A little while later, Tomari, stealthily returned to the house casually carrying the loaded and cocked shotgun. He walked silently up the timber stairs and snuck around the verandah where he peered through Rascher's bedroom window. The priest, in some pain from his illness, lay with his eyes shut. Raising the gun to his shoulder and taking aim at the priest's chest through the window, Tomari squeezed the trigger and one barrel of lead shot was discharged into the body of Matthäus Rascher. That was the signal for Tomari's co-conspirators to begin the massacre.

Rascher did not immediately die. Covered in blood, he had the strength to get up and run from the room to another part of the house where he was found by a shocked Sister Anna who was cleaning with some native helpers as was her usual Saturday morning duty. Tomari had by now entered the house and fired a second shot into Rascher which finished him off. Sister Anna, born Katherina Utsch, locked herself in the adjacent dining room and was herself shot through the head after Tomari smashed open the door. Joseph Bley, a brother doing some carpentry under the house, heard the commotion and came up to investigate. Seeing the bloodshed and Tomari holding the gun, he immediately made for the bush but was cut down with a tomahawk by another native before moving only a few yards. Bley was finished off with a shot through the head from Tomari.

Tomari's accomplices swung into action with their tomahawks and clubs. Another brother, also a carpenter, Edward Plaschart, had his skull split by a tomahawk. When his body was found he still held a pencil and foot-rule in his hand. Brother Johann Schellekens was cementing the stairs leading into the newly built church which was to be officially opened in a few days. He was similarly axed to death. Four other sisters on St Paul's mission were killed in gruesome fashion with axes and clubs: Elizabeth Rath (Sister Agatha), Katherina Holler (Sister Agnes) and Wilhelmina Balka (Sister Angela).

The conspirator, who earlier that morning made his way to the outstation a few kilometres to the west, sprung into action on hearing the distant gun fire. He decapitated Henri Rutten, a Trappist priest, who became the tenth European victim. The mission stations were then ransacked and the bodies of the victims were further mutilated after death, particularly that of Matthäus Rascher, who was unrecognisable.

An unrecorded number of natives who had previously shown support for the mission were also killed in the mêlée.

Two boys, Tande and Toherman, witnessed the catastrophe and fled the slaying. They carried news of the disaster to the coast. Following the river, they raced north along a well-worn jungle track and informed the mission staff at Vunamarita who got word by boat to the German authorities at Herbertshoe further around the peninsula. Had the boys been caught by Tomari's insurgents they would have certainly been killed.

Some hours after the St. Paul massacre, a second attack on Saturday afternoon was mounted by Tomari's men to murder the manager of the *German New Guinea Company* who was operating a plantation at nearby Massava. Two further attacks were repulsed by force on the Vunamarita mission itself.

Tomari had control of the St Paul mission for three days until a party of over fifty armed men from the coastal plantation entered St. Paul the following Tuesday to discover the bodies of the slain still laying where they had fallen. Eight of the missionaries were buried together that same day in an extraordinary funeral service. Armed police faced the jungle and each white man present held a loaded gun. The officiating priest, Fr Kleinditschen, presided over the funerals with a rifle at his feet. The next morning at around 4 am another attack was mounted on the mission by hundreds of natives who were repulsed by gunfire. At 7.30 am Matthäus Rascher was given a separate funeral service and buried within the church itself. During his service a now reinforced army of natives[5] attacked the mission and were yet again repulsed by force. The Trappist monk, Rutten, was buried at his mission outstation.

A state of war was announced shortly after by the German authorities in New Britain and at the same time martial law was declared in expectation of a more widespread native uprising that might affect the entire colony if left unchecked.

Reprisals followed swiftly. The main suspects were rounded up, tried and summarily executed by firing squad. Tomari was decapitated after he was killed and his head mounted on a post as a warning to other colluders. Some natives implicated in the massacre then turned on their own and returned to the police, presenting them with the heads of their co-conspirators. Several punitive expeditions were mounted by the German authorities resulting in an imprecise number of further executions, certainly in the hundreds.

This was a dark period in the history of New Britain. Within a few months after the situation calmed sufficiently, both the German authorities and the Missionaries themselves were keen to restart the mission with renewed vigour and see their work continue.

News of the massacre filtered slowly down to Australia via the steamers that travelled to and from the islands every few weeks. Initially the events were recounted by Hubert Linckens who was the German priest responsible for the Catholic missionary presence in the area. He was the Provincial of the Northern (European) Province of Missionaries of the Sacred Heart and by chance happened to be visiting the mission sawmills near the Torio River on the Gazelle Peninsula at this time, about a day's journey from Vunamarita by boat. Linckens saw first-hand the aftermath of the massacre and, with the missions being his responsibility, conducted his own investigation into what had occurred.

Australia's unique geographic and geopolitical position concerning New Guinea meant that European missionaries travelled through Sydney on their way to and from the missions. Sydney also served as a convenient supply base for materials needed by the MSC missions which could not be acquired locally. These included medicines, books, food, clothing, tools and building supplies. The New Guinea missions were a fairly large operation,

> *The Order of the Sacred Heart... has twenty-six head stations and thirty branch stations in the various islands, and the staff totals eighty-four workers. Of these are thirty priests, thirty-six brothers, and eighteen sisters. They have in all 12,000 native converts...*[6]

In fact, the missions relied so heavily on material supplied from Australia that it was the responsibility of a Sydney-based missionary priest to acquire, package and send-up goods in a timely and cost-efficient way. The person doing the job at this time was the newly ordained Archibald Shaw.

Archibald's job necessitated personal visits to the mission territories as well. On a visit to New Britain only months before the massacre he had met each of the slain missionaries, and like all the missionaries and indeed the general public in Australia and Europe, the horrible events left an indelible impression on him. He returned to the New Britain mission, in his role as mission supplier or *procurator,* in the months following the massacre. On this visit he accompanied ten replacement missionaries who had been sent out from Europe, via Sydney, to re-establish the mission.

◆ ◆ ◆

The tragic story of the Baining massacre, as it came to be known, has been retold here from a variety of contemporary press accounts.[7] Today, the missionary victims are remembered annually by the brothers, priests and sisters of the Missionaries of the Sacred Heart and the Cistercian Orders, (or Trappists), who were profoundly affected by the untimely deaths of their own. However, the events of 1904 are not well known today outside these congregations. Similarly, the hundreds of native victims killed in Tomari's rebellion and in the reprisal attacks by the Europeans were unrecorded and have been forgotten.

With a background as a postal telegraphist and having familiarity with developments in the fledgling field of wireless prior to the 1904 massacre, Archibald Shaw, the young MSC procurator-priest, began to develop an interest in the new science and foresaw its application within the foreign missions. He entertained the possibility that one day wireless might allow remote missionaries to stay in contact with larger towns for a whole variety of purposes but, essentially, to ensure their safety and security and to prevent an incident on the scale of the Baining massacre from ever happening again.

By his own account Archibald acknowledged that this massacre was a pivotal event that changed the course of his life. He told a newspaper nearly a decade later that this was the reason which lead him to pursue the study of wireless.[8]

There were other reasons too that wireless would be an indispensable tool for mission work. Communicating back-and-forth with distant missions was traditionally done by mail with a two or three week delay. A return letter might be received a month later. It was a long-winded and often frustrating process, fraught with misunderstanding, particularly as the European missionaries were not native English speakers. The missionaries ordered their building material, medicines and food by mail from the mission supply house in Sydney called the *procure*. Orders were placed in either French, German or poor English and their lack of consistency was at times a source of great frustration for Archibald, who as procurator had to interpret them. There was a similar frustration for the missionaries too if incorrect goods arrived months later. The implementation of instant communication between missions and the procure would bring a much needed efficiency to the ordering process.

Aside from the technical challenges of implementing wireless there was always a lack of funds available to sustain the missions and Archibald was continually looking at ways to supplement the mission budget from other income sources. He had a fledgling idea that if wireless sets could be made for the missions, he might be able to supply wireless to other markets as well. The profits from such a venture could then be used to help fund the missions.

Following the re-establishment of the St. Paul mission during the latter part of 1904, Archibald's obsession with wireless lead him on an extraordinary and consequential journey.

New Guinea, New Britain and other areas in the Pacific where colonialists and indigenous interacted, were unstable and frequently dangerous places. The indigenous inhabitants and colonial settlers had for centuries been on a slow collision course since European explorers first sailed to the area. In the early 1900s many Aboriginal tribes in Central Australia had yet to see white men and, similarly, indigenous groups in Central Africa, South America and the inland parts of New Guinea remained insulated from Western thinking and scientific understanding. When native groups, who held tightly to their ancestral ways, eventually did come into contact with white-people they saw technologies that were *indistinguishable from magic*[9] and found the challenges of adapting to strange Western ways, often by force, disconcerting and threatening.

The Baining massacre occurred on the Gazelle Peninsula which is located on the northern tip of New Britain, an island off the New Guinea mainland. It was just one flashpoint where two culturally opposed worlds collided. The sea-borne traders who often made undocumented first-contacts were frequently uneducated and even outcast from their own society. They carried firearms into this frontier-land for their own protection and inevitably violence was a predictable outcome whenever an uneasy situation escalated. In New Britain this happened too when European expeditions attempted to penetrate through the jungle to the inland.

♦   ♦   ♦

In the year that Thomas Edison patented the phonograph, half a world away in the United States, cannibal tribes in New Britain were feasting on missionary teachers,

> *In April 1878, four Fijian teachers… recently installed inland from Ratavul in Blanche Bay (New Britain), were murdered and eaten, because the local 'big man', Talili, feared he*

would lose his monopoly over the supply of European trade goods to the interior.[10]

A year after this 1878 massacre, Joseph Swan and Thomas Alva Edison developed a working electric light bulb and later, when the Baining massacre of 1904 was taking place in New Britain, Englishman John Ambrose Fleming invented the first electrical vacuum tube, or valve, which was based directly on the Edison bulb of 1879. The *thermionic valve* (or *Fleming oscillation valve*) was later used as a 'detector' in early wireless telegraphy, or as a 'rectifier' for converting alternating current into direct current. Despite only being an incremental development, it took some twenty-five years for the electric valve to be developed from the first practical light bulb. Several decades later this invention was to revolutionise wireless communication and came to replace earlier electro-mechanical components which wireless was then based. Valves are some of the earliest components of modern electronics. But we are getting ahead of the story.

Industrial science had entered a golden age in the West; something which Archibald Shaw was not unfamiliar with. Simultaneously, in other parts of the world, civilisation was painfully and sometimes violently coming out of the stone age.

Wireless Science: On the Shoulders of Giants

An Incomplete History

What made Western science and industrial development so successful was that its progress relied on improvements to inventions made by people who had come before. For example, Edison did not invent the light bulb in isolation. Somewhat forgotten are the twenty-two pioneers of electric lamp research before him. Industrial science is full forgotten heroes. Many developers registered patents to protect their discoveries. Edison's system was recognised as superior because it worked reliably and was commercially viable despite its similarity to the patents of others.

PROLOGUE: BETWEEN TWO WORLDS

Joseph Swan used carbonised paper filaments for his bulbs as early as 1860 but needed a better vacuum and didn't have a reliable power supply. Because of this his lamp was inefficient and the filament short-lived but it operated on a principle identical to Edison's bulb. Contributions from people like Sir Humphry Davy, as far back as 1802, James Linsday, Alexander Lodygin, Heinrich Göbel are now largely forgotten.

An essential precursor to the functioning light bulb was a pump that could create a decent vacuum. This device remains one of the most important stand-alone inventions of the modern era. Its significance cannot be underestimated. Had it been developed two centuries earlier, a trip to the moon may have been possible in 1769 instead of 1969.

The first vacuum pump was invented by Otto von Guerick around 1654 and improved over subsequent centuries. Without a vacuum the hot filament quickly oxidised and broke. His invention was based on earlier work done by Evangelista Torricelli, Gaspara Berti and Galileo Galilei which was based, in turn, on the siphons and suction pumps of an Arabic inventor, Al-Jazari, from the thirteenth century. Pumps of a similar type had been used by ancient Romans to move water but by the mid 1870s they came into their own as efficient and practical machines to move air. By 1904 a mercury vacuum pump was developed which could easily produce a reliably hard vacuum.

People like Crookes, Geissler, and a host of others, began using these pumps to suck air out of glass tubes which had embedded electrodes through their walls. From about 1869 they tinkered with the evacuated tubes and connected high voltage electricity to the electrodes to produce beautiful light displays or discharges in the tubes. From these discoveries Wilhelm Röntgen, in 1885, *accidentally* stumbled upon x-rays and, two years after that, using similar technology, John Joseph Thomson discovered the existence of the electron at Cambridge University.

Since Fleming's discovery, fragile and expensive electric valves, encapsulated in glass bulbs, were used endemically for the next sixty or seventy years until their function was taken over by modern solid state devices like silicon transistors and diodes. Today these cheap and durable components are ubiquitous in almost every device powered by electricity.

There was another critical invention which made progress in wireless science possible and changed the world in ways no one could ever foresee. It is a favourite of science enthusiasts young and old. It is the machine used produce high voltage electricity, essential to run the early wireless transmitters. As a young boy I built one myself using an old car ignition coil – just as children would have done a hundred years ago. The device is known by many names: induction coil, Righi coil, Ruhmkorff coil or just simply, the transformer.

It provided a supply of high voltage and was used for decades to power Crookes' tubes and x-ray tubes; it was used for arc lighting, for quack medical therapies, and it provided the spark used to ignite petrol in the newly developed internal combustion engine. It also created the spark for the very earliest wireless transmission systems in what were known as *spark-gap* transmitters. The earliest wireless transmissions could not send voice or music, only coded messages using the dots and dashes of Morse code. The induction coil was the *principal* component of early wireless transmitters. They had a completely electro-mechanical design and were used for about twenty years before being superseded by the real electronics of electric valves. It was this spark-gap technology that Archibald was to work with, develop and later manufacture in Australia's first wireless factory.

There were many contributors to the theoretical development of the induction coil; people like Michael Faraday, Joseph Henry and William Sturgeon, but it was a Catholic priest working out of *St Patrick's College*, an enormous seminary school in Maynooth near Dublin, which is now part of the *National University of Ireland*, who developed the first practical machine and is credited with its discovery. His name was Nicholas Callan.

The Maynooth seminary is best known for educating large numbers of Irish priests who were sent around the world, including Australia, to fill the lack of local religious recruits and to serve large parishes where priests were few. Nicholas Callan was the inaugural Professor of Natural Philosophy at Maynooth and one seminarian who studied under him ended up in Australia. He became a Vincentian priest. His name was Joseph Slattery.

PROLOGUE: BETWEEN TWO WORLDS

Slattery arrived in Sydney with seven other Vincentians in 1888 and by chance, travelled on the same boat as Patrick Moran, then the Archbishop of Sydney, who was returning from a trip to Rome. Later, Moran ended up being a supporter of Archibald's endeavours in wireless.

A week after arriving in Sydney, Slattery and the other Vincentian priests travelled to Bathurst and took over the administration of St. Stanislaus' College, a boarding school for boys in the Central West district of New South Wales which still operates today. There he taught natural science, later to be called physics, until his departure from the college and from teaching altogether, in 1911.[11]

A modest man with a stern disposition, Slattery also experimented with x-rays. He is credited with taking the first diagnostic x-ray in 1896 less than a year after Röntgen's discovery which was used by a Bathurst doctor to locate and remove lead pellets from a boy's hand, the result of a shot-gun accident, which would otherwise have been amputated. Subsequently, Slattery was called upon to provide x-ray services from his laboratory in a small room at the school, making it the first radiography clinic in Australia. When the x-rays were taken, a *cold-cathode tube* was used and the patient had to hold very still for upwards of 20 minutes; all the while being exposed to the rays. The equipment was powered by messy liquid cells and the exposed glass negative was developed using the same chemicals and techniques that ordinary photographic negatives were processed with.

The original cold cathode x-ray tube used by Slattery was improved in 1913 when William Coolidge put the filament of an electric light bulb inside a traditional x-ray tube. These *Coolidge tubes*, using a hot cathode, made more free electrons available for acceleration under high voltage and hence a stronger x-ray beam. With the new tube the strength of x-rays was more easily controlled and the exposure time drastically reduced making for clearer results, with more comfort and safety for the patient. No one knew of the dangers of extended x-ray exposure at this time.

Slattery experimented with spark-gap wireless with the same induction coil he used for generating x-rays. In 1904, while holding down a full-time teaching position, he obtained an Australian distance record for land-based wireless transmissions. This occurred between his school which was located on a rise in West Bathurst and the nearby village of Kelso. Unusually, later in life, and in contrast to Archibald, he held little regard for his own scientific accomplishments in either x-ray or wireless, seeing them as unimportant and inconsequential to the work he did as a priest. However, Slattery's experiments in wireless were a major influence on Archibald when their paths eventually crossed.

Around the same time, another character in this story, Edward Kirkby, a jeweller-watchmaker by trade and later an instrument-maker and inventor, was giving public displays of x-rays and wireless in Williamstown, Victoria. Soon Archibald was to cross paths with Kirkby as well when he moved to Sydney and they became friends.

Four years after the birth of Archibald, an intuitive Italian, Guglielmo Marconi, was born. Unable to pass the entrance exam for the Italian Naval Academy and having failed the exam to enter Bologna University,[12] he was, not long afterward, able to put himself up against the expertise of scientists and engineers two and three times his age. To the surprise of several established scientists, Marconi lodged the first patent for wireless communication using the newly discovered Hertzian Waves. A few years later he was jointly awarded the Nobel Prize for Physics in 1909, with Karl Braun, in recognition of his contribution to the development of wireless telegraphy.[13]

During his acceptance speech Marconi freely admitted that there were aspects of his invention that could not be satisfactorily explained.[14] He repeated this decades later at the inauguration of Vatican Radio which he installed in 1931. When Pope Pius XI asked him how wireless worked he said,

> *You should actually be better placed to answer that question. You are closer to God. I don't know the answer.*

The penultimate industrialists of the time were Americans like Andrew Cornelius Vanderbilt, Henry Ford and John D. Rockefeller: sometimes referred to as the *robber barons* because their business practices favoured monopolistic behaviour. In 1876, Thomas Edison, known as the *Wizard of Menlo Park*, established a large laboratory in

New Jersey. He differed from the Barons in that he saw invention and technological development as a means to help regular Americans rather than being a cause for driving them into poverty through extortion and rampant capitalism.

Edison had one foot in the camp of industry and was often backed by the barons' money; the other was in research and development. Whilst his most famous inventions were the commercial electric light bulb, the phonograph and the motion-picture camera, he actually registered over one-thousand patents in the course of his working life. He was inspired by a host of diverse interests from iron-ore refining, to children's toys, mass housing, rechargeable batteries, electric vehicles and rubber production. The number of patents registered by the career-inventor was seen as a reliable measure of their success and Edison had plenty.

Like Marconi, Edison lacked a formal education and did not progress beyond the first grade at school. He was largely home-schooled by his mother and later succeeded in his endeavours because of his curiosity driven *self-education.* He hired the best scientists and engineers to develop his ideas and was unceasing in his experimental perseverance. He lived a life of invention by his own maxim:

> *Our greatest weakness lies in giving up. The most certain way to succeed is always to try just one more time.*

One of the most significant inventions to come out of the 1800s was the telegraph; a device where coded messages, comprised of dots and dashes, could be sent instantly between distant cities and towns along metal wires strung between wooden poles. Morse code was named for its developer, Samuel Morse. The telegraph continued to be used in various forms until the late twentieth century. Edison was taught the code at the age of fifteen by a station-master as a favour for saving his two-year-old son from being struck by an oncoming freight train.

Edison taught his future wife Morse code so they could communicate privately at family gatherings and he even proposed marriage to her in code. She responded in Morse by tapping out *yes*. The couple went as far to nickname one of their children *Dot* and another *Dash*. Later entire telegraphy systems were adapted for wireless using Morse's code or variations of it.

Archibald Shaw knew the code too. Even though he was born in a remote bush-town, the fast-paced developing world with its new science and interesting machines was a familiar presence. Archibald wanted to be part of it. He learnt Morse code and became familiar with the telegraph technology of the time during his training as a postal-telegraphist.

In some regard, the future activities of Archibald Shaw's *Wireless Works*, the factory built behind the mission procure building in the Sydney suburb of Randwick, were to mirror the Edison approach albeit on a smaller scale: diversity of interest, collegial development and an onsite manufacturing capability. The United States had a market big enough to sustain large well-funded industrial research and development laboratories and many Australian inventors and industrialists, like Archibald, were drawn to America for this reason. Some well-intentioned Australian manufacturing enterprises were not able to survive because the local market was too small or they were squeezed out by larger competitors.

The nineteenth century saw great progress in pure science and practical applications of newly-found scientific principles took-off in the sheer number and variety of electro-mechanical machines and contraptions devised during this period. You did not need to be an inspired genius to succeed as an inventor – you needed a creative mind, some intuition, curiosity, experimental persistence, and the courage to think up and try something that no one had done before – without being put off by inevitable failures along the way - just like Edison.

Archibald Shaw had all these characteristics but his life was complicated by its own set of circumstances and it became increasingly complicated as time went on. He came under constant pressure from multiple fronts. As the years rolled on the pressure on him increased.

He was lucky enough to have a modicum of education. The final decades of the nineteenth century was an amazing time to be a curious student, an experimenter or a tinkerer. The era was a true golden-age of discovery and fostered much experiment and many thoughtful scientists and ambitious industrialists. It was not without a good deal of quackery and a few cranks either.

What made Archibald unique was not that he was a priest engaged in science. There were a handful of priest-scientists around and over the centuries there had always been a tradition of priests embracing science. His distinctiveness was that he became a priest-industrialist. This was a rarity indeed. There was something dissonant about this combination. It conflicted with the generally accepted role of priest as pastoral care provider, particularly within Catholic orders like the Missionaries of the Sacred Heart where a vow of poverty was taken by all members of the society.

Archibald Shaw was a man who had a foot in two very different worlds: the Western world of scientific development and the simple hand-to-mouth existence of village life in the remote mission territories which, as a young missionary, he dedicated his life to serving. The missions were a place where foreigners were viewed with fascination and fear and where the law-of-the-jungle sometimes trumped the rule-of-law that administrators, often violently, struggled to impose.

When he left his job as a young postal telegraphist to commence religious studies, Archibald chose the life of a missionary priest. He adapted easily to mission life and knew well the trials and tribulations of his colleagues. Later, when he moved into the role of scientist-industrialist, he endeavoured, at least initially, to remain faithful to his first calling, the missions.

This is his remarkable and astonishing story.

II

Boyhood in Adelong

If anything is remembered of Archibald Shaw it is either through his association with the *Shaw Wireless Works* established in the early 1900s at the northern end of Dutruc Street, Randwick, or because of the vague, mysterious and scandalous circumstances of his death in the middle of 1916.

Archibald's story is barely known today even by his family's descendants. In fact, as sometimes happens when a stranger conducts research into another's life, I found myself passing on details which were previously unknown. The community of Roman Catholic priests among whom he spent most of his life, now three or four generations past his time, similarly know little of the story. The descendants of the woman he loved knew nothing of him either.

The evidence shows his childhood and that of his siblings was one of struggle. Despite or perhaps because of early challenges he was forced to face, Archibald was a popular and well-liked person. What has come to light and presented here has been pieced together from a variety of sources. It is the story of his early years based on primary sources as much as is possible. Whilst limited in some detail, it is doubtful if further information about this period will come to hand.

Archibald was born John Archibald Shaw in a wooden hotel owned by his parents in Tumut Street, Adelong, a small mining town at the foothills of the Snowy Mountains in New South Wales on December 16, 1870. Today Adelong is reasonably close to the modern capital of Australia. In those days Canberra had not yet been founded and the area was just scrub and grazing land. The centre of Australian Government at the time and capital of the then British Colony until 1927 was Melbourne. Adelong was a backwater. It was several days' journey from either Sydney or Melbourne, the principal cities of Australia.

Adelong township developed from gold mining and timber milling. It became a significant gold-producing town from the late 1850s and was home to a large Chinese population with some remaining in the area after the gold rush. Miners and fortune hunters came from all over the colony in the hope of striking it rich. Large steam-powered stamping batteries thumped day and night separating gold from quartz. The batteries continued even as smaller independent miners moved away after the more easily recovered gold was removed. Today the fields around Adelong support the grazing of sheep and beef cattle.

During the gold mining years fortunes were made, mostly by the store-keepers, and lost, mostly by the miners, but one such miner drawn to the area for gold struck lucky. He was a Scotsman, Charles Shaw, Archibald's father. Born in the village of Newhills near Aberdeen on January 24, 1832, he was baptised a Presbyterian. Charles travelled to Australia when he was seventeen years of age and mined gold in Adelong from 1858 until 1866. This was toward the end of the rush. According to the contemporary press, he was *extensively engaged in mining pursuits*.[1] He had enough money aside from gold mining to buy a hotel and a few blocks of land by the time he met his wife, Catherine.

Charles married Catherine Scanlen in Adelong on June 8, 1865. She was a first-generation Australian from Irish immigrant Catholic parents who lived at South Creek near Windsor in New South Wales. Their wedding was held in Charles' home. Her family later settled in the Campbellfields area, now known as Campbelltown. Her family name is memorialised in an Ingleburn street, *Scanlen Way*, near where her half-brother, Patrick Scanlen, had land. He was a grazier who was also involved in local government. Neither Charles nor Catherine were able to write their names at the time of their wedding, leaving only their witnessed mark, a cross, in the marriage register.

Charles was publican of his first hotel, *The Pride of Galway*, from 1867 until 1868.[2] It stood where the *Royal Hotel* stands today on the corner of Tumut and Campbell Streets. After crossing the bridge over Adelong Creek from the north it was the first hotel that travellers passed before properly entering the township. By the end of 1868, Charles had sold this hotel to purchase another up the road on the western corner of Tumut and Neill Street; the *Adelong Hotel*. This was the Shaw family home as well. It sat on some four acres, a much

Charles Shaw and Catherine Shaw (nee Scanlen), Archibald's parents.   *Credit: B. Clark*

larger site than their previous hotel[3] which allowed room for future development and expansion. A private home stands on the site today and the block has long since been sub-divided. Both pubs were simple affairs made from wood. Though the Adelong Hotel was only single-story, it had accommodation facilities at the rear which were improved over the years by the Shaws.

Archie, as he was known as a boy, was born in one of the rooms of the Adelong Hotel. By this time Catherine already had three daughters to Charles: Blanche Amelia (then aged about four years), Mary Frances (aged about three) and Bessie, or Elizabeth, (aged about one). In 1873, a few years after Archibald's birth, another child arrived to Charles and Catherine, Charles William Fraser Shaw.

The family were active participants in Adelong life. The elder Charles played the violin in public on occasion and sang.[4] He held athletics, race days and wood-chop events in the grounds of the hotel, followed by evening dances in the hotel ballroom.[5] In 1873 he chaired a public meeting at the courthouse in an effort to reopen the hospital at Adelong.[6] By 1875 Charles also operated a billiards room from the hotel having successfully applied for a billiard license.[7] Catherine and Charles had horses which were raced at various tracks around the district - Adelong, Gundagai and Tumut - and Charles acted as steward and starter for the Adelong horse-race meetings.[8]

One particular horse was entered in the Adelong Cup held on Valentine's Day, February 14, 1874. There is no record of how it faired but it was ominously called *Scandal*, a play on Catherine's maiden name. The year before this horse had won the Maiden Plate in nearby

Charles Shaw in the yard of the Adelong Hotel. Credit: B. Clark

Tumut.⁹ The name was to serve as a harbinger for the young Archibald, but no one knew it at the time.

When Archie was a little over three years old Guglielmo Marconi was born on the other side of the world into a life of wealth and privilege - in stark contrast to life in Adelong. The self-taught Italian radio pioneer brought about a technical revolution that changed long distance communications forever. Many decades were to pass before Marconi's invention connected with Archibald's world.

The Shaw children were brought up in their mother's religion, as Roman Catholics. They received their primary education at the newly built Adelong Public School. In 1879, when Archie was in second class he received an end-of-year General Proficiency award. His sister Mary received the same being in Upper Fourth Class, and Bessie received a special prize for needlework.¹⁰

Young Archie Shaw, c. 1876.
Credit: MSC Archive

The streets of the town were dirt, transport was by horse and cart, and the currency was the Great British Pound. Life was pretty rough. The leading technical innovations in the town were noisy steam engines that powered the few surviving gold stamping-batteries and saw mills of the district, and the electric telegraph system that connected the post office of the little town to its neighbours and to the larger inland town of Wagga Wagga via overland wires.

There is record in the press of June 1876,[11] which reported on the most miniscule local events, of a four-and-a-half-year-old Archie being taken by his father to *Sydney Hospital* in Macquarie Street for surgery on a dislocated ankle bone. Whether this came about by a birth defect or accident is uncertain but the operation resulted in one leg being slightly shorter than the other, giving him a permanent limp.

Four months after this trip to Sydney, the first of several tragedies were to befall the family and the world of the Shaw children began to fall apart.

On Thursday, October 5, 1876, aged 44, Charles Shaw died of *extreme exhaustion caused by intemperance of several years' duration*.[12] He was an alcoholic and, as a publican, one of his own best customers. Archibald was just 5 years old.

Sometimes funerals give an indication of the regard in which the deceased is held. This was certainly true for Charles. Some four hundred people attended. He was described as being *honest and straightforward, held in esteem, generous to a degree and, in mining, he was enterprising and energetic*.[13] The shops in Adelong closed on the day as a mark of respect. Charles was a Freemason and a member of the Order of Oddfellows,[14] both large organisations in Adelong – the latter even having its own brass band. The funeral service was conducted by a Presbyterian minister and followed by a Masonic service with a graveside hymn. He was buried in the general section of Adelong cemetery.

In addition to the hotel, Charles owned various parcels of land around Adelong at the time of his death which, by December 1878, were transferred over to Catherine.[15] This included fourteen acres spread over several blocks on the outskirts of town and five building blocks within the town.

After her husband's death Catherine continued to operate the hotel and worked hard to increase its value whilst at the same time raising five children. She had a reputation for cleanliness and quality accommodation.[16] [17] She made improvements to the hotel and furthered its income by refurbishing the buildings at the rear of the property into private apartment style accommodation.[18] She continued to hold entertainments and dancing on the premises with visiting troupes, regularly employing the band of a local man, Mr Parker, known as the *blind musician.*[19] As reported in the March 16, 1878, edition of the *Australian Town and Country Journal*, she intended to erect a completely new hotel near the bridge on Tumut Street.[20]

The children, particularly the older ones, were enlisted to support their mother's work in running the business and probably felt the weight of obligation and responsibility in giving up their own freedoms to do so.

Catherine proved to be a capable and creative business woman. In the December of 1879 she purchased two booths at the Adelong Racecourse for £12/15s each. In addition, she paid a further £12 for a twelve-month *Right of Tattersall's* to the Adelong races. This created another income stream for the family as the right allowed her to have the general business of the race club, (such as the issue of bookmakers' licenses, owners and jockeys' tickets and settling of accounts etc.),

The Shaw Children: Charlie, Archie, Blanche, Mary & Bessie c. 1879.   *Credit: MSC Archive*

conducted on the premises of her Adelong Hotel.[21] [22] She organised refreshment booths at local sporting events[23] and the hotel served as a booking agent for *Cobb and Co.* coach runs around the district and beyond.[24]

Catherine was no slouch after her husband's death - a virtue certainly witnessed by her children. However, she may have kept the children unaware of the police charges she faced in May of 1880 for permitting card-playing in the hotel during the early hours of a Sunday morning. For lack of evidence the case was dismissed.[25]

Catherine was forthright in defending her business even when she did not always win. Once she employed a Chinese cook who happened to smoke opium. When the cook, Charley Sin Poo, became ill after a session with an opium pipe, he arranged for a substitute to take his place cooking in the hotel kitchen. The replacement had no idea how to go about it and Catherine duly withheld some of his wage. Not only did she have to assist him but, when the matter was heard in court, she was ordered by the judge to back-pay his wage in full and pay the court costs as well.[26]

Catherine's business was well supported by the townsfolk following Charles' death. The Adelong Masonic Society, known as the St Clair Lodge, of which her husband was a founding member, continued to hold luncheons on her premises. She would cater for upward of thirty members and decorate the dining room for these functions.[27]

Four years after the death of their father another tragedy shattered the lives of the Shaw children. On Tuesday, November 9, 1880, Catherine herself died unexpectedly after a short illness leaving the children orphaned.[28] She was just thirty-seven years old. The formal reporting of Catherine's death was left to her eldest daughter, Blanche Amelia, who, being only fourteen years old, travelled to the larger neighbouring town of Tumut to register it at the Court House. Tumut was about half a day's horse-ride away. As part of the registration process she stated the names and ages of the surviving children: Mary, the second eldest was thirteen years old; Bessie was ten; Archie was nine years and eleven months, and Charles was seven.[29] In the space of four years the children had lost both parents and their grief must have been severe.

Catherine is buried separate from her husband in the Catholic section of the Adelong cemetery.

The five children initially came under the custody of John Causon. On December 1, 1880, Causon was granted letters of administration for Catherine's estate. She died intestate. He was also appointed guardian of the children.[30] John Causon and his wife were sponsors (or Godparents) at the baptism of the youngest Shaw child, Charles William Fraser.[31] Perhaps they had some similar association with the other children. Causon was a miner and chairman of the trustees for the common land around Adelong.[32]

Now, little more than a month after Causon was granted control of the estate and guardianship of the children, for reasons that are unclear, these duties were passed onto Catherine's half-brother, Patrick Scanlen. This occurred on February 5, 1881.[33] Patrick was a grazier at Campbellfields, about seven kilometres north of Campbelltown. He was at various times an alderman and mayor of the municipality. Neither of the guardians were able, or prepared, to put up the bond necessary for the settlement of Catherine's estate which was commonplace at this time, so it was passed over to the Curator of Intestate Estates. By 1898, some *eighteen years* after her death, Catherine's estate was finally settled and whilst she had significant assets including land and a gold mining lease,[34] she also held significant debts. After the repayment of debts the remaining £95/2s/10d was divided amongst the surviving children.[35]

It is not known how the children were looked after on a daily basis following their mother's death but it appears the boys did not leave the district of Adelong and Tumut. A photograph survives of Archie attending nearby Tumut School. The three girls may have come under the care of Catherine's sister, Mary-Ann Carr,[36] who lived at Nemingha near Tamworth, or may have been farmed out to other relatives. There is evidence that Bessie moved to Nemingha.

John F. McMahon, a Missionary of the Sacred Heart priest who undertook the first serious Shaw research in the early 1980s, maintained that there was, *a tradition among some of the living descendants that the children were brought up by relatives, that times were very hard for them, and that they knew the pinch of poverty.*[37]

Tragedy was again to strike the Shaw children. Bessie lost her life in 1882 through an unfortunate accident. At thirteen years of age she fell backwards from a hay-loft at Nemingha whilst collecting eggs.[38] In the space of six years the Shaw family had halved. The impact on the surviving children was devastating.

Evidence survives for Archie's younger brother staying in Adelong after his parent's death. An 1886 record shows Charles Shaw being charged by the police at the age of fourteen for breaking into and stealing from an Adelong shop with another boy. Someone had enough faith in him to put up a £100 surety that the young boy would return to court at a later date for a sentence hearing.[39] By 1899, the young Charles was still living in Adelong and performing in concerts as a singer and actor.[40] A prominent theatre building remains in Adelong from this period. Later he pursued acting professionally and conducted travelling shows, enlisted in the AIF[41] during World War I at the late age of forty-two, serving in the United Kingdom. When he returned to Australia he became a publican like his father.[42] [43] [44]

There is evidence also that the family of Walter and Olieve Hoad from Yarrangobilly and Adelong had an association with the young Archie Shaw, likely acting as primary carers. It is recorded by their daughter Evie Hoad, in testimony given after Shaw's death, that Archie was known to her father, Walter, as a boy[45] and he would occasionally visit them as an adult. The Hoad family shared the elder Charles Shaw's membership of the Masons' and Oddfellows' fraternities.[46] Such groups acted as locally administered social welfare agencies. In modern times they have largely been superseded by government funded social security departments. The Masonic and Oddfellows' lodges saw the care of deceased members' children as an essential duty and a central reason for their existence.

Years later Archibald himself implies in correspondence that he stayed in the Adelong area after the death of his parents. He writes,

I was born in the saw-mill districts of Australia and lived

there til 19 years.[47]

In all likelihood, he worked in some capacity with timber either in the forests or in the mills during his early youth. Later in life he was able to make use of this experience when he became involved in the operations of some very large-scale timber businesses.

He was just under twelve years old when he lost both parents and a sister. It is difficult to contemplate how the deaths of these significant people would have shaped the young boy.

By his fifteenth birthday Archie had secured a job working as a messenger boy at the Adelong Post and Telegraph Office.[48]

III

From Messenger Boy to Religious Novice

Archibald's teen-years are the least documented. There are a smattering of newspaper stories that mention him in passing but lack enough detail to build a comprehensive profile. They provide a limited idea of what he was doing and hint a little at his personality.

On March 12, 1886, the *Adelong News*[1] section of *The Gundagai Times* reports,

> *Master Archie Shaw, the eldest son of the late Chas. Shaw, has been appointed messenger in the Telegraph Office, in place of Master Harry Smith, who was lately promoted to Tumbarumba.*[2]

The fifteen year-old Archie worked for the Postmaster-General's Department (PMG) for the next six years. The PMG oversaw postal and telegraphy services throughout all of Australia.

Beginning as a messenger boy, Archie rode a push-bike around the town to deliver telegrams. In his early years at the post office he watched the telegraph operators at work and assisted them maintaining the apparatus. In his spare time he learnt Morse code. He was taught the need to respect the privacy of recipients' telegrams and to hold secret the contents of messages he carried. He held a position of trust. At the same time, he had a privileged view into the operations of many local commercial enterprises and held an intimate knowledge of the joys, sorrows and personal business of people in the town he served. The Adelong Telegraph Office gave him a window into a world much bigger than he had ever known.

Telegraphy was at the cutting edge of communications technology during this period. People who worked in the industry were well respected. A job with the PMG was stable and provided a reliable income. It offered the young Archie learning opportunities and a career path with promotions for life if he wanted it.

In March 1886, Archie was temporarily transferred to the Telegraph Office at Tumbarumba, again to replace Harry Smith, who this time had taken a promotion to Silverton, just north-west of Broken Hill. With Smith's original move to Tumbarumba being a promotion, we can only assume that Archie was now no longer a messenger boy but a telegraphist. This is confirmed in newspaper reports from May, 1890. To become a telegraphist he was required to pass examinations in the theory and practice of telegraphy. He had to demonstrate a fluent proficiency sending and receiving Morse code at speed and without error and he had to display the technical competence necessary to keep the telegraphy apparatus working properly.

Working as a telegraphist was a dream job for a kid from the bush with a technical disposition.

The next time we hear of Archie is in a newspaper story from June, 1899. With a sense of relief the Adelong reporter records,

> *We have at last obtained telephonic communication with Reedy Flat, Mr. Archie Shaw having gone up to fix the battery.[3]*

Batteries in those days were messy, wet-cell affairs, sometimes consisting of many hundreds of glass 'jars' connected in series and parallel configurations, made with various metal electrodes immersed in copper sulphate and corrosive sulphuric acid solutions.

Electrical voice communication along wires was starting to become popular around this period too. So-called *telephone lines* carried voice messages without the need for a telegraphist and were beginning to operate concurrently with the telegraph, though over much shorter distances.

By May 1890, the nineteen-year-old Archie had permanently left Adelong and was working as one of the assistant operators in the

Telegraph Office at Wagga Wagga. This was the largest office outside a capital city and a major junction for various country lines. For its time, the equipment was sophisticated. Multiple telegraphic messages could be sent simultaneously along a single telegraph line.[4] Not only were personal and business messages sent but newspapers relied heavily on reports relayed from distant places telegraphically. For the first time a little of Archibald's demeanour is revealed in this report by an Adelong newspaper correspondent,

> *The friends of Mr. A. Shaw, late messenger in the Post and Telegraph office here, will be pleased to learn that he has been appointed assistant operator at Wagga, being chosen for the position from a large number of applicants. Mr. Shaw is a native of Adelong, and during the time he has been in the office here he has made himself a host of friends by his civility and attentiveness.[5]*

In another press report made on December 24, 1891, we learn that Archie, still stationed at Wagga, displays impressive artistic talent,

> *For some years past the officials of the Wagga Telegraph Office have adopted the custom of issuing a typical Christmas greeting card, and these productions have always been, from an artistic point of view, highly creditable. It is, moreover, a noticeable fact that Wagga, in following this practice of sending kindly greetings to the electricians scattered all over Australia, speaks on behalf of New South Wales, no other station having as yet vied with her in this interchange of professional courtesies. Creditable as have been the cards issued heretofore, they are, it is fair to say, completely left in the shade by the elaborate and ornate picture containing this year's Christmas greeting. The design was prepared as a pen and ink sketch by Mr. A. J. Shaw, one of the operators, who is, unquestionably, the possessor of great artistic talent. The picture contains so many distinct features, all treated in a style of such perfect finish, that a lengthy description would be required to do justice to its merits... A scroll in the corner of the picture gives very clearly the names of the*

present official staff... [6]

A poorly preserved copy of the above artwork is held in the National Archives.[7]

At the beginning of 1892 Archie, now twenty-one years old, left Wagga to start in a new position as one of several telegraphists at an equally busy station in country New South Wales - the Postal and Telegraph Office in Goulburn. Several eulogistic and complimentary speeches were made during his farewell from Wagga and he was presented with a travelling case as a parting gift. He and another colleague, being transferred elsewhere, were accompanied to the Wagga Railway Station together with *a large number of friends... to bid them bon voyage.*[8]

Archibald's move to Goulburn changed the course of his life.

♦   ♦   ♦

On Monday April 4, 1892, Archibald resigned from his position as telegraphist with the Postmaster-General's Department to begin studies toward the Roman Catholic priesthood. He officially joined[9] the *Congregation of the Passion of Jesus Christ* on Sunday, May 15, 1892, four months after his arrival in Goulburn. He was one of five postulants who took the 'black robe' of a novice during an investiture ceremony held in a small chapel at Mary's Mount on the outskirts of Goulburn.[10] [11] [12] A Father Alphonsus presided over the ceremony in the presence of a Bishop Lanigan.[13] The monastery in Goulburn, or *retreat* as it is called by the religious order, was part of a large farm operated by the congregation, generally just known as the *Passionists*. As the name suggests, the spirit of the congregation is derived from devotional practices centred around the suffering and death of Jesus. They also hold a reputation as impressive evangelising preachers.

The main building that was once owned by the Passionists is no longer a monastery. It can still be seen today on a rise north of the township. Overlooking farmland plains, it has since been converted into self-contained flats which are independently and privately owned.

The original use of the building is evident from its architecture and the chapel is still easily recognisable, annexed to the northern end of the building. A prominent driveway lined with original trees is still present. However, the surrounding farmland, once quite extensive, has been subdivided into smaller building blocks in recent years for the construction of new homes for the expanding city of Goulburn. Street names like *Monastery Drive* and *Mary's Mount Road* hint at the original size of the place and its early usage.

It seems a strange turn of fate for the young Archie to be working as a telegraphist one day and taking the robe of a religious novice the next. He was surely entertaining the idea of religious life well before moving to Goulburn. He may have been influenced by the sermon of an itinerant Passionist preacher in Wagga at some point during his time there in the Telegraph Office. (The Passionists are known for conducting parish retreats and missions). Regardless, it would seem the purpose of his move to Goulburn was to enter the order, on a kind of exploratory basis as a *postulant* or aspirant, with a foot in both worlds for awhile. He may have lived at Mary's Mount monastery with the other postulants from the January of 1892 prior to his investiture. His move to the Goulburn Telegraph office wasn't a promotion. It was a swap with another employee, a Mr W. B. Turner, himself a native of Goulburn. It is likely that Archie was living the life of a postulant from his January arrival and considering his vocation to religious life whilst continuing to work as a telegraphist in Goulburn. He may have supported himself at the monastery whilst he was working by contributing some of his income for food and lodging.

To stretch the point of speculation a bit further, Archie's exposure to this particular religious congregation, set up specifically toward devotion to a *suffering* Jesus, may have held a resonance with him and given him a profound sense of belonging. Loss and grief had been a significant part of his childhood and his siblings' lives when he was a youngster back in Adelong.

In Catholic religious orders it was customary for a novice to take a different name as a kind of acknowledgment of the new life that they professed commitment to and as a reminder that their old life had been left behind. The name given to Archie on the Sunday he received the Passionists' black habit was *Brother Placid*. There were four others entering with him, and each took a religious name which they would be known by until their ordination as a priest. After the investiture ceremony at the Mary's Mount Chapel, the five brothers travelled to the training house or *novitiate* which was located near the original Passionist church in Despointes Street, Marrickville.[14] Here they were to *enter on a course of philosophy for two years, under the care of the Rev. Father Clement.*[15]

Father Clement was *Clement Caine* from Lancashire.[16] When Brother Placid and the other brothers arrived at the novitiate, Caine had only been ordained a priest barely three years and had been in Australia only for the last two.[17] He was twenty-seven years old, just six years older than Brother Placid. He was appointed to teach philosophy and theology to the new novices. He had previously worked in England in a brief missionary role.

Archibald did not remain with the Passionists long. According to the limited archives of the period,

> *Brother Placid was voted unsuitable for study for the priesthood on October 11, 1892, but he was offered the chance to become a Brother with the Passionists, which he accepted, [and], as he never made Profession a year after, it is assumed that he left the congregation during the year of novitiate.*[18]

Jeff Daly, the archivist who re-discovered Archibald's Passionist record goes on to say,

> *My own thinking, not based on records, is that he missed out on being a priest with us possibly on poor academic grounds, rather than [his] limp... This was sometimes the case with suitable students who had difficulties with studies. The study demands on a brother were much reduced at that time. If the physical disability was the reason, this would have hindered his acceptance as a brother as well.*[19]

This hypothesis might be valid but unfortunately there are no surviving records to corroborate it. Furthermore, a letter from a Monsignor Navarre written later is contradictory and indicates Archibald's limp was in fact the reason he left the Passionists.[20]

Having left the Passionists, Archibald next appears in the historical record arriving on Yule Island as a lay-missionary on February 22, 1894.[21] Yule was a mission station of the Missionaries of the Sacred Heart,[22] off the southern coast of what was known as British New Guinea in those days. He must have begun an association with the MSCs in Sydney, possibly through a Fr Peter Tréand. He was still known as Brother Placid at this time on Yule Island. The MSCs are a missionary society founded by French priest, Jules Chevalier, forty years earlier in Issoudun, a town about two hundred and twenty kilometres south of Paris in central France. At the time of Archibald's arrival on far-off Yule Island, the other missionaries were native French speakers with limited English.

Archibald may have come to recognise he would be happier and more productive offering his ability and skills to the more practical endeavours of the Missionaries of the Sacred Heart on their remote missions rather than through the more intellectual, evangelistic-style preaching and parish work that the Passionists were engaged in. He thrived on the remote island and made himself more than useful. He had a reputation for directness and took a pragmatic approach to mission life. He became someone whom the mission superior, Monsignor Louis-André Navarre, relied upon heavily and he was spoken highly of in correspondence.

Regardless of the path he walked between 1892 and 1894 and the reasons for doing so, what becomes clear is that Archibald definitely wanted to pursue a religious calling as a priest and he was not going to let rejection from one order stop him following this calling with another.

IV

Missionary on Yule Island

Some geographic and political background will help to understand the disparate world Archibald Shaw had entered as a missionary.

New Guinea, that is the whole land mass and surrounding islands immediately to the north of Australia, was inhabited by hundreds of separate and frequently warring tribes which had distinct ethnographic differences - some with fearsome reputations. Stories of cannibalism[1] and strange witchcraft and sorcery practices were relayed by early explorers, convincing the European mind that the place was completely uncivilised and very dangerous. Impenetrable mountain ranges, forbidding river systems and thick jungle canopies made the interior almost impossible to explore.

A border was established by early Dutch colonists, running north-south through the middle of the island; the land to the west becoming known as Dutch New Guinea, a former territory of the Dutch East Indies.[2]

The eastern side was sub-divided between the British in the south and the Germans in the north who established 'protectorates', or colonies, on the land they claimed. A boundary line running roughly east-west along several groups of mountain ranges acted as a natural kind of geographic barrier, effectively dividing the eastern portion of the country in two; a northern part and a southern part.

The British New Guinea Protectorate was established in 1884 partly in response to the wild and unsuccessful attempts of the scheming *Marquis de Rays*[3] who attempted to claim the whole area in the name of the French and colonise the Bismarck Archipelago as well. The mountains on the mainland provided a natural division between north and south which was formalised as a boundary by an Anglo-German agreement on April 6, 1886. The border was then properly surveyed and mapped. The southern part was called *British New Guinea*, and the northern section, under German control, was known as *Kaiser Wilhelm Land*.

Kaiser Wilhelm Land extended into the waters to the north-east and included the islands of the Bismarck Archipelago. Somewhat confusingly, the archipelago's largest islands, named New Britain and New Ireland, were actually under German control. They were named as a result of earlier historical claims. The Germans referred to these islands as *Neu-Pommern*, often called *New Pommerania* by English speakers, and *Neu-Mecklenburg*.

A diverse mix of colonialists, adventurers, social-outcasts, plantation developers and competing missionaries of all denominations flocked to both New Guineas, often clashing with the indigenous tribes in staking a claim for their own particular interest, be it land, resources or their own brand of Christianity. It was very much frontier territory.

When Archibald Shaw arrived on Yule Island which is located about a hundred kilometres north-west of Port Moresby, the interior of the country, with its wild mountain ranges and dangerous river systems, had only been explored sporadically by missionaries. Later attempts at exploration were made, not all that successfully, by larger colonial-funded expeditions or through private business operators looking for natural resources to exploit.

The MSC Society, under control from their French motherhouse at Issoudun, had been running a mission station on Yule Island since July, 1885, in 'competition' with the *London Missionary Society*, a congregational assembly of Protestants: Anglicans, as well as a Presbyterians, Methodists and Baptists who viewed British New Guinea as their own ecclesiastical territory.[4] The various denominations were quick to baptise natives and establish religious allegiance amongst their followers.

In 1889 Louis-André Navarre was the French-speaking Catholic Bishop of the British New Guinea mission territories. He lived on Yule

Island which had become the administrative centre for MSC missions throughout the entire British Protectorate. He was addressed by the title *Monsignor*. By 1891, eight mission out-stations, each relying on the central station on Yule for logistical support, had been set up on the mainland and the whole population of the island, some two-hundred and fifty people, were baptised in a great ceremony on Christmas Day that year.[5] The MSC mission on Yule was very successful if measured by religious fidelity and counted by the number of baptisms from the indigenous population. The early MSC presence on Yule is fondly respected by locals to this day. When Archibald arrived in 1894 the mission was well developed with a staff of about twenty.

Archibald adapted easily to mission life. He developed a fluency in French sufficient to teach English to the young French, Dutch and Belgian seminary students who were in their final period of study and would soon be ordained on Yule Island.[6] He continued to practice his drawing and painting. Right up until the 1980s, one of his religious artworks, a copy of a Heinrich Hoffman original, was photographed hanging in the chapel on Yule albeit in an unrestored state. The painting is longer there.

His fluency with language and his general usefulness made him an indispensable secretary to the bishop, Navarre. Monsignor Navarre regularly writes to Jules Chevalier in Issoudun, reporting on matters concerning the mission and missionaries on the island. When speaking of Brother Placid, he gives reliable insight into Archibald's character and we learn a little of what he was up to,

> *Brother Placid, the young Englishman,[7] of whom I spoke to you in my last letter is teaching English while waiting for you to admit him as a novice. He also serves me very well for my letters in English.[8]*

And a few months later, Navarre again writes to Chevalier,

> *I think I forgot to give you the names of the father and mother of the young Englishman who is with us and wants to enter the Society, but has need of a dispensation because he took the habit with the Passionists but did not take vows. He is a truly exemplary young man and of robust health and is*

the only one who has not suffered from the painful effects of acclimatization.[9]

Archibald formally breaks his earlier association with the Passionist order whilst on Yule Island. Navarre continues,

He is pious and, without having extraordinary intelligence, he succeeds in everything. He doesn't waste a minute; learns Latin, French, Kanak and teaches English to all scholastics and fathers. I notice that the defect which made him leave the Passionists is less with him than with Father Karseleers... I hope the Council will not refuse me this English subject... [10]

On March 9, 1895, Swiss born priest Fr Peter Tréand, who for most of his career was to serve as the parish priest of Randwick, NSW, writes to Fr Genocchi, the superior on Yule Island, at the request of Monsignor Navarre,

Bishop Navarre wants me to tell you about a young religious brother whom I knew - and who - at the end of his first vows - left his Congregation - in the hope that he could be accepted into our Mission in New Guinea. - Of course, we gave him no sure hope. - He's acting of his own free will. He is 21 years old - knows Latin and French - has his diplomas - has completed his philosophy.[11]

In fact, by 1895 Archibald was nearly twenty-five years old. Monsignor Navarre had petitioned church authorities in Rome, who had oversight of all Catholic religious congregations, to establish a novitiate[12] on Yule Island in 1894. The authorities in Rome were slow to approve Navarre's request but a novitiate did eventually start operating on the island by 1896 and Archibald was accepted as one of its first novices by the MSC General Council in Issoudun,

Seeing that I have asked for and obtained from Rome permission for him [Br Placid] to enter our Society in the missions in spite of one leg being shorter than the other. Nevertheless, he limps less than Fr Karseleers. This brother should finish his novitiate in October.[13]

Archibald's limp is identified here as the reason he left the Passionist congregation. Physical impediments were viewed as a potential liability for a religious congregation taking on a new aspirant. However, the community on Yule already had one priest with a similar impediment who was capable of pulling his own weight and carrying-out his duties. On this basis, the decision to accept Archibald with a lesser impediment of the same nature would have been an easy one. Navarre continues,

> *This brother with the endorsement of the fathers here is one of the most judicious, clear-sighted, pious and zealous in the mission. His character is upright and frank... If it has not done so I beg the Council to be good enough to accept him. He is indispensable to us for all matters English.*[14]

On September 24, 1896,[15] two years after his arrival on Yule, Archibald's application to join the MSC was formally approved and he was accepted as a member of the Society. In a ceremony in the Yule Island chapel he made his first commitment by a profession of vows - a step closer to be later being ordained a priest. He continued to be known as Brother Placid.

Navarre recognised the sense in sending Archibald to Sydney after his profession for further theological studies, suggesting to Chevalier months before,

> *In spite of the great services he does for us, I think for the greater good of the mission he should go to study theology at Randwick under Fr. Tréand.*[16]

However, certain developments and considerations outlined below complicated this plan and resulted in Archibald being sent to the MSC mission on Thursday Island, off the tip of Cape

Msgr Louis-André Navarre, Bishop of New Guinea
Credit: MSC Archive

York instead, to complete his studies. Navarre wrote to Chevalier on October 29, 1896,

> *When I received the Council's authorisation to receive the temporal vows of Br. Shaw, the secretary added a note: 'the Council [in Issoudun] has decided that this brother will do his studies in Sydney', but at the time we had already held a council meeting at Port Leon [on Yule Island] concerning the brother and had decided he would do his studies on Thursday Island, and when I received this letter, the brother had already commenced his studies in the latter locality.[17]*

Thursday Island was chosen for Archibald to study mostly because of a conflict he, and nearly everyone else on the mission, had with one Fr. Jean Genocchi.[18] Genocchi had unpopularly changed the mission program by allocating undue time for personal reflection and private study for the missionaries, instead of using this time for formal catechetical instruction of the natives on Yule,[19]

> *Having destroyed our whole organization in the mission and having set up in its place a system of idleness, Fr Genocchi has forced to discourage a great number of our missionaries and played a large part in the departure of several and of others who will still leave.[20]*

In the same letter, Navarre spells out to Chevalier Archibald's unique response to the destructive action of Genocchi which created further friction between Genocchi and Archibald,

> *This brother [Brother Placid], who is very intelligent and very insightful, saw at once the faults and defects of Fr Genocchi and did not hesitate to tell him [directly] his opinion when pushed; from this moment on the Father could not bear him and the brother led an exemplary life; he had no hold over him and so took other steps to rid himself of him. He [Genocchi] told him repeatedly that he [Archibald] was not made for New Guinea. This was the one brother who for a year had been without fever which was looked upon as something extraordinary. However, he later developed it*

more severely than the others.

When the doctor-magistrate found him during strong attacks of fever, he also said that he was not made for New Guinea. Brother [Placid] was little impressed by this judgement. But I told him that for the 18 years I have been in the tropics, I have nearly always been sick and the doctors repeated to me that a stay in the tropics was incompatible with my temperament. I continued in work that many in Europe told me not to do, but since this brother is very humble and mortified he said to me: I believe as a matter of fact that for me to do good here I will have to suffer a lot but it does not matter if I win souls for God. From this point this was the position he took when Fr. Genocchi would speak.[21]

The explanation to move Brother Placid over to Thursday Island was principally a result of Fr Genocchi's continuing conflict with Archibald. These reasons are spelled out by Navarre when he later reported back to Chevalier in France. Navarre continues,

But Reverend Father, when we took council as to where the brother should do his studies, Fr Genocchi was in Sydney and the brother [Placid] had come to us to explain his fear if he went to study in Sydney: 'Fr Genocchi is there and is almost certain to send me back and set my superiors against me'. This reason has caused a lot of weight in the decision we have taken. But other members of the Council have observed that even if Fr Genocchi were not in Sydney it would not be good for the brother to go there for his studies.

He has a very positive and practical mind, considering ideas from their practical and useful point of view. In all probability he would then come under Fr Vandel as his teacher and it is said this good father is essentially [too] subtle [or esoteric] in his teaching and would discourage Brother Placid.[22]

Archibald Shaw made his perpetual vows with the Missionaries of the Sacred Heart on September 27, 1899.[23]

It was decided that Fr Joseph Guis would teach Archibald

theology and philosophy at the catechist school recently built on Horn Island, immediately to the east of Thursday Island. This school was part of the Thursday Island mission located in the Torres Strait off Cape York, the northern most point of Queensland.

Guis had a military history and had served in the French army for three years. He reached the rank of lieutenant before entering the MSC congregation to work as a missionary. He was well educated, a writer, and musically talented.[24] Fr Guis and Brother Placid formed a close working friendship that began on Thursday Island and lasted until Guis' premature death in 1913. Navarre continues in the same letter,

> *In a month the catechists' house will be finished and Fr Guis and Brother Alexis will receive pupils there. Brother Placid will go there also but separate from the other pupils. Fr Guis, who will have some free time, will teach him Philosophy and Theology. Fr Guis has a very clear and practical method and has a lot of patience. It will give him a chance to go over his books, and he is moreover a model missionary who edifies everyone at Thursday.*[25]

But Guis did not formally teach Archibald on Thursday Island for long. The efforts of Monsignor Navarre to convince the General Council that his studies should continue on a remote island mission station did not materialise beyond the period that Archibald had already spent with Guis. The General Council decided instead the best place for Archibald to be a seminarian was in Sydney.

By April, 1897, Archibald Shaw had left Thursday Island by steamship and entered Sydney Harbour after a short voyage. He then made the hour-long journey from Circular Quay to the Randwick Presbytery of the Missionaries of the Sacred Heart.

Archibald, as Brother Placid, front far left, with students from the indigenous catechist school on Thursday Island, c. 1897. *Credit: MSC Archive*

Unrestored oil painting of St. Cecilia by Archibald. Photographed in the 1980s. In possession of the Quigley family. *Credit: MSC Archive*

The boy Jesus at the Temple. Detail from an oil painting by Archibald which was hanging in the chapel on Yule Island up until at least the 1980s when this photograph was made. The painting is a copy based on the work of contemporary artist Heinrich Hoffman.

Credit: MSC Archive

V

Priest and Procurator

On October 18, 1897[1], Fr Peter Tréand, regarded as one of founders of the Australian province of the Missionaries of the Sacred Heart,[2] returned to Sydney from Europe on the *Prinz Regent Luitpold*. The ship had left from the Italian port of Genoa several weeks earlier. Tréand had been representing the Australian Missionaries of the Sacred Heart and the missionaries of New Guinea, New Britain and the Gilbert Islands at the General Chapter of the order held at the MSC headquarters, the General House, in Issoudun, France.

He travelled with a large entourage of French and Dutch missionaries and had some new recruits in his care as well. These included eight priests, six brothers, six sisters and two aspirants or postulants. Some were to study at the newly built monastery in Kensington.[3] Within a few days, thirteen of the party; the six sisters, three priests and four brothers, departed from Sydney to swell the ranks of the island missions. They travelled north with Monsignor Navarre who was the Bishop overseeing the British New Guinea mission territory at the time.

Another member of Tréand's entourage was a young French MSC brother, the twenty-three year old Fernand Edmund Arnoult, born in 1873 in Bar-Sur-Aube about one hundred and ninety kilometres south-east of Paris. Whilst studying at Kensington monastery, Arnoult and Archibald met and so began a lifelong friendship. Arnoult will come up repeatedly at key points later in Archibald's story.

On the boat also with Tréand was one Francis Xavier Gsell

who had been ordained the year before. Gsell was born on the border region between Germany and France in the Alsace area which, in the course of seventy years, had changed hands four times between the French and Germans. He identified himself sometimes as French and sometimes as German[4] when required but preferred to be known by his provincial ethnic Alsatian heritage. Given this background, he would have been an ideal candidate to serve in either the French speaking MSC missions of British New Guinea or the German MSC missions in Kaiser Wilhelm Land. But he ended up in neither place and spent most of his later missionary life amongst the Australian aborigines of Bathurst Island. He was later installed as Bishop of Darwin.

Gsell was keen to be a missionary. However, it would be a few years yet before the young priest would actually travel to the missions himself. He came to Sydney firstly to learn English and then to take up a new post teaching dogma and scripture at the recently opened Kensington monastery[5] where Archibald finished his studies toward priesthood.

When Archibald first came down from Thursday Island he was based at Randwick for about a year and a half[6] and it was there he came under the tutelage of Gsell when he arrived a few months later. Fr Tréand was the superior at Randwick. Archibald's expenses as a seminarian for that period, some £60, were being borne by Msgr Navarre anticipating his return to Yule Island after his ordination.[7] Gsell was about the same age as Archibald[8] even though he was his teacher. Archibald had sounded Gsell out before he was appointed his instructor and both thought well of the idea, so I suppose it would have been a relatively pleasant period for both.[9]

Fr Vandel writes from the Kensington monastery to the MSC founder, Jules Chevalier on August 30, 1898,

> *Monsignor Navarre spent four months here last year; he left here a Brother Placid who for eighteen months has been eating at our table and taking lessons from Fr Gsell.*[10]

Archibald was still recovering from a tropical illness during his studies. This came as no surprise as almost all missionaries would come undone by disease at some point. An ill Brother Placid is identified by

Fr Vandel living at the Kensington monastery in November, 1898[11] - part of a group of seven convalescing missionaries.

By December, 1898, Gsell was also the coordinator of supplies for the mission territories, working out of the Randwick presbytery and Archibald may have come under the influence of other teachers like Frs Buckley, Tréand and Vandel. According to Gsell's autobiography, the job of procurator was a dispiriting time for him[12] as it also would be for Archibald who followed in the job some years later. By 1899 both Gsell and Archibald had moved from Randwick to the new Kensington monastery where Archibald finally finished his studies. Gsell was replaced by Father Emile Merg who became the next procurator.

On March 14, 1900, Fr Gsell finally headed for the missions and left for the Yule Island mission by the steamer *Moresby* having finished his tutelage of Archibald. Frs Peter Tréand and the novice master, Jean-Marie Vandel, gave positive testimonials concerning Archibald's suitability as a priest which was required by the General Council of the MSC in Issoudun in the months preceding his ordination. This is the only evidence that they acted as educators of Archibald.

It is difficult to establish with any accuracy how long Archibald's seminary studies actually took and there is no surviving record of his capacity as a student during this time either. Whilst he spent about three years in Sydney before ordination, his studies during this period were irregular. The view held by John F. McMahon, the first Shaw researcher, was that his studies were truncated to about eighteen months.[13] Fr Vandel writes a testimony for Archibald about a month before ordination describing him *as a very fine religious.*[14]

Archibald continued to engage in artistic pursuits whenever possible and is recorded supervising some remarkable decorations in preparation for the consecration of the newly built church at Randwick in September, 1899.

> *The altar decorations were artistic and brilliant. Behind the High Altar, reaching almost to the roof of the sanctuary, was a perfect network of dark green ivy leaves, and beautiful design consisting of three large crosses, stars and hearts, in which were fixed hundreds of candles. The decorations*

were designed and carried out by Brother Placid, M.S.H., assisted by the ladies of the Altar Society.[15]

The consecration ceremonies at the Randwick church were concluded by *Reverend Father Clement* who preached an evening sermon to an *immense congregation on Devotion to the Sacred Heart*[16]. Curiously, Fr Clement was the Passionist priest, the very same Clement Caine from Lancashire whom we met earlier in the story. He taught Archibald philosophy and theology at Marrickville when he first entered religious life.

Caine must have had some friendship with the MSC to be invited to preach at the consecration of a church belonging to another congregation. Perhaps it was through this friendship that a recommendation was made for Archibald to continue his vocation as an MSC after he left the Passionists.

Having finished his studies by the end of January 1900,[17] Archibald was finally ordained to the priesthood on Pentecost Tuesday, June 5, 1900, by Cardinal Moran in the chapel that is now the library at St. Patrick's College, Manly. He was twenty-nine years old. James Redden from Port Augusta was also ordained during the same ceremony.[18] He was now known as Father Placid Shaw and continued to serve the Catholics of Randwick for a short time after ordination. Soon he abandoned the name Placid and was known henceforth as Fr Archibald Shaw or *Arch* to his confreres.

Archibald was the first Australian-born MSC to be ordained. This warranted some celebration after the service and acknowledgement that the MSC presence in Australia was beginning to put down roots and grow. Fr Jules Vandel, Superior and novice master at Kensington, wrote to the then General Secretary in Issoudun, Fr Meyer, on June 16, 1900,

> *Father Shaw has been ordained a priest at Manly, at the seminary, by the Cardinal, [Moran], on Pentecost Tuesday... [The Feast of the Sacred Heart] will be a great feast. It is our first Australian ordination – in four or five years, others will follow.*[19]

The day after ordination Archibald said his first mass in the little chapel inside the Kensington monastery and a couple of Sundays later on June 24, 1900, a High Mass was held in the Randwick Church for the Feast of the Sacred Heart. Archibald was the principal celebrant. This was his first public mass. Later that same day, before an evening Benediction, he preached his first sermon.[20] Amongst these 'firsts', no one was to know, that sixteen years later, another would be added to the list. He would be the first Australian born priest in the order to die. But in the meantime, much was yet to happen.

♦   ♦   ♦

After his ordination Archibald did not return to Yule Island. However, the local MSC Council were not keen to see his mission experience wasted and he was made *procurator* for all the MSC mission territories on July 31, 1900. This was ratified by the General Council in Issoudun[21] who kept a close eye on the operation of MSC communities throughout the world and had to approve various appointments. He took over from Emile Merg.

Missionaries from Europe travelled through Sydney on their way to the mission territories and sick island missionaries were given respite from their duties in Sydney when required. Frequently missionaries developed a variety of serious tropical diseases like dysentery, malaria, encephalitis and blackwater fever that, in the absence of doctors, could not be satisfactorily treated on their missions. Even with the medicines available at the time these conditions often remained chronic. Sick missionaries would be sent temporarily to Sydney for treatment or convalescence. It made logistical sense to have the supply depot for the missions, the *procurate*, located in Sydney as well.

The job of procurator came with its own unique responsibilities and difficulties. A procurator had to be financially adept, a nimble administrator, a good negotiator, an accurate accountant, and he had to be creative in finding the material items ordered by the distant missionaries so that they could do their job. He had to find the means to pay for what was sent and arrange to have the requested items

Archibald Shaw c. 1911

Credit: MSC Archive

despatched in a timely fashion. He also had to accommodate visiting and convalescing missionaries and show them a degree of compassion.

Orders from the missions received at the procure were made out in either French, Dutch or German, depending on the language of the mission bursar placing the order, and would take weeks to arrive in Sydney. Similarly, the goods ordered would take some time to be found and shipped; sometimes several months. There was a certain amount of stress that came with the procurator's job and a certain amount of tension between the procurator and the distant missionaries was inevitable, particularly if orders were delayed by misunderstandings, misinterpreted by language or cultural differences, or if they were unable to be properly funded.

To complicate matters, when Archibald began in the job, there were four MSC mission territories serviced by the procure and each had their own accounts: Yule Island in British New Guinea, largely staffed by French MSCs, the Gilbert Islands, part of the British Western Pacific Territories, the Marshall Islands, and the New Britain mission in the Kaiser Wilhelm Land, principally staffed by German MSCs.[22]

Despite the size of the operation, the procure was operating out of Randwick presbytery at this time, adjacent to the newly built church.

Another significant fact about the procure is that it was not under local MSC oversight or control. The procure, and therefore the procurator, was directly under the control of the Superior General in Europe. Things had been operating this way since the General Council decided so on October 26, 1892.[23] This made sense from the point of view that the mission territories themselves were also under direct control from the MSC General House.

So it was to the MSC Secretary General and later Superior General, Fr Eugène Meyer, in far-off Issoudun, that Archibald sent accounts to and took directions from. This was an arrangement Archibald enjoyed and did not want to give up. Not only did it give him a certain independence in carrying out his duties but it relieved him of immediate accountability because there was no one local to whom he was subordinate.[24] Later, this independence from local oversight became a significant factor contributing to the financial problems Archibald and the procurate found themselves in. However, for the present, and despite the challenges of the job, it was an ideal situation, especially from Archibald's perspective.

Bishop de Boismenu, during a visitation from the General House reported back to Europe that,

> *Although Fr Merg has given excellent service to the mission, we have in Sydney Brother Placid who is as well-advised as Fr Merg in business matters, more obedient, more flexible, more interested, just as devoted and, above all, held in high esteem by both superiors and confreres. I am sure he will be well received by the three vicar apostolics...*[25]

Correspondence from Archibald during this period highlights the difficulties and stresses he endured in the job. Nevertheless, he continued in this position for the next seven years.

VI

Difficult Years

Before Archibald became procurator for the mission territories after his ordination,[1] he was likely assisting Emile Merg in the role, at least from the end of January, 1900, when his studies had finished.[2] Then the procure was operating from Kensington monastery.[3] Additionally, Archibald was also put in charge of the monastery grounds.[4]

One year later on January 1, 1901, Australia formalised its own constitution when the six disparate British colonies making up Australia at the time were united into a single *Commonwealth of Australia*. Under a plaster dome in Centennial Park *Federation* was proclaimed, only two kilometres north of the Randwick church and presbytery[5] where the procure office was now operating from. It was a time of great nationalistic pride.

That same year, in Europe, the French Government passed the *Law of Associations* for a variety of political reasons. This resulted in the suppression of clericalism and the expulsion of religious congregations from all over France. Following the implementation of the law, the Missionaries of the Sacred Heart moved administration of their order to a house in Hiltrup, near Münster, in Germany in 1901. This became the Provincial House for the Northern Province which oversaw most of the MSC operations in Europe. However, a discrete MSC presence was maintained in Issoudun by Chevalier himself, the MSC founder, until he was evicted in 1907 when the French Government assumed ownership of all church property.

The early years of Archibald's priesthood saw him considered for a leadership position on the Australian MSC Council in addition to his assignment as procurator. His practicality was seen as an asset over his inexperience and relative youth. However, the role was given to a more senior priest, Fr Joseph Bach.[6]

Half a world away in Africa, the discovery of gold and diamonds was increasing tensions between British colonialists and Dutch-Afrikaner settlers, known as Boers. Contingents of Australian soldiers and mounted riflemen were raised to support British forces in a conflict that dragged on in South Africa for years. Soldiers from New South Wales were encamped at Kensington Racecourse awaiting deployment. Here they trained and prepared for the Commonwealth's first overseas war. Little more than a decade later the same racecourse was used as the Australian camp for soldiers taking part in the Gallipoli campaign of the First World War. Kensington racecourse is not to be confused with Randwick Racecourse. It stood until 1951 on land now occupied by the lower campus of the University of New South Wales.

The soldiers camped at the racecourse needed a Catholic chaplain and Archibald was given the task.[7] The camp was a relatively short walk from the procure. For Archibald, visiting the soldiers was probably a welcome break from mission supply work. It is not known for how long he conducted this chaplain service.

In the months after Federation Archibald read about surprising developments in the field of wireless telegraphy. His interest was natural given his background as a telegraphist. Toward the end of 1901 Guglielmo Marconi sent the first wireless transmission, a *Morse code* signal, from Poldu in Cornwall to Newfoundland in Canada, a distance of about three thousand five hundred kilometres - a remarkable achievement and a new record.

This distance record was a significant milestone for wireless science because it showed that radio waves, which were known to only travel in straight lines, must have followed the curvature of the earth in order to travel the vast distance across the Atlantic Ocean. The explanation for the phenomenon relied on an idea that the upper atmosphere served as a reflector just as the earth or the ocean surface did. The waves still travelled in straight lines but bounced many times between the earth's surface and the ionosphere, the reflective layer in the upper atmosphere. Archibald would have mulled over these breakthroughs as he thought about bridging the distant mission stations via wireless. Communication between foreign countries was either by hand-written letters, which took many weeks or sometimes months to be delivered - or by cable telegrams, which were received immediately but only between stations connected by long undersea cables spanning continents. These cable stations were mostly built in the larger coastal settlements. The missions were as remote in the early 1900s as an astronaut today would be on the dark side of the moon.

From 1902, when the procurate operated out of Randwick presbytery, Archibald had only a minor role in regular parish duties. Superior General Eugène Meyer notes after his visitation to Randwick in 1902,

> *Fr Shaw, Placid, fulfils the functions of Procurator of the Missions: he appears to be a good religious, is faithful to his exercises of piety, to the exercises of rule, is good child, never smokes and does not drink either wine or liquor.*[8]

Some money from parishioners in Randwick was made available for the mission procure. However, this was an insignificant fraction of what was required to keep the missions running. The bulk of the money came out from France, Germany and Rome and required careful accounting. Even so, the amount sent was never enough to keep the mission accounts operating out of debt. Consequently, Archibald was constantly looking for ways to save money and generate it through local fund-raising endeavours. J. F. McMahon notes,

> *A great deal of capital investment was tied up in the new missions: churches, convents, presbyteries, dispensaries, schools – all had to be built with materials bought elsewhere. In addition, there was the need to keep the missions supplied with food, clothing and medical supplies... There was never enough money available.*[9]

Whilst the work of the procurate was consuming, it fostered an entrepreneurial bent latent in Archibald. An early effort to raise money saw him produce painted artworks for sale, some as large as nine square metres. He produced these successfully for a limited time, though the money they brought in was well below what was needed. There is mention of him selling two paintings, one of St Cecilia and another of the composer Beethoven, for 50 guineas each (a little over £52 around this time).[10] Some of his confreres thought the role of priest-artist was incompatible with the calling of an MSC priest and frowned on the idea.[11]

He created some original portraits too: one of Peter Tréand survives and is hung in the MSC Provincial house at Coogee. His larger paintings were copies of old masters and frequently of biblical scenes. Two used to hang on the first floor of Kensington monastery but were destroyed when a severe hailstorm ripped through the suburb on April 14, 1999. Few of his paintings can be located today.

Archibald writes about this period some years later,

Realizing (sic) that the Procure was carrying a heavy debt which was always increasing and seeing the impossibility of getting no funds from Europe, it was up to me to get funds from somewhere; I have a faculty for drawing and painting and therefore I tried to get funds in this way; it displeased the senior fathers of the province and I gave it up.[12]

Operating with only limited funds, the procurator was obliged to implement a certain economy without reducing the quantity or quality of goods sent.

Procure work created significant strains and made the job one of the most difficult and thankless in the society, especially when trying to interpret orders from a missioner whose mother tongue was not English. The demands placed on Archibald become abundantly clear when reading his letters to the Superior General to whom he was directly reported. The letters are archived today in Rome. Archibald answered to both Fr. Arthur Lanctin, until 1905, and then Fr. Eugène Meyer who took over and remained Superior General until 1920. Meyer was based in the MSC General House in Rome.

Fortunately much of the correspondence giving accounts of the mission finances and procure business from Archibald to the Superior General has survived as it was archived in Europe. However, most of the letters sent in reply back to Archibald from either Lanctin or Meyer have not. Still, from the tone of Archibald's letters and despite being only a one-way record of conversation, it is apparent that there is an excellent working relationship between Archibald and his superiors in Europe. Whilst most of the correspondence deals with the minutiae of the procurator's job, some of it gives particular insight into how Archibald operated and how he was perceived by his own confreres locally and in the distant missions. This was often in an unfavourable light.

The following excerpt from a letter of Archibald to Meyer represents a small part of a lengthier account.[13] The letter appears to be in response to complaints passed to the General House from the New Guinea mission which Archibald had a fair bit of trouble keeping happy,

> *I met Frs Julien and Gsell at Thursday Island in January. I feel too pained to speak of my interview with Fr Gsell so I will not speak of it. But one thing I protest against is that when anything was wanting at Yule Island, he usually said that he ordered the thing at Sydney but that I did not send it. I have always sent the things ordered by him except on one occasion. I did not send all the ironmongery because there was no money in the bank but I always sent the food that was ordered. I will give you one example of this.*
>
> *When I met Fr Gsell in January he gave me a written order to be sent from Sydney. He told me that he was ordering many things from Thursday Island; among these things he would order kerosene and on this written list from Sydney he did not put kerosene. At the beginning of May I got a letter from Fr Cros asking why I did not send the kerosene ordered by Fr Gsell, that through my neglect the mission would be without kerosene for 6 weeks. Fr. Gsell informed Fr Cros that he gave me the order for kerosene – This is a lie. He gave me no order, there is no kerosene either on his written list.*
>
> *I may state the Fr Gsell never took a copy of his orders*

sent to Sydney so that he never knew what he really did order – of course then he blames me.

I spoke to Fr Julian and asked him was the mission content with me. He astonished me by saying that I had no right to spend £40 buying a gold set of teeth for a mission sister that was at Sydney. I simply laughed at him; as I had bought no teeth for any sister whatever.

He informed me that he had heard this on the mission! What next!...

Msgr Allen also writes to Fr Tréand that I reported that you, as Visitor, had made my charge in the procure impossible for me. This I deny absolutely. I never said such a thing. On the contrary my Dear Father you gave me courage and lightened my charge for since your first visit Fr Tréand has left me entirely free of all other work.

There is increasing frustration in Archibald's tone as he responds to the litany of complaints made against him,

So I am all very easily (sic) to manage all the missions, the Dutch mission also. Msgr Navarre writes to me by last boat a long and furious letter protesting against my administration. He also says that there is a difference of £1,200 between his accounts and my accounts and wants an immediate explanation. I have checked my accounts. They are right. What am I to reply to such accusations[?] - simply nothing. Fr Gsell said in his letter my account were (sic) right – you yourself know how the accounts at Yule were kept. Fr Cros is now Econum [Bursar] at Yule. I think things will be easier now but his first command [i.e. French], is not free from faults.

I will give you an example –

Copy: part of Fr Cros' Order   Remarks of Procure

1 sac bouchons. . . . .   How many required?

DIFFICULT YEARS

Cirage pour souliers . . . . . . What quantity?
Vin rouge 8 tonneaux . . . . . . Large or small? Sometimes they want large and sometimes small ones
Souliers assortis . . . . This is very vague and most difficult for the procure. What quantity and what sizes?
3 sac de café . . . . What quantity?
Huile pour machines . . . . . . What quantity?

This will show you how mistakes are made. Fr Cros is new in his charge and I don't complain against him. I have written him at length explaining what I want.

New Britain is a mission 6 times more complicated than New Guinea and there are never any mistakes made simply because the brother Dominic gives all the possible particulars he can in making his orders.

One more remark my Dear Father. Yule Island sent down the boiler of their steamer saying they wanted new brass tubes and a new covering. This was all the order. I got it mended and sent it back. They sent it back again asking why I had not put a chimney on it and they further said all the tubes were not brass.

I got no order before about the chimney. I swear all the tubes are brass. Bro Phillip also certifies this. They complain of the expense which is £48. They say every engineer they have asked says it is too dear. This is sickening. I got an expert engineer to value the work and he says the price was reasonable. I can never please New Guinea. They never say what they want.

There's a defensive tone in Archibald's correspondence from this period. It was probably his self-justifying stance and forthright demeanour that made him the right man for the job. One can only assume the ferocity of complaints made against him. In another letter to Meyer he writes,

This last boat I received a long sharp letter from... the

> *superior [on the mission] reprimanding me for waste and he says he has reported my carelessness to your good self. But down there everything that goes wrong is the fault of the procurator. Somebody must be blamed so I get it.*[14]

Given that Archibald's correspondence only provides access to one side of the story, it is easy to feel sympathy for him and think the system of ordering material from mission procurate would make it difficult for anyone in the role. A note from Fr Vandel to Meyer, who knew Archibald from his days as a student at Kensington, may lead us to think otherwise. It reveals another side to Archibald's character,

> *I don't think the missions will ever be satisfying to Fr Shaw. He is of a rough and capricious nature who starts off with great enthusiasm in the beginning and then runs out of steam, who lacks attention to detail, who does as little work as necessary, who makes fine plans – sincerely - but his nature cannot carry them through for long. We all know him for that. All the missionaries passing through leave here furiously opposed to him – he does not busy himself with them; there is no affability, no eagerness to help, no sympathy... he is too independent in this office. Certainly there is no perfection in this world but a procurator without devotedness and sympathy for missionaries passing through – that I can hardly comprehend. I think you will have to present us with a better candidate later.*[15]

The following part of a letter between Archibald and Fr. Meyer is interesting also. It indicates there was discussion from as early as 1903 about removing him from the procurator role. It shows Archibald has a degree of sympathy and compassion extended to him from his superiors in Rome and it also shows he possessed that remarkable attribute seen frequently in politicians and some high-level achievers. He had the capacity to carry-on regardless of criticism and despite what anyone might have thought of his work,

> *I hear from all quarters that there is going to be a new procurer at Sydney in my place. Deo Gratias.*[16]

DIFFICULT YEARS

My Dear Father, it will be a pleasure for me to be relieved of my present charge. I will do all in my power to aid my successor if needed.

I have no explanations or no protest to make. If my superiors judge me unfit it is their duty to discharge me.

Fr Merg will return [in] the middle of July. When he went to the Gilberts, [Gilbert Islands], the Governor, Mr Campbell, returned to the islands on the same boat. The Captain told me that he would have liked to throw them both overboard, for from the first day they both got fighting and destroyed the harmony of the boat...

I think to be a good procurer a man must have some bulldog fighting qualities: then others will be quiet and he will have rest himself.

Do not worry about me Dear Father. I am quite hardened now and can endure their torments.[17]

Archibald enthusiastically continues his letter to Meyer and proceeds to give him a comprehensive lesson in the economics of timber milling in the missions – a subject Archibald had some familiarity with as a youth in Adelong. The New Britain mission relied on profits from the milling of timber out of a large forest on the Torio River to support itself. He sets before Meyer a business plan for the New Britain mission. His thinking seems in keeping with the character analysis provided by Vandel earlier; he was a man with big dreams. Archibald's proposal is a grandiose idea and it displays an inspiring entrepreneurial bent.

If successful his plan would hold a promise of eventually eliminating the missions' financial challenges. Aside from plantations, the timber available in the mission territories was potentially the most valuable and readily accessible natural resource. If harvested, milled and sold efficiently, the forest timbers, in Archibald's eyes, were key to making the mission financially independent. He writes to Meyer,

Notes on the New Britain Mission

I stayed 6 weeks in New Britain – [from] November til [the]

end of December. I visited all the missions, plantations and sawmills.

Plantations: there is no chance of revenue from the plantations worth speaking about til 3 years...

I gained good experience in New Britain in every branch of my work.

Since I have returned to Sydney I have economized [sic] to the value of £89 in two shipments, New Britain is a mission different to New Guinea as regards procure work. There is organisation there. I brought many samples which I find are equally suited for the mission which will make a saving of 1/3 the price.

For example, Tobacco. This mission uses 15 tons of tobacco a year. The price of good tobacco is £100 a ton; 15 tons a year = £1500

Now I have been able to procure damaged tobacco at [just over half that price] which the natives accept without any comment; they do not see the difference. 15 tons of damaged tobacco costs £840 per year.

<u>Result</u>: A saving of £660 in one year on tobacco alone. I tried some of the tobacco at Yule Island and I got the usual formula as a reply: 'all the fathers are angry with you for sending such tobacco'. On many other things: blankets, knives, axes etc. I can save a good lot. When Mgr Couppé has a credit I will get these things direct from England in quantities for one year – which will mean a saving of one-third the present cost.

I cannot do this yet as I must have a good credit of say at least £2,000. I estimate that I will save £800 this year for [the] New Britain mission.

<u>Sawmills</u>: the machinery is first class... the position of the machinery is also good. It is in the centre of the timbers; ... the timbers (woods) are first class; the organisation at present is weak to very weak.

The Timbers: I brought down 16 specimens of timber to Sydney and had some tested by the Government Railway

DIFFICULT YEARS

Dept., 14 of these passed the tests, 3 of these received 1st class certificates (which means they are good for railway work and blocking[18] the streets).

Two of these timbers are most numerous at the saw mills.

With the Government Certificate these 3 timbers will enter the European Market from Sydney which means that there is always a good market; for England and Germany have been buying the timbers for over 20 years and will still continue. Africa has now started buying which has brought the market a little higher.

<u>*Capacity of the Sawmill*</u>: *the mill can cut 30,000 feet of timber a day. If organised tightly there will be no difficulty of cutting 20,000 feet a day.*

The timber at Sydney is selling for 10/- for 100 feet.
The expense of cutting and freight to Sydney will be 4/- for 100 feet.
20,000 feet cut in 1 day at 10/- per 100 ft = £100
20,000 feet expenses cutting etc 4/- per 100 ft = £40
Nett profit a day = £60

Working the mill 4 days a week at £60 profit a day amounts to £240 a week. In three months or 12 weeks: profit = £2,880

This is not exaggeration but careful calculation of every circumstance. There is timber at this rate of cutting on the Torio River for 20 years. In Australia saw mill timbers run 22 trees to the acre which is considered good. In New Britain saw mill timbers run 31 trees surpassing Australia.

I was born in the saw mill districts of Australia and lived there til 19 years. I never saw such a forest of timber as there is in New Britain.

<u>*Present Organisation*</u>: *It is weak.*

<u>*Mgr Couppé thinks to work the mill with the brothers and natives*</u> *– He will fail – He is tenacious in his opinion.*

> *He must fail first. Then we can organise properly.*
>
> *He must have at least 5 white men who have spent their lives at this work and a good organising manager who has been at this work all his life. The expenses of £40 a day include these men.*
>
> *[The] Reason of this is that no merchant will buy timber for the European Market if the timber is not cut just exactly and this is a special trade in itself. No man not having at least 5 years' experience in mill work is fit to cut for the European Markets.*
>
> *Not only that, with men of the world working for wages, you can depend on a certain amount of work being done in a certain time. This is important because you can not regulate the boat that comes to take the timber away otherwise. But Msgr will see this as he has practical sense when once the mill is started to work.*
>
> *I do not think that we will be getting any revenue from the mill til February next year.*[19]

Archibald writes to Meyer again on July 6, 1903, spending a considerable part of the letter again in defence of his position and responding to various criticisms,

> *The specimens of timber sent by him [Msgr Couppé] to Sydney have received good reports and a secure market for all our timber is certain. Cash paid at Sydney. But Msgr will not be ready till January to send timber to Sydney....*
>
> *I still receive many general complaints from New Guinea and Gilberts [Gilbert Islands] about my neglect of duty but they specify nothing. They always say that they don't receive their accounts but I have always, from the beginning of my charge, sent them 2 times a year. In turning up the old letters from New Guinea I have received letters acknowledging receipt of the accounts and then, six months later, I receive letters blaming me for not sending them. I wrote a rather stiff letter to Msgr Allen complaining of the injustices of some complaints; my stile [sic] of letter pained*

> *him very much and he complained of my insolence. I asked him to give proof of some accusations made against me. I am very sorry now that I wrote and I, on receipt of his letter, wrote [again] and begged pardon for my letter. It is useless for me to try and vindicate myself...*
>
> *Some accusations they make against me are really absurd. I will not worry repeating them to you my Dear Father. I may say that Msgr Couppé on Jaluit [Marshall Islands], do[es] not complain... I will do everything the different missions ask and try my utmost that things may work in accord. At the same time I think it will be hopeless in trying to secure complete peace. And I ask you my Dear Father in your charity if you consider [me] unfit for my charge, do not hesitate to change me and if you consider it your duty to reprove me at any time, do not out of kindness to me, omit to do so; I will receive your reproofs as coming from a kind Father and to my own interest...*
>
> *Trusting my dear Father you are all well.*
> *I am Dear Father your obedient son in C. J.*
> *A. Shaw*[20]

By November of 1903 the sawmill under the management plan of Monsignor Louis Couppé did fail as Archibald predicted. He used Couppé's failure as an opportunity to begin the implementation of his own plan,

> *I spoke to you about Msgr Couppé going to manage his sawmill with the brothers. Well he tried: Now he has changed his mind and I have sent him down last October a thoroughly reliable man understanding the sawmills perfectly. Last mail Msgr told me that the Government of New Britain had handed him a large order for timber. I know the man*[21] *very well that has gone down to New Britain, so I am confident that I will receive a good substantial amount for the timber sold in December or January...*[22]

In the early days, Archibald's relationship with his confreres, under the trying circumstances of providing for the missions, was never easy but not without humour. Occasionally this was conveyed through in his letters,

> *I am in trouble with the shipping company since the return of Fr Merg. He got fighting with them and the concessions they made to me have now been withdrawn. I will have more trouble with them yet. Fr Merg was handled rather roughly by the Captains of two boats: one refused to take him as a passenger; the other swore at him all day long. Fr Merg asked me to complain to the company so I saw the Captain that swore so much. The Captain said, "Father I did swear at him, but that man [Fr Merg], would make the almighty swear at him".*[23]

From mid-November to the end of December, 1902, Archibald spent six weeks in New Britain visiting he says, *all the missions, plantation and saw mills.*[24] He spent considerable time assessing their needs and prioritising funds. He also used this time to explain to the local bursars what was expected when they placed an order for material with the procurate in Sydney.

Only six months before Archibald's visit, on April 3, 1902, a great tragedy befell the family of a young German plantation owner in New Britain, Rudolf Wolff, whose wife, infant child, and the native carer of the child were tomahawked to death by disgruntled natives in what was a misunderstanding over the sale of a portion of land.[25]

In the weeks before the massacre, Wolff, who had been dismissive of the tension, was warned of the seriousness of the situation by a German Missionary of the Sacred Heart priest, Fr Eveline. Immediately after the initial deaths, some two hundred natives were killed in reprisal attacks by the police before the murderers themselves were killed. Such a disproportionate response to the massacre was instigated by an inexperienced German magistrate and sparked the inter-tribal Varzin War ending in May, 1902.[26] The war occurred in the Varzin Mountains of New Britain.

No doubt during Archibald's visit to New Britain the missionaries were still reeling from these gruesome events. The Varzin Mountains are quite close to the Baining MSC mission and the coastal head-stations. The slain German family were Catholic.

The massacre was symptomatic of an instability and fragile co-existence existing between natives and white settlers.[27] During his visit to New Britain Archibald became intimately familiar with the details of the slaughter as he listened to missionaries from his own congregation recall the events.

Little did he realise that ten missionaries whom he knew personally would themselves be massacred two years later in circumstances that affected him profoundly.

VII

Inspiration from an Island Massacre

In 1903 Archibald supplied four missions from the procurate in Sydney: the Gilbert Islands, Marshall Islands, New Guinea and New Britain. He operated separate accounts for each mission. He reported directly to Father Eugène Meyer and continued to do so after Meyer became Superior General in 1905.[1]

The job of procurator remained challenging and the complaints from missionaries were relentless. Archibald continued to have support from the tolerant Superior General as seen in this excerpt from Meyer to Tréand, the local superior at Randwick,

> *Encourage Fr Shaw and support him all you can. Be a father who carries on his shoulders all your religious – as in his heart.*[2]

However, by 1903 the decision had been made to replace Archibald with his seminary teacher, Francis Gsell. He was recalled from Yule Island for the role. A notation in the *Province Minute Book* states,

> *We have sent Fr Gsell to Sydney to take the place of the procurator. Since he has a sense of economy he could make a good procurator for the procure has only to make a good [choice] of merchandise and Fr Gsell knows what is needed. I have written to Fr Lanctin*[3] *to ask him to accept this change.*[4]

As Gsell made his way to Sydney from Yule via Thursday Island, quite by chance, he met Archibald on the steamer *Moresby* and something very strange happened. Remember, Gsell already had a taste of being procurator and was later to describe the job in his autobiography[5] as *dispiriting*. A conversation ensued between the two which resulted in Gsell abandoning his new appointment before it even started. He returned immediately to Yule Island on the next steamer!

Navarre, who was one of Archibald's strongest advocates only a decade earlier, shares a growing sense of frustration with Archibald, and recognises that lack of financial oversight is becoming a cause for serious concern. He reports to Meyer on June 1, 1903,

> *He [Fr Shaw] is at Thursday Island returning from New Britain and meets Fr Gsell who is on his way to Sydney. Fr. Gsell, instead of continuing his voyage returned to Yule and 'told me that he would lose his vocation if he had to live in Sydney'. What passed between them? Fr Shaw is disgusted in spirits – he said. He does these things without interest and in spite of good sense. As a matter of fact, his report of last year is riddled with mistakes – and all to our disadvantage. When we receive our goods the suppliers send us at the same time their bills, that is to say the sum total of goods but on Fr Shaw's report these same bills are considerably overcharged – or rather they concern goods that have not been received or ordered; are we going to pay for goods which have either been sent to another mission or even to one of the Sydney houses? The fact is we have suffered a loss of 26,000 francs. I have asked for Fr Shaw for explanations on this point: I don't expect to get an answer, he never replies to observations made to him... we have no one overseeing over Fr Shaw. Fr. Cros will himself go and buy for us in Sydney...*[6]

For the time being and in the absence of another suitable candidate, Archibald continued on as procurator.

Then, on August 13, 1904, the massacre of ten missionaries in the Baining district shattered the MSC world. Repercussions from this tragedy were felt for decades throughout missionary societies of all denominations; even by ordinary citizens in Australia and the European states regardless of religion - but especially amongst the people of Germany. Up to this time the supply of missionaries to New Britain came from the church in Germany.

The events in Baining deeply affected Archibald as well. Together with other massacres that occurred in New Britain and the Yule Island region in the years before Archibald's first arrival,[7] they were later recorded as one of the key factors leading Archibald to pursue wireless.[8] The Baining massacre was close to home. It occurred on a mission he supplied as procurator and he knew all the slain missionaries from previous visits.

Like other missions of the period, the New Britain MSC outposts were, from about 1898, organised around a larger central station which offered community support for the missionaries and guarded against prolonged periods of missionaries working in isolation. Outstations, typically within a day or two travel time by foot from the central station, were occupied on a temporary basis for days or weeks at a time. The missionaries would then move on to another outstation or return to the central station.[9] St. Paul mission station in the Baining hill country was about five kilometres south-west of the larger Vunamarita mission on the coast.

The MSCs first established a mission at Vunamarita from their main central station at Vunapope, located near Herbertshoe, (now Kokopo), about twenty kilometres south-east of modern-day Rabaul. Fr Hubert Linckens, founder of the MSC house at Hiltrup near Münster, was then the Provincial of the German Province which included the missions in the German Protectorate of New Britain. By chance he was visiting New Britain at the time of the massacre and became the go-to man for the press who were seeking commentary on the incident. Vunamarita mission had been established in attempt to bring peace to two rival races; the *Tolai* and the *Baining* according to an account written by Linckens.[10]

The Tolai, who numbered between thirty and forty-thousand people were united by a single language. They had displaced the Baining from the fertile coast and pushed them southward towards the mountains where life was harder. Both races were organised into several smaller tribes. The stronger and more war-like Tolai made frequent raids upon the defenceless Baining. They hunted them for enslavement as workers, either using them for their own purposes, or passing them on to work in plantations run by European settlers or on the surrounding islands. Linckens makes the point too that the Tolai slaughtered the Baining on occasion for cannibal feasts.

The mission at Vunamarita was located in Tolai territory amongst the slave traders. The primary intention of the missions was to introduce Western Christian values into the local culture. Under the direction of Monsignor Louis Couppé, the missionaries took steps toward preventing the trade in Baining slaves and freeing them with the support of the German administrators. They also acted against underage marriage and polygamy, treated disease, ran orphanages, taught natives to read and write, and introduced Christian theology into a strange world of sorcery, magic and medicine-men.[11]

> *Couppé's plan of conversion was to collect these former slaves, as well as orphans and the illegitimate children of white settlers, feed and clothe them, and then educate them in Catholic orphanages. Later they would be settled in self-supporting peasant-communities in the interior and through inter-marriage and instruction, provide the core of a new Christian people in New Guinea.*[12]

Like the colonialists, the adventurers, the businessmen and the plantation owners, missionaries of all denominations shared a belief that Western values, and Christian values in particular, were superior to existing codes of tribal morality. Yet the colonialists, who *selectively* adopted Christian values with varying degrees of commitment, shared a naivety and to some extent an ignorance of the effect their colonial presence had on the native population. This is more obvious in hindsight. Few could anticipate the immense tensions and consequences of the conflicting morality and profound cultural changes which were inadvertently introduced by the presence of Europeans.

Whilst the raids of the Tolai on the Baining continued, the MSCs established further missions south-west of Vunamarita in an attempt to protect and offer places of refuge for the vulnerable Baining. The large St. Paul mission station was a model self-supporting community for Baining tribes-people who had been freed from indenture to the Tolai. A bookish and gruff German MSC priest, Fr Matthäus Rascher, was in charge.

Rascher was an interesting character. He was an ethnologist who spent considerable time learning multiple native dialects and publishing his findings in Europe. He even collected items of natural and cultural significance and sent them back to the newly established mission-museum set-up by Linckens in Hiltrup, Germany.[13] The abrasive Rascher had difficulties dealing with people from his own cultural background, let alone tribes-people who had a completely different mindset. He chose to ignore recent warnings which were passed to him from sympathetic natives that his life was under threat.

The large mission village consisted of separate orphanages for boys and girls, a school, a newly constructed church and small homes with several acres of land for the so-called 'freed slaves' to work under the direction of the MSC fathers, brothers and sisters. It was set-up as an industrial village. The mission was completely staffed by European missionaries but supplied materially from Australia by Archibald and the procure in Sydney.

Several kilometres to the west of St Paul, across a fast flowing river, a small mission station at Nacharunep was manned by a Dutch Trappist priest, Fr. Henri Rutten.

Several accounts of the Baining massacre of August 13, 1904, made their way to Sydney via steamer in the weeks afterward and the shocking details were published in the press in Australia and internationally. Updates continued over the following months as new information came to hand. Not unusually, the accounts varied somewhat depending on who was telling the story, particularly in respect of what the principal cause was. The gist of what happened is as follows,

> *... a Baining man, Tomari, after fourteen years as ward of the mission, found himself at variance with Church policy and alienated from the way of life now expected of him. Tomari*

wanted to divorce his wife, a mission convert, in order to marry his lover, Sa Vanut, who was already wife to another man.[14]

Both Tomari and Sa Vanut fled to a nearby village and were humiliatingly brought back to the St. Paul mission for punishment. This incident initiated the massacre but historians are unanimous that this was just the spark which ignited pre-existing tensions,

Tomari had planned to attack the mission station on 7 August, 1904, but the attack had to be put off at the last moment because of the arrival of the New Guinea Company plantation manager, who was well armed. The opportunity came again on 13 August. On that morning... Tomari asked for Rascher's rifle in order to shoot pigeons for the mission's kitchen. While Rascher, feeling unwell, lay on his bed, Tomari stole up to the priest's window and shot him in the stomach. It was the signal for conspirators to fall upon the rest of the missionaries. Three brothers and five sisters were cut down with axes as they went about their daily tasks; at the same time on a lonely station at Nacharunep some kilometres west of St Paul, Baining people murdered a Trappist monk, Fr Rutten, as he sat reading his breviary.[15] *Those Bainings who were regarded as particular supporters of the priests were also killed, though several managed to escape to the coast and raise the alarm.*[16]

There were simultaneous but thwarted attacks on other white-owned plantations in the district.[17]

In contemporary newspaper accounts, Hubert Linckens, speaking as MSC Provincial of the New Guinea Mission, was understandably anxious to play down the behaviour of Rascher himself in events.[18] Accusations that the massacre was induced by the missionaries using corporal punishment on Tomari and on Sa Vanut were denied absolutely by Linckens,[19]

He [Tomari] was simply scolded for committing adultery, but the girl concerned was given the usual punishment of

flogging by the police, who rely on this punitive method as being the only means of enforcing the law.[20]

When reflecting on the massacre twenty-five years later, Linckens' version of events had not shifted. He writes with the same authority Western colonialists and missionaries assumed when they first entered the country, leaving no doubt where to lay blame,

The motives of this carnage were the savage instincts of these cannibals, full of hatred against the progress of religion, the true civilisation in their country, as was judicially proved in the long official enquiry that followed[21].

Largely due to Linckens' version, and because of the legal threats he made to silence the Jewish press in Europe[22] who were publishing critical accounts from the Islands which blamed the missionaries themselves for the catastrophe, the murdered missionaries came to be known as the 'Baining martyrs'. This was followed by a cause for beatification and canonisation made to the Vatican which officially commenced in 1932. By 2010 the application had stalled. The Rome-based *Congregation for the Saints,* was unable to establish whether,

Those who killed the missionaries were acting out of hatred of religion (because the missionaries had opposed a case of adultery in the mission) or for cultural, political motives (because they saw the missionaries as agents of a foreign power who were opposed to their culture).[23]

A preliminary investigation into the cause of the massacre prepared by an MSC Brother, L. Dorfler of the German *Mission House* in Hiltrup, identified as early as 1926, that Rascher's public humiliation and punishment of Tomari and his lover, Sa Vanut, was the principal trigger,

At Rascher's behest, both were brought back to St Paul on the end of a rope, where Rascher proceeded to beat Tomari for his sins while a nun dealt the same punishment to Sa Vanut.[24]

With the benefit of hindsight and the availability of primary sources the reality of cause examined over a century later is more nuanced than was made known at the time.

Historian, Peter Hempenstall, presents the most complete analysis of the circumstances leading to the massacre. Based on Rascher's behaviour he argues, the natives would have had difficulty differentiating whether Rascher was the head of a Christian mission or the local leader of a secular government in priest's garb. He was a difficult man, clashing both with his own confreres and the natives. He administered corporal punishment; he represented the imposition of a new order (German occupation) with its European buildings, new moral codes and Western work ethic. He supervised the construction of roads by natives - work which they detested - and *he was the local paternalistic head of a new priestly regime which likely appeared in opposition to traditional tribal chiefs.*[25]

Inevitably with the arrival of the missionaries came pressure to abandon tribal customs that were in conflict with Christianity, such as the Baining death-cult for example. This had been passed down tribal lines for generations. German colonial historian, Horst Gründer, argues that the Tolai cleverly manipulated both the gullible Baining and Tomari himself into murdering the missionaries in order to restore the death-cult along with the old order that existed between the two ethnic groups.[26]

As recompense to the MSC for the massacre, large tracts of Baining land were confiscated by the German administration and handed over to the MSC mission for plantation use. This immediately increased the viability of the New Britain missions.[27] However, it had negative repercussions for the local Baining economy. Consequently, the Baining now saw themselves as victims of both the Tolai *and* the German administration which fuelled tensions further. Cultural conflicts persist to this day between the Tolai and Baining.[28] It is remarkable that the MSC mission at St. Paul was able to restart at all, only a few months later, unmolested.

As shocking as the Baining incident was, it did not end on August 13. Deaths continued for months in the form vicious reprisal attacks orchestrated by the authorities as a form of social control.

Sixteen natives were captured and shot when the initial police troop arrived from the German administrative centre at Herbertshoe,[29] now Kokopo, after the alarm had been raised by the two boys who ran down to the coast from St. Paul. A further eighty natives were rounded up and shot in the weeks following.[30] No one knows how many died altogether but it could well be several hundred based on the number of natives that were killed in reprisal attacks after the Wolff family massacre two years earlier.[31]

Road construction using forced native labour in New Britain   *Credit: NSW State Library*

On the same afternoon as the massacre, by coincidence or otherwise, a schooner owned by the missionaries, the *Pearl*, became detached from its mooring. A storm blew up and the boat was destroyed on rocks near the neighbouring island of New Ireland with all its cargo on board. The financial loss was estimated to be about £2,000.[32] The captain of the boat had just been employed by Archibald and commenced a two-year contract with the MSC. Now, having no boat to sail, he chased Archibald to Sydney for a pay-out. This gave Archibald another reason to return to New Britain.[33] As he explains to

INSPIRATION FROM AN ISLAND MASSACRE

Meyer,

> *I have just returned from New Britain after a 3 months' stay there. I have had much trouble with the Captain of the New Britain schooner 'Pearl'. He was only on the boat a month when she was wrecked. His engagement was for two years. He came to Sydney and brought me before the court for 2 years wages, £400. Our advocate said that the Captain would gain the case against me and he advised me to get away to the Islands quietly before the case was brought to the court and stay there until the Captain got employment on another ship. This I did, now all is quiet again and I am back at my work.[34]*

Archibald had an unusual familiarity with massacres. He was acquainted with the details of the Europeans killed on Yule Island[35] in the years before his arrival there as a postulant; he was in New Britain months after the Wolff family massacre and the ensuing Varzin War of 1902. He arrived in New Britain again, four months after the Baining massacre witnessing its aftermath and, aside from keeping out of the sea-captain's way, used the trip to accompany the new missionaries who replaced those who were murdered.[36]

Whilst important, the cause of the massacre is not what concerns us in telling the Archibald Shaw story. More relevant is the effect the massacre had on the man himself. It convinced him of the value of wireless as a means of protection for missionaries and as a way to enhance the safety of the missions generally. On a very practical level, wireless would also offer the benefit to communicate directly, in real time, with the missions from as far away as Sydney. He could use it to facilitate mundane matters expediently: take orders from remote mission bursars and get instant clarification on orders which were unclear or incomplete, without waiting weeks for the back-and-forth of letters carried by steamer. Wireless would make life safer and his job easier. It might even calm the complaining missionaries who were unhappy with his service. He certainly would not have to write long-winded letters to his Superior General addressing the litany of complaints made about him.

The events of the Baining massacre and its aftermath indelibly affected Archibald. Many years later, a newspaper account records his own first-hand comments on the matter,

> *While I was doing missionary work in Papua... a party of our people was massacred. Only twelve miles away was another party connected with our mission, who would have been strong enough to have rescued them from the horrible torture which precedes cannibals' feasts. If those two parties had been connected with wireless there would have been no massacre... So when Marconi's system was placed before the world I made a study of it and became efficient...* [37]

VIII

Fr Shaw's Road

On a small beach at Woody Point in Redcliffe, Queensland, lies the slowly disintegrating wreck of an old iron-hulled boat. It sits where it was beached in 1958 after a long and distinguished history. This is the final resting place of the *Gayundah*,[1] once operated by the Queensland Maritime Defence Force and later the Royal Australian Navy before it was sold into private ownership. At 9.30 pm on April 9, 1903, it sailed from Brisbane into Moreton Bay under the command of Captain William Creswell. A bamboo pole was attached to the foremast supporting a wire aerial which transmitted the first wireless messages over a distance of about twenty-four kilometres from a ship at sea to the Australian mainland. A transmitter built by the Marconi company was used. The receiving station was set up in the grounds of St Mary's Church, Kangaroo Point[2], then adjacent to the Naval Stores. The press carried the story and several earlier failed attempts as well. The message was received in Morse code and read,

> *Gun drill continued this afternoon and was fairly successful. Now off Mud Island. Blowing squally, cold and raining - prize firing tomorrow. Marconi insulators were interfered with by rain but easily rectified and communication since has been good. Good night.*[3]

Earlier, longer distances had been obtained over water by ship-to-ship wireless experiments. For example, the HMS St George and HMS Williamstown established a distance of thirty-seven miles for

Wreckage of the *Gayundah* at Woody Point, Queensland, from which the first successful Australian ship-to-shore wireless communication took place in 1903.   *Credit: M Ryan*

Plaque at Kangaroo Point, Brisbane, commemorating the reception of wireless from the *Gayundah* in the Naval Yards adjacent to St. Mary's Anglican Church.   *Credit: M Ryan*

wireless in May, 1901, according to a report in the Melbourne *Argus*.[4] Much longer distances over water were reported from overseas manufacturers of wireless plant.

From around 1905 wireless was more than a novelty. It was being used for practical purposes. The sets and their associated power supplies were large and cumbersome, requiring skilled engineers to set-up and operate them. All communication was undertaken in Morse code so it was necessary for the operator to have a competent mastery of Morse. Archibald read the press accounts of these events and may have thought, like many others, that it was unfortunate the newly formed Commonwealth had no capacity to locally manufacture and supply its own wireless plant.

Generally speaking, the measure of a country's defence capability at the beginning of the twentieth century was gauged by the size and effectiveness of its navy. Naval vessels with wireless sets would be able to communicate with each other and their base. They would have a distinct advantage over those that could not. It was obvious then that the Navy would be particularly enthusiastic about seeing wireless plant installed aboard their ships.

In 1904 the *HMS Diana* located at Suez, Egypt, intercepted wireless signals from the Russian navy forewarning the English of the Russo-Japanese war.[5] This was the first time an intercept like this was successful. *Forewarned is forearmed* and the message played a tactical part in the eventual Japanese victory, demonstrating the power of wireless. This marked the beginning of what is known in military circles today as *signals intelligence*.

Whilst wireless was being developed elsewhere, Archibald continued in a parallel world as the mission procurator from Randwick presbytery; ordering goods, sending them north to the missions by steamship, receiving sick missionaries for care, filing accounts and preparing statements. He still had no local overseer and continued to be directly answerable to the MSC Superior General, Eugène Meyer in Rome. The mission accounts remained in significant debt as Archibald's earlier schemes to generate funds had only limited success,

At the end of this year Gilbert [Islands] will have perhaps a

> *debit of £400 and New Guinea £250 Debit. Father Linckens is arranging to remove the New Britain Debit by the sale of one of the plantations there for about £10,000.*[6]
>
> *He gives an exceedingly pessimistic account of New Britain finances. I am glad he passed by and saw for himself; he knows now exactly how matters stand. The saw mills seem to be at present a failure. Although I think, were they in other hands than the mission it could be made a success.*[7]

Complaints about Archibald's performance in the role of procurator had subsided for the moment and, despite the constant struggle to find funds, there was a period of calm,

> *As regards myself and [the] procure, everything is going along alright; as far as I know I think the missions are satisfied. Fr Linckens seems to be satisfied with the way I do business; he however wishes to have a separate procure; separated from the houses at Sydney.*[8]

By March, 1905, Archibald became distracted by a serious family matter. His sister Mary and her husband both took gravely ill and, not being able to work, were unable to feed their five children who were still at school. Mary was going blind and suffering from a general breakdown in health. She was only thirty-eight years old. Her husband, William, had a lung condition and, according to the doctors, had no hope of recovery. Archibald was trying to support the family financially from his own meagre resources which he just could not do. He made overtures to Frs Tréand and Meyer that he leave the procure and conduct parish missions elsewhere which would provide him with a larger stipend,

> *They have five children, the youngest is four years old. The children are unable as yet to do anything to help their parents. They have no one to aid them but myself. I feel that in conscience I am bound to help them.*[9]

If the Superior General was not enthusiastic about letting him participate in parish missions, Archibald suggests he could temporarily leave the MSCs and work as a diocesan priest under a bishop,

> *I have no desire to be relieved of my vows. I am extremely happy in my vocation...*
>
> *I must come to their help. I cannot see my family starving any longer. This matter is very urgent as the condition of my family is extremely painful. They have disposed of their household furniture little by little and there is nothing left to sell.*[10]

The urgency is clear. It is even evident in the quickly written hand of his three-page letter dated March 30, 1905. Archibald concludes with,

> *I cannot state how long this necessity of aiding my family will last but I think it will be a few years... try to get me a decisive answer one way or the other as this is most urgent.*[11]

Meyer's response has not survived but the response from the mission bishop was pragmatic. In October, 1905, Fr Navarre writes to Fr Meyer,

> *I have been warned that Fr Shaw is on the point of leaving the Society to become a secular priest in the diocese of Adelaide. If the news is true who shall we appoint as Procurator in his place?*[12]

Precisely how Archibald spent the remainder of 1905 generating cash to support his sister and her family is uncertain. However, his friend Fernand Arnoult, an MSC brother managing the recently purchased farm attached to the monastery at Douglas Park, may have played a part in his plan. Like Archibald, Arnoult was a practical man, later identifying himself as an engineer.[13] As farm manager, he installed a steam-operated pump to move water from the Nepean River into tanks on the farm[14] and previously worked for five years in the missions[15] – probably operating the remote MSCs Torio River saw mill in New Britain on Archibald's recommendation. However, Arnoult had become dissatisfied with religious life.

Around this time two things happened. It is not clear from the historical record the circumstances of how they transpired, or the order in which they happened, but the course of events seems to run as follows:

The first was that, somehow, possibly through benefactors or timber merchants he was acquainted with, Archibald became involved as *one of the principals* in the operation of a large saw-mill in the Bobin district around Dingo Creek north of Wingham in New South Wales.[16] As he had no money himself, I suspect he earned shares in the company or was paid in shares by offering various services to the company. The dividends or pay from his involvement in this business may have been diverted to support the needs of his sister's family. If there was a surplus of money perhaps he might have passed it on to the mission accounts, though there is no record of this.

He did have some experience in timber milling as a youth in Adelong and displayed considerable entrepreneurship formulating a business plan for Meyer concerning the mission's forests on the remote Torio River up in New Britain, which to date had not been fully implemented. He used this early experience to contribute to the operation of a large New South Wales based saw mill operation - the Bulga Sawmill Co. Limited.

This saw-mill was one of the biggest operating in Australia at the time and was funded by a consortium of shareholders which included some of the country's prominent businessmen and businesses like *Anthony Hordern & Sons,* for example. The operation was valued at some £100,000 at one point[17] and operated several mills at various times; one near the hamlet of Bobin just off what is now called the Bulga Road, and another in a level paddock north of Wherrol Flat, just before Carparra Creek. Such was the quantity of timber and availability of markets that there was even talk of constructing a private railway line from Bobin to Wingham to transport timber from the mills.[18]

Whist little is known about Archibald's involvement in the Bulga Timber Mill Company, to be speculative, it would seem his interest was motivated by the intention to help his sister's family who were in desperate need. Just how successful his efforts were is uncertain but their dire situation is never mentioned by Archibald again. They were perhaps living off the dividends of Archibald's shares in the business. In various ways Archibald's help to the family continued through into the following years as we will see.

Moving freshly-cut hardwood logs from forest to mill, and from mill to town or a railway siding, was done by large and heavy steam crawler-tractors, or traction engines, which damaged local roads so much that they needed constant upkeep. For efficiency the crawler-tractors had to take the most direct route to the mill towing their loads. Archibald is recorded constructing a significant road, then known as *Fr Shaw's Road,* some three and a half kilometres long with the assistance of labour from the mill and local landowners. The road included several timber bridges and culverts and made the journey from the timber mill to the main Bulga-Wingham road more direct. The road today is known as Gunyah Road[19] and is located east off Bulga Road near Bobin in New South Wales. Sadly, the history of the road and Archibald's presence in the area is largely unremembered.

Gunyah Road today leads past a property called *Gunyah.* This was the home and also the nickname of 'Gunyah' Green whose real name was George William Green. He was a carpenter and a high-quality furniture maker with an international reputation.[20] Some of his creations survive today in the Wingham district and in Sydney's Powerhouse Museum.[21] The road provided a short-cut from his property to Bobin village. Green set-up one of the mills for the Bulga Sawmill Co. on his own land before handing it over to be run by the company under the management of Archibald's friend, Fernand Arnoult.

The mill was set up just off Back Creek Road east of the Bulga Road and the road made hauling timber from forest to mill easier. The steam tractors used other local roads, Little Back Creek Road and Warrawillah Road to drive the sawn timber to the main road which led into Wingham.

Alfred (Fred) Richards worked as a driver on a traction engine for the Bulga Saw Mill Company as a very young man. He remembers Archibald,

> *... Father Shaw – a priest of massive proportions who also owned a sawmill... He and his brother once borrowed a pair of the good Father's trousers in which they clad themselves – together, one lad in each leg – and walked away only slightly hobbled. Fred hauled logs to the town or the railway siding,*

taking a full day. The creeks by the roadside provided the water for the boiler and wood picked up along the way was used to stoke the fire.[22]

Archibald's relationship with Gunyah Green was significant. Aside from being a carpenter and noted timber worker, Gunyah Green was also a prolific inventor. One of his more enduring inventions was an anti-rattle catch[23] used ubiquitously on railway carriage windows for decades after it was first patented. Green was granted eleven patents which are recorded by IP Australia[24] from 1907. These represent a diverse range of interests. There are claims in other sources of more.[25]

During the period that Archibald built the road going to Green's property, followed by Green setting-up the mill for Archibald's company to use, it is likely that Green may have mentored Archibald in the technicalities of patent registration. Gunyah Green used Wilfred Spruson[26], a patent attorney in Sydney, to register each of his patents and Archibald used the same patent attorney for the registration of his own wireless series of patents formulated later in 1910 and again in 1911.

Gregory Blaxland, grandson of Gunyah Green, recalls,

His brain was always active and he held many patents – his inventions included an automated seed drill, a harvester, constant mesh automotive gearbox, washing machine [and] swivel headlamps for motor cars. A wooden model of his washing machine (hand driven in this case) stood near the backdoor of our home at the end of the Kaiser's war and, as there were five children, it was much in use.[27]

An odd dispute concerning *Fr Shaw's Road* is the reason it remains in the historical record. In 1921, five years after Archibald's death, one uncooperative land-owner, James Brown, was gating-off access to the road and attempting to charge a 'toll' to another settler living further up the road, a Mr Clayton,[28] for travelling through three portions of his land which the road passed. The settler refused to pay and in response Brown burned bridges and destroyed culverts that were on the road making it impassable. There was a court case and a paper trail left which identified the damage occurring on *Fr Shaw's*

Road. Without this incident no record of Archibald's road-building enterprise would have survived.

The details of Archibald's involvement with the Bulga Sawmill Company were not known to his religious superiors. If there was some knowledge, there is no recorded opposition. No obvious financial benefit was passed into the mission accounts from the Bulga business. I can find little historical financial information on the company at all, except that it had rights to some twenty-thousand acres of forest – referred to as *Fr Shaw's 20,000 acres* in one press account.[29] The timber was hardwood, mostly *tallowood*, which was sold to a large market in Newcastle and was ideal for use as railway sleepers. None of this is recorded in MSC correspondence or mentioned in MSC archival material.

Another account of *Fr Shaw's Road* has it operating for some 18 years before 1921.[30] This is unlikely as Archibald was fully involved in the procurate, the dispute with the sea-captain and the resettlement of the New Britain missions at this time. However, a year later, he

Steam tractors operated by the Bulga Saw Mill Co. at Bobin, NSW.   *Credit: Arnoult Family*

Steam tractors were renowned for damaging roads and retrieving a bogged traction engine was no easy task. *Credit: Arnoult Family*

had the time and moreover, because of the dire situation of his sister's family, he had the motivation to make this timber enterprise work.

The second significant event occurring around this time is that Archibald's good friend, Fernand Arnoult, had left the society of the Missionaries of the Sacred Heart and religious life altogether. He was installed as the manager of the Bulga Sawmill Co. Ltd.. This would have been done on Archibald's recommendation and supports the idea that Arnoult was the unnamed man recommended to manage the Torio River saw mills in the business plan he sent to Meyer years before the Baining massacre.[31] Arnoult lived for a while in the nearby hamlet of Bobin whilst working as manager of the mill. In 1914 he married a local Wingham girl, Ruby Thompson, and settled on a farm in nearby Mooral which was a few kilometres away from one of the company mills at Little Back Creek near Bobin. Archibald's influence in the Bulga Saw Mill Company continued for many years.[32]

The friendship between Arnoult and Archibald did not wane

either. Over the years, Fernand Arnoult became associated with many of Archibald's endeavours. He was born in France and began training there as an MSC brother. As an idealistic twenty-three year old he travelled to Australia with the returning Fr Tréand in 1897, who brought out fifteen other missionaries on the same boat including Francis Gsell. They were bound for the mission wilds of New Guinea and New Britain.

From the beginning of 1906 Archibald has returned to the MSCs in Randwick and is working out of the procure in the presbytery adjacent to the church. Records from the period suggest he was still completely distracted from doing his job properly. His loyal and ever-patient supporter of many years, Superior General Meyer, became irritated and penned an abrasive line to Fr Tréand in Randwick when Archibald failed to send timely accounts of the missions to him,

> *[This is] unpardonable on the part of Fr Shaw. Tell him so from me.*[33]

Timber cutters from Bobin Mill, Bulga Sawmill Company, 1912. Fernand Arnoult is seated holding a shotgun.   *Credit: Arnoult Family*

By the middle of 1906 Archibald's mission statements had been brought up to date. In the interim, Fr Linckens, the German provincial, had given supply of the Marshall Islands Mission to a private shipping company, *Justus Scharff* of Sydney.[34] So now Archibald was only responsible for supplying three missions instead of four. Around this time the New Britain saw mill on the Torio River surprisingly started to turn a profit,

> *... New Britain has sent me during this 6 months moneys amounting to £2,688 for sales of timber. They are on the side of prosperity now and I would not be a bit surprised that in 3 years they will have paid off the debt at Hiltrup... I am sure that the saw mills alone could keep the missions in money for the next 10 years...*
>
> *The German Govt. are going to build during this 12 months and have informed the mission that they will need £6,000 worth; they have now already timber cut to the value of £4,000. Fr Linckens laughed at me when I said there was a lot of money in the saw mills. This credit of £2,688 from New Britain will open his eyes. In this money there is a little copra sold also but most of it is timber.[35]*

However, Archibald was not happy. The same old frustrations that developed between procurator and missionaries several years ago were re-surfacing. Accusations of inaccurate accounting were met with documented rebuttals but it was something else that caused Archibald the most pain. He wrote of this in brooding correspondence to the Superior General from his Randwick presbytery,

> *... what is hard for me to support is the New Guinea Mission continually say I am leaving the Congregation. Msgr Navarre himself only the other day told Fr Gsell that he would perhaps not find Fr Shaw at Sydney as he had already been accepted by a bishop in Australia; 3 years ago, when they wanted to get rid of me from the procure they wrote and spread the same report that I was leaving the congregation. This is cruel for me Dear Fr General. I have no desire to be their procurator. While I am so I will act according to*

conscience.

The procurator has as many superiors and critics as there are men passing to the missions. It is one of the most disagreeable positions in the congregation and when a man kills himself with work for them, he does not even get ordinary politeness and justice at their hands...

In conclusion dear Father I say that I will do my work with conscience and if at any time you deem me unfit for the work and relieve me of my charge you may be sure you will give me no offence; you will make me very happy. The work is very easy to me as I had a commercial education before I entered; but I have to deal with men very often who do not know what they are doing or what they want and then they expect me to supply them this.

I also intended to speak of the state of things here too – they are bad – so much so that you would hardly believe me...[36]

For both Archibald and the distant missionaries, it was clearly time for a change. Very soon there would be a new procurator and a new location for the procure. Archibald too would follow a different path and take his priesthood into unchartered territory.

IX

The First Workshop

Archibald first met Joseph Guis as a twenty-four year old postulant on Yule Island in 1894 during the first year of his association with the Missionaries of the Sacred Heart. Guis was only twenty-five years old himself and had just been ordained the year before. His native language was French, having been born in Marseilles on December 13, 1869. He had served three years in the French army and was a lieutenant before leaving to become a missionary priest.[1]

After many years of mission service and suffering from an array of tropical disorders, Guis was appointed Mission Procurator by the General Council in April, 1907.[2] Archibald was appointed his assistant. Archibald welcomed the appointment even though it was a demotion for himself. In accepting the job Guis wrote to Eugène Meyer,

> *I think I can do the work, above all with the very devoted help of Fr Shaw who does his work very conscientiously as far as I can see.*[3]

In reality the job was reasonably shared between them: Guis dealing with the missions and having ultimate responsibility for finances, whilst Archibald, with his English mother-tongue, continued to deal with local purchases, shipping companies and the bank. He sent regular accounts to the Superior General in Europe.

There had been talk for awhile about establishing a separate procure with rooms set aside for recovering sick missionaries; acting as a kind of sanitorium, separate from the Kensington monastery and parish presbyteries. The expense of transporting and keeping sick missionary priests and brothers was significant, approaching two-thirds of the missionary budget,[4] and thus far this expense had been borne by the local MSC communities. This was unfair given their own financial commitments and particularly as the visiting priests were mostly from overseas provinces. A separate procure and convalescent home would relieve the local church of some financial burden and pass the expense of keeping the sick onto the procure itself which was mostly funded by the overseas provinces that looked after the mission territories.

A large two-story Italianate house called *Ascot*, on a fairly extensive block of land at 4 Dutruc Street, Randwick, was purchased for £1,850 by the MSCs early in 1907 and used for just this purpose: firstly as the procure and then as a rest-house for missionaries travelling to or coming down from the missions. Archibald had moved the procure office from Randwick presbytery to Dutruc Street whilst awaiting the arrival of Guis who was on his way down from New Guinea to take charge. The place came to be called *Mission House*. It was big enough to accommodate several visitors at any one time and held a picturesque eastern outlook from the upper-story verandah toward Coogee Beach about a kilometre away.

Archibald wrote to Meyer soon after moving into the new premises and gave updates on the condition of the visiting missionaries. He expresses happiness in his new home and in his new role. He may even hint at some personal melancholy or depression,

> *My Dear old Father General,*
> *... We are living very quietly here...*
> *... As regards myself I am very happy. I'm having my own way; perhaps that accounts for it. However, I get serious sometimes so cheer up Dear Fr General, there is still a bit of hope for me.*
>
> *Write soon and don't write serious letters – I don't like them – I sometimes pray for you, knowing it won't harm you at all...*[5]

Both Procurator Guis and his assistant were still directly accountable to Fr Eugène Meyer, the Superior General in Europe and did not have a local superior to keep an eye on things. Archibald must have felt a great sense of relief at having the burden shared and not having to solely bear criticism from the dissatisfied missionaries which seemed to be an indelible part of the procurator's job.

Whilst the sale of timber from the Torio River mills in New Britain assisted the funding of more ambitious mission activities, the growth of the missions themselves demanded a constant supply of funding which kept up financial pressure on the procure. It remained operating in a constant state of debt. The occasional painting Archibald sold sporadically brought in some money but this was an unreliable and insignificant source.

In his recorded memoirs wireless pioneer Ray Allsop,[6] the son of a racehorse trainer, recalls an unusual development next to the new procure, as a child growing up in Randwick,

> *It was in 1908 when two timber masts first appeared in the land around Ascot in Dutruc Street, Randwick, to support an antenna used by Fr Shaw for an experimental wireless set.*

Archibald's oil portrait of Peter Tréand, c. 1907.
Credit: A. Shaw, Tréand House

Allsop was a curious individual who began his career in wireless as an apprentice at Archibald's factory at Randwick. He acquired his own experimental wireless license at the age of thirteen[7] - but we are getting ahead of ourselves.

Back in May, 1907, Archibald found himself in Bathurst, New South Wales, for the funeral of Archdeacon[8] D. J. D'Arcy. He travelled there with Fr Tréand. The funeral was held at Saints Michael and John Cathedral in the middle of the township.[9] D'Arcy had been a benefactor to many causes, amongst them the Darwin mission run by the Missionaries of the Sacred Heart.

A few years earlier, in February, 1904, the bell tower of the Bathurst Cathedral was the scene of a remarkable wireless demonstration by Joseph Slattery, the Vincentian priest from nearby St Stanislaus' College.[10] It is unlikely that Archibald was not aware of this at the time of the funeral. If he wasn't, he would learn of it when he returned to Bathurst the following year with Fr Tréand to run a month long 'mission' as a kind of *thank you* for Archdeacon D'Arcy's benevolence to the MSC order.[11] In such missions the priests would thank parishioners for donating money, explain what overseas mission life was like, how the missions operated and how their donations were

Joseph Slattery's contribution to x-ray science is commemorated on this 1995 postage stamp, together with Thomas Lyle and Walter Filmer.
Credit: Australia Post

being put to use. Their sermons and presence in the district would probably elicit more donations. Whilst there is no record of a meeting, it is highly likely that Archibald paid a visit to Slattery's laboratory and was inspired by his work.

Slattery made a significant contribution to wireless science during this period.

Joseph Slattery was an Irish Vincentian father who was master of natural science (physics) at St. Stanislaus' College, a boarding school on the edge of Bathurst. In February, 1904, with his students as assistants, he arranged an experiment which successfully demonstrated the transmission and reception of radio waves. This was done first over short distances within the school grounds, and then over longer distances to a receiving station located a little over a kilometre from the school. The school was located on a convenient hill with line-of-sight vision to the tower of the cathedral in the centre of Bathurst where a galena crystal receiver was set up. Wireless messages were sent one-way only and the students receiving the messages communicated their success or failure back to the transmitter at the school by a kind of flag semaphore designed specifically for the experiment. The flag signals were viewed by a spotter at the school looking through a telescope.

Given the success of the demonstration, experiments resumed the following day and, still using line-of-sight semaphore to confirm the received signals, the distance was increased dramatically to about three-thousand eight-hundred metres. The receiver, a kind of early 'crystal set' was connected to a *twenty-two foot pole to act as a support for the aerial wire.*[12] This time the arrangement was set up in the yard of Fr Flanagan's presbytery on a hill in Boyd Street, in the neighbouring village of Kelso, on the other side of Bathurst, but still in line-of-site to St Stanislaus' College. In 1904 this became, for a short time, an Australian distance record for wireless signals received over land.

Slattery is also credited with producing the first diagnostic x-ray in Australia[13] and in July, 1896, the press were reporting on a surgical operation which saved the hand of a boy, Eric Thompson, who had accidently discharged a shotgun through it. Instead of removing the entire hand as was initially proposed, the doctor, aware of Slattery's experiments, sent the boy to the school for an x-ray where the position of each lead pellet was able to be identified and individually removed.

It is no coincidence Slattery experimented with both x-rays and wireless. The principle component for both systems relied on the same device - an *induction coil* - the machine which stepped-up low voltages to very high voltages. This created an electric spark if the electrodes were brought close enough together or would give a sharp jolt to anyone touching them. Slattery had a head-start on many of the experimenters tinkering with induction coils in x-ray and wireless. He was taught by the man who invented it.

Slattery studied in Ireland at the large Maynooth Seminary College under Professor Nicholas Callan, also a priest. Callan had invented the iron-core induction coil in 1836, some improved wet-cells for supplying the primary current and an electromagnetic crane. He had also developed a form of galvanisation to prevent iron from rusting.[14]

A quiet man with a stern demeanour, Slattery was generous with his time and gave public lectures to the Bathurst Scientific Society was demonstrating x-rays as early as 1896.[15] He demonstrated wireless from 1900[16] at the Bathurst Technical College Union; a building which still stands in William Street.

Slattery imported most of his large equipment – his thirteen-inch induction coil and a high vacuum mercury pump – from London. Like many experimenters of the era, he had to make other components himself: the large glass batteries of liquid cells to power the coil, coherers, Geissler tubes and x-ray tubes. He successfully improved x-ray tube design - an effort that was acknowledged by Röntgen himself, who discovered x-rays by accident in November, 1895. Röntgen was subsequently awarded the Nobel Prize in Physics for doing so.

Archibald would have been inspired by a demonstration of Slattery's progress in x-ray generation and wireless production. This may have been the reason wireless aerials were seen by Allsop near *Ascot* as early as 1908. Whilst the science behind both x-ray and wireless was developing, discoveries and improvements were concurrently being made by amateurs and enthusiasts; almost anyone who had some technical competence and access to the right equipment or who could turn their hand to building the apparatus.

One such experimenter was Edward Hope Kirkby. Kirkby was a watchmaker and jeweller by trade and became adept at developing and manufacturing electro-mechanical apparatus to serve specific purposes. He developed timing systems for the Victorian Football Association, for Victoria Park Racecourse in Sydney and the Australian Jockey Club at Randwick. Aside from watchmaking, he became an instrument maker or, in the parlance of the day, a *manufacturing electrician.*

Between 1889 and 1913 he had registered several patents[17] for inventions and improvements over the years relating to mechanical automatic fire-alarm systems and pole-mounted street fire alarms which were in use before the telephone became ubiquitous. These instruments allowed people to directly notify the fire brigade of a fire by dedicated telephone lines. Most of Kirkby's patents show clock like-mechanisms interfaced with relays and switching circuits. Several public buildings in Melbourne[18] were installed with fire-alarm mechanisms made by Kirkby. On moving to Sydney, he continued to manufacture electro-medical apparatus like x-ray machines and Finsen lights - an ultraviolet light used in the treatment of the skin disorder *lupus.*[19]

Edward Hope Kirkby, c. 1910, founded the first factory on the Wireless Works site in a timber workshop used to manufacture his patented fire alarms. He partnered with Archibald to begin the first incarnation of the Maritime Wireless Works and offered manufacturing capability and construction expertise to the fledgling company.

Credit: Brian Kirkby

Aside from his work on fire alarm systems, Kirkby also turned his hand to making wireless equipment and gave entertaining public demonstrations of x-rays and wireless, like Slattery and several others around this time. However, neither he nor Slattery took out any wireless patents.

The existence of radio waves was first proposed by James Clerk Maxwell as early as 1865. He was a mathematician working on problems associated with electro-magnetism and light. He came to see light and similar forms of radiation as having two constituents: an electric component and a magnetic component. Whilst he deduced that wireless waves existed, he could not find a way to produce or detect them. Heinrich Hertz did that later in 1887. Progress quickly followed. The early practical development for applications of invisible wireless waves involved many people: Edouard Branly, Alexander Popov, Karl Braun, Guglielmo Marconi, and a litany of others.

Scientific papers published in Europe and America found their way to Australia and announced the most recent discoveries to an eager academic and populist readership. People in Australia like Professors Richard Threlfall at the University of Sydney, Thomas Lyle in Melbourne and William Bragg at the University of Adelaide, read the journals and repeated the experiments by either making their own equipment or importing apparatus that could not be made cost-effectively. The principles of electro-magnetism and wireless were soon part of the curriculum in technical colleges everywhere. It was at one of these colleges, the Bendigo School of Mines, that Edward Kirkby picked up a prize for a course in *Electricity and Magnetism* as a twenty-seven-year-old student.[20]

There is no surviving record explaining how Archibald became educated in wireless. He received technical training as telegrapher in the post-office, he mixed with people who had expertise and competence in wireless and, at the time of his death he owned several books on the subject. Many experts at the time were self-educated, like the young Ray Allsop who obtained his experimental wireless license as a boy.[21] Even though wireless could be easily demonstrated, it remained little understood – Marconi himself admitted this – and, by experiment, it was continually being improved. Experience seemed to be the best teacher. Archibald states,

> *I had a knowledge of electricity and engineering before I entered the Order... and [was] determined to use my knowledge in the engineering line to create money for the Procure.*[22]

Joseph Guis explains Archibald's interest in wireless in May of 1911,

> *Like so many others, Branly and Marconi's invention interested him but, better than many others, he became interested in it in a practical way and, having fully understood the theory, became master of the practice and has already perfected existing systems in several ways.*[23]

Whilst spark-gap wireless technology was new, it was not complicated in theory; certainly nothing like our modern iterations of radio. Today, radio sets use hundreds, sometimes thousands of components mounted electrically on special insulated boards. In the 1900s, spark-gap wireless used around ten components and sometimes less. However, even with the right equipment, making the technology of a primitive transmitter and crystal receiver work efficiently in a practical sense required a lot of experiment, a lot of fiddling around, a good deal of patience and a lot of trial and error.

It was probably at Randwick racecourse[24] where the paths of Kirkby and Archibald first crossed. They became friends and an arrangement developed that was to benefit them both. Archibald writes,

> *I was working on wireless and had no tools to make the instruments I needed. I went to an electrical engineer, an old friend of mine, a Mr Kirkby, who had a shop with his three sons. They were earning their living making electrical instruments. He too was working on wireless but had no success or a place to put up an 'aerial'.*
>
> *He said he'd gladly make up the instruments I needed if I would help him and let him work with me at night. I designed the instruments and he made them up.*[25]

THE FIRST WORKSHOP

This account is corroborated by Joseph Guis, Archibald's immediate superior, writing to Fr. Field, a visiting priest from the MSC General House in Rome,

> *After the first tests, Fr. Shaw needed to build the necessary instruments for new experiments and new improvements. But he didn't have a penny, and not a lot of experience as a construction engineer. So, he ended up with a young engineer-electrician, who out of love for science and friendship for Shaw, gives him 3 or 4 hours of his time every evening. Together they experiment, and they succeed beyond their expectations.*[26]

In an unusual arrangement, Kirkby and his sons are living at *Ascot* with Archibald during this period on the understanding that their rooms may be required for use by convalescing missionaries at any time. It was the land surrounding *Ascot*, previously sitting idle, which was turned into an income earning asset for the MSCs through the friendship that developed between Archibald and Kirkby. Archibald continues the story,

> *In no time at all success crowned our efforts. Kirkby then asked my consent to make up these instruments for public use and, if he sold any, I would get half the profit. He also asked us to rent him a corner of our land and he would put up a shop and pay rent. Fr Superior [Guis], and myself, finding that the shop was a simple affair and costing only £61 to build, decided to build it ourselves and get £2 a week rent for same.*[27]

Guis clarifies the reason the procure decided to construct the workshop,

> *We said no to Mr Kirkby who wanted to build a workshop on this land, because the fact of building a house would have given him almost a right to the land itself, something to which I could not consent. The procure itself has therefore taken charge of the erection of the workshop, which thus remains the complete and absolute property of the procure*

The first workshop constructed by the MSC Procurate behind *Ascot* was rented to Edward Kirkby shown far left. Various clocks and fire alarm cases can be seen on the rear bench and wall. *Credit: MSC Archive*

Charles Kirkby, Edward's son, assembling wireless equipment at the rear bench in front of stacked fire alarm cases. *Credit: MSC Archive*

or the congregation. We just rent the land and building to Mr Kirkby.[28]

In addressing any criticism that Kirkby could be seen to be profiteering from the manufacture of Archibald's instruments, he offered to share half the profits of his own inventions with Archibald,

> *But even in this case one might have found it exorbitant that Kirkby profited half. To make it fair, Kirkby more generously still, gives to the procure half of the real and tangible profits of his own inventions and labour. It is a pure gift he gives us...*[29]

Archibald's wireless plans are two-fold. He foresaw the sale of instruments designed by himself and manufactured by Kirkby under their profit-sharing arrangement would significantly reduce the debt of the procure. He also envisioned that wireless telegraphy would soon be employed as a means of instant contact with missionaries in the distant territories; something that was previously impossible. Guis explains,

> *... both Fr Shaw and I have been attracted to the idea of providing our missions with wireless telegraphy. In the beginning it was just a confused idea; but this idea quickly took shape and form as improvements were made. When we saw that the thing was working better than we could have dared hope, we came to the conclusions that this telegraphy could at the same time be a source of income for the Congregation in general, and more particularly used for the Procurate and the Missions.*[30]

It was the partnership with Kirkby that gave Archibald his initial success in wireless. Archibald then became determined to explore the potential wireless had to revolutionise the operations of the missions and to use it to relieve the MSC procure of financial shortfalls.

X

Company Business

The procure's arrangement with Edward Kirkby, his sons and their employees was mutually beneficial. By June, 1909, Kirkby was operating out of premises at 222 Clarence Street, Sydney.[1] He had dissolved his business partnership with Wormald Brothers in Melbourne at the end of August that year.[2] Sometime between then and before the April of 1910,[3] Kirkby left Clarence Street and had moved into *Ascot* at 4 Dutruc Street, Randwick. He now had a place to manufacture his fire alarms whilst the procure received an income of £2 rent per week from his company workshop. In addition Kirkby and Shaw worked together on wireless and split the profits on the sale of devices they manufactured.

Archibald explains the rental arrangement of the workshop to his superiors,

> *The procure has signed no lease for same whatever, and the men were informed that at any day... we might need the land and they are quite willing to rent the shop under these conditions but considering the way we are situated for funds it is a blessing for the procure to have this £104 a year extra.*[4]

The idea of a Catholic priest involved in a business enterprise with the purpose of making a profit did not sit well with traditionalists in the MSC order and the wider Catholic community, yet others readily accepted the idea. Joseph Guis argued a compelling case, particularly when the religious vow of poverty came into the discussion. He maintained that if it was admissible for the congregation to take on debt to run the mission procure, then it should be equally valid for them to accept a means to remove debt which Archibald's business venture promised,

> ... *Kirkby is offering him (Archibald) a share of what the instruments will bring in. We have accepted this from the outset. It was a matter of taking or leaving; either from the instruments or from the profits... Kirkby agrees to carry all the risks; it was very generous on his part, seeing that Shaw, without working (except by using his brain), without any pain, without risks, will receive his share whilst Kirkby runs all the risks... To make it more just, Kirkby most generously gave to the procure that portion of the real and tangible profits he has made... That's a straight-out gift he has made to us. Since when have we refused gifts?...*[5]

Archibald was aware that the unusual arrangement could bring criticism. He pre-emptively sought permission from the MSC Superior General in Rome and Cardinal Moran in Sydney who both gave their support for his venture,

> *I am aware that some of the fathers do not like me working [on] wireless for fear it might bring trouble through the Cardinal disapproving of it. I thought it my duty to see the Cardinal on that point telling him everything and that perhaps it might bring in a little money. He was delighted and gave me his blessing... He also hoped that I would make it a life study as he wished all his priests to be leaders in science and to help in every way the working classes.*[6]

With Guis' permission, being the superior of the procure, Edward Kirkby and the men in his employ together with Archibald and some others, formalised their arrangement and registered a business. They called it the *Maritime Wireless Telegraph Company Limited.*[7] The business operated more widely than the name suggested. It was a broad-range electrical manufacturing business, albeit on a relatively small scale. At the time of its inception Kirkby was still mostly making

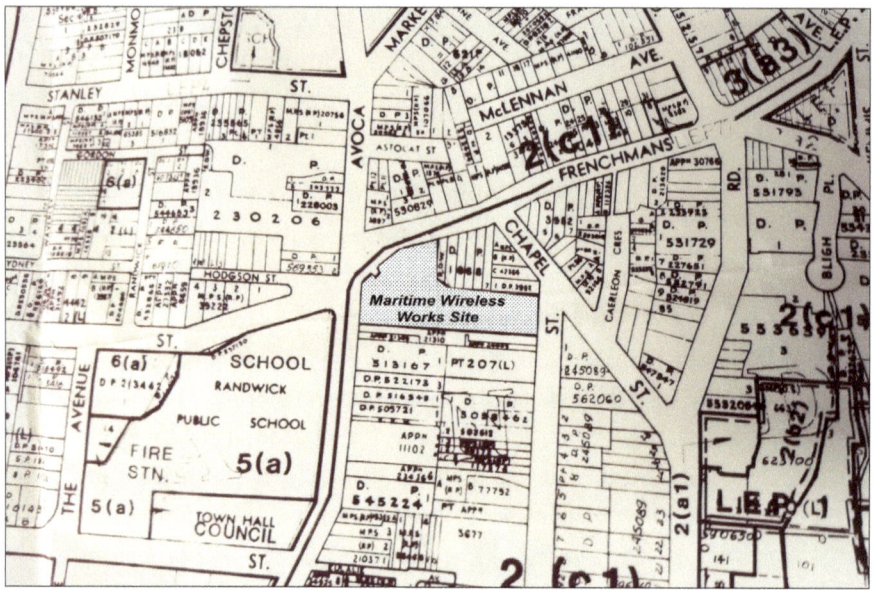

Location and extent of Maritime Wireless in Randwick, NSW, from 1912.

fire alarms and x-ray equipment under the new company name and did so until at least the end of November, 1910.[8]

The company registration took place on November 4, 1910, with a capital of £5,000 in £1 shares. The principals held one share each. The signatories were listed as: A. J. Shaw, E. H. Kirkby, M. A. Mulrony, C. Kirkby, G. T. Stowe, F. W. Marks and G. Kirkby. The directors were listed as: A. J. Shaw; F. W. Marks; E. H. Kirkby, G. T. Stowe and M. A. Mulrony.[9]

About a month before the founding of the Maritime Wireless Telegraph Company, Archibald registered two provisional patents in an attempt to increase the value of the company by creating some 'intellectual property'. Patent 19394, *Mineral Detectors for Space Telegraph Receivers* and patent 19395, *Spark Gap Apparatus for Space Telegraph Transmitters* were published in the Melbourne Herald, October 4, 1910.[10] The former patent may have been inspired by some work conducted by a co-worker, Reg Wilkinson.

A lot was going on locally with wireless in 1910. Edward Kirkby had an association with two early wireless pioneers Walter Hannam and Reg Wilkinson. On Easter Monday, March 28, 1910, together with Lieutenant George Taylor of the Army Intelligence Corps,[11] they demonstrated the advantages of using wireless in a military context during army exercises held on a military range at Heathcote. Two-way wireless contact was established from a tent located near Heathcote Railway Station to a second station set-up in a rocky cave, known as *Spion Kop,* about two and a half kilometres to the south-west.[12] The event is memorialised today on a plaque in Veno Reserve not far from Heathcote station.[13]

Earlier, in March of 1910, George Taylor established the *Institute of Wireless Telegraphy* at the Australia Hotel, 117 Pitt Street, Martin Place in Sydney.[14] The disappearance of a ship called the *Waratah* in 1909 somewhere off the coast of South Africa resulted in the tragic loss of six-hundred lives. The ship had not been not fitted with wireless. This tragedy is cited as the principal impetus for the group's formation.[15] Though the loss of ships and lives was, unfortunately, a relatively common reality around this time, for the first time wireless offered the possibility saving lives during incidents at sea. Taylor was also a publisher of several weekly journals.[16]

Very soon after the Institute of Wireless Telegraphy became the *Wireless Institute of Australia* and served to promote wireless education amongst its membership, and to protect the interests of wireless experimenters and amateur operators throughout the Commonwealth. The organisation continues to operate today and is recognised as the oldest association of wireless operators and experimenters in the world. Walter Hannam became its first secretary and Wilfred Spruson, the patent attorney who was close to Cardinal Moran, was its first treasurer. Spruson, who had earlier registered all of Gunyah Green's patents – Archibald's associate in the Bulga Saw Mill business – was later to register Archibald Shaw's three subsequent wireless patents and several patents from other inventors that originated from the Maritime Wireless factory behind *Ascot* in Randwick.

Addressing the inaugural meeting of the Institute of Wireless Telegraphy, George Taylor proclaimed,

> *...investigations of wireless were today on the verge of an arena of wonder. They were like explorers of a strange new*

country, where every step was a discovery. But as success could only be achieved after many failures, there was need of mutual cooperation between investigators to avoid making the same mistakes, and to climb together when any successful discovery would be achieved. The time was approaching when this age would not again have the stigma of a Waratah going out into the unknown without a wireless connecting link.[17]

Taylor promoted a collegial approach to invention and development, something that was innately nationalistic, during a period when Australia's two largest wireless distributors were promoting foreign manufactured plant from the Marconi and Telefunken companies. It was this collegial approach that became the hallmark of Maritime Wireless's endeavours in Randwick as well.

That same month, Archibald still conducted his priestly duties but spent an increasing amount of time developing the business. He had given the last rites to William Johnstone[18] who was a resident[19] at the *Little Sisters' of the Poor*, two blocks north of the mission procure where he would frequently say mass. The Little Sisters operated a home which cared for the elderly and infirm. Johnstone had lived to one-hundred and six years of age and had an unfailing memory. In his youth he served as a naval lad and for five years was the personal servant to Napoleon Bonaparte before making his way to Australia on a whaling ship.[20]

Kirkby's associate, Walter Hannam, went on to travel with the geologist, Douglas Mawson, on the famous Antarctic Expedition of 1911[21] as his chief wireless officer. Reg Wilkinson was to work for a short period with Archibald on wireless at Randwick, as his 'assistant' in some accounts and as his 'partner' in other accounts. It was Reg Wilkinson who probably pioneered the geophysical application of wireless which detected mineral ores using a kind of resonance. Wilkinson gained his experience in wireless telegraphy from the United States.[22]

A newspaper article of the period claims, that around May of 1910, Wilkinson accidentally discovered that ore traces in the earth

Walter Hannam operating the Telefunken Wireless from Cape Denison, Antarctica, 1912.
Credit: Frank Hurley, Mitchell Library

could be detected by wireless. The methodology used for Wilkinson's mineral ore detector is vague and there does not seem to be much scientific follow-up at the time but a similar technique is used today in modern mining and geological mapping applications.

The same article identifies Wilkinson as an *electrical engineer* and Archibald, perhaps self-deprecatingly, as *'a bit of an engineer'*.[23] The account maintains that the wireless installation at Randwick was *'the work of Fr Shaw and Mr Wilkinson'* who, together, *'make their own machinery and instruments'*.[24] Whilst they may have designed the instruments, it is more likely that manufacture of them was deferred to Archibald's original partner, Edward Kirkby.

The ordinary layman showed an immense interest in science during this period. This was driven by some unusual and widely seen natural phenomena during 1910. At night *Halley's Comet* was brilliantly lighting up the night sky. In fact, by mid-May, around the time of Wilkinson's discovery, the earth was passing through the tail of the comet and it was at its brightest. Earlier in the year a separate comet, visible during the day, and duly called the *Daylight Comet*, instilled wonder, fear and an intense curiosity about the natural world and for science in general.[25]

By the middle of 1910 the Maritime Wireless Works, operating from a shed in the backyard of *Ascot,* had developed a wireless capable of reliable communication with ships at sea over a distance of two-hundred and eighty-five miles. The station was in regular contact with the US Navy-trained wireless operator of the *Makura,* Marion Alvin Mulrony, who became one of the original shareholders and directors of Maritime Wireless. As a young man with significant electrical experience, Mulrony worked for several years at the Wireless Works as manager. He had been an electrician in the United States Navy and came to Australia with prior patent registrations and a letter of introduction from famed scientist and engineer Alexander Graham Bell, inventor of the telephone.[26]

The *Makura* utilised American designed Armstrong wireless equipment manufactured by the United Wire Service Company. It could communicate over distances up to one-thousand nine-hundred miles. Archibald's Maritime Wireless Telegraph Company was still perfecting the science and working to improve the range of their equipment. Perhaps storm damage to the original wooden aerial masts at Randwick was the reason for the limited range of the station in July, 1910.[27] Archibald explains,

> *I may state that the timber merchants gave me timber to build my masts and as I was already doing good work in wireless and on that account got a certain amount of publicity so that when a storm came and blew down the masts people came and offered me money - Catholic and Protestant – to put up a steel tower. Fr Superior permitted me to accept same and I received a sum of £43. The men of the shop put some other money to help and myself and the men built the steel tower. It cost in all £91 - the balance was paid by the men in the shop.[28]*

Safety at sea was the most critical application for wireless. Both military ships and merchant vessels promised a large untapped market. Historically, once a ship left port it was at the mercy of the elements and a few never saw land again. No wonder sailors had a reputation for being superstitious. If a ship without wireless came into trouble the crew would shoot a flare into the air which might attract the attention of a nearby vessel or, if the passengers or crew survived a shipwreck they might put a message in a bottle with little more than a slim hope of rescue. These were remarkably inefficient and unsatisfactory safety-nets. Wireless provided a new era of security and protection for ocean travel.

When Maritime Wireless commissioned a large generator to power the machines in the workshops at the Randwick site, enquiries came from the municipal council to see if the company was also able to supply the power needed for electric street lighting in the area. The idea of installing electric lights at the MSC's Douglas Park monastery powered by generators made at Maritime Wireless was also entertained,[29] as was the manufacture of a completely Australian-built aeroplane to claim a £10,000 prize offered by the government.[30] But the future of the company envisioned by Archibald and the founders, was in the provision of engineering services and, separately, the manufacture of wireless.

Wireless was frontier territory. Most experimenters were struggling to make existing systems more efficient. Directional or beam antennae, capable of concentrating radio energy in a particular direction, had not yet been developed. Tuning or the ability to filter wireless energy into a narrow range of frequencies was a science in its infancy and most transmitters wasted much of their energy by operating over a very wide bandwidth. This caused serious interference problems and made it very difficult for an operator to hear one particular station over another. Tuning offered the promise of directing energy into a specific part of the wireless spectrum and, at the same time, increasing the range of the transmitted signal.

However, in 1910, with only rudimentary tuning, signals got through to a distant receiver based largely on the power that was made available to the transmitter's spark coil. The more power that was available, the more range a station had – and, of course, the more interference a station would generate. Wireless operators had great trouble discriminating one station from another amidst all the noise.

The Wireless Works steel tower and factory buildings at their zenith c. 1913. The stone transmitting room is shown, right, behind Ascot just out of view. *Credit: Low Family*

Some experimenters attempted to overcome these inefficiencies by making the dots and dashes of the transmitted Morse signal sound like a musical note. This system used a rapidly *spinning* spark-gap which was able to be better heard by the operator of a distant receiver. The Americans had devised the following operating strategy to help reduce interference: the first half of every hour was given over to naval communications only. The second half of each hour was used for commercial wireless traffic (wireless telegrams) and for experimenters; and so the pattern would repeat. The Australian Government took a different approach: they regulated wireless by licensing experimenters and by imposing limits on the amount of power they could use.

It was the naval and merchant maritime market that had the greatest need for wireless and Archibald's company was fervently trying to tap into it; hence the use of the word *Maritime* in the Company's name. However, wireless for the missions remained paramount in Archibald's mind as well. The *Molong Argus* reports that contact from Sydney to the missions was occurring by June, 1910,

> *An illustration of the use of wireless has come under notice in Sydney. Father Shaw, of the Sacred Heart Order, Randwick, has established a station to communicate with the Missions in New Guinea and other Islands of the Pacific, and has invented a transmitter which enables him to send messages two-thousand miles. An installation is being made in the islands with a view of transacting the business of the Missions in Sydney...*[31]

The wooden masts supporting the wire aerials that were blown down in the storm were re-erected temporarily whilst the imposing new steel mast was being built. This was designed by John Paton, an engineer from the firm that supplied the steel, *Holdsworth, MacPherson and Company*. The tower was assembled by the factory hands which then totalled about twenty-seven men and boys.[32] It took about three months to construct and was completed in February, 1911, making it the tallest aerial structure in Australia at the time and likely the tallest man-made structure in the southern hemisphere. It was located directly behind *Ascot* in Dutruc Street, the highest point in Randwick.

The impressive tower was fifty-two metres tall and a mast of twenty-four metres was perched atop, making the whole structure some seventy-six metres tall.[33] The steeple of the nearby Randwick church was only thirty-three metres high and the tallest building in Sydney, the newly built *Culwulla Chambers,* which still stands today on the corner of King and Castlereagh Streets, was only fifty metres high.[34] The antenna tower symbolised an optimistic future for wireless and for the Maritime Wireless Telegraph Company in particular.

An observation deck was reached after a twenty-five minute climb up a series of eight metal ladders which were permanently attached to the tower. The platform was built close to the top providing impressive views in all directions. The structure could be seen by ships miles from the shore. Nearly one kilometre of wire was used in the aerial itself. This was attached to the upper part of tower and formed form two round cages which ran down to the new wooden masts located at the east and west of the tower. Each wooden mast was about forty-six metres tall.

The imposing tower, antenna and associated infrastructure made the Maritime Wireless Telegraph Company the best equipped workshop of its type, housing the most powerful wireless station in Australasia. More workshops were constructed and fitted-out with lathes, enlarged work areas, wire winding machines, metal presses and screw-making machines. A powerhouse was installed to generate electricity from a suction-gas generator. There was also an accumulator-room which housed batteries powerful enough to run the equipment and transmitter throughout the night if necessary.

Around this time, Fernand Arnoult, the young missionary brother who arrived in Australia decades before with Fr Tréand and who was Archibald's friend in the seminary and throughout their missionary adventures in New Guinea, also worked at Wireless Works briefly, if only to assist his friend. He may have helped with the tower assembly or used his engineering brain in the construction of the larger workshops. The *Wingham Chronical and Manning River Observer* reports,

> *Mr Arnoult took a deep interest in wireless telegraphy, and was associated with ... Rev. Father Shaw, with long distance wireless messages. Mr Arnoult assisted in erecting the experimental station at Randwick...*[35]

Subsequently a foundry was added to the Randwick site, together with carpentry workshops and metal-stamping machines. It appears that Edward Kirkby continued to operate his business under the banner of the Maritime Wireless Telegraph Company yet somewhat independently.[36] He continued to manufacture his *thermostat system of fire alarms* onsite using the available plant and machines. The new transmitting tower with its increased generating capacity resulted in a wireless station now having an effective range of about two thousand miles.[37] The landmark site came to be known colloquially as the *Randwick Wireless Station* or more simply, the *Wireless Works*.

The Wireless Works offered the opportunity for apprentice-aged boys to learn various metal, electrical and carpentry trades and it gained a reputation as an engineering trade school. Ray Allsop, manufacturer of the *Racophone* cinema amplifier and an early radio pioneer, was given his start by Archibald at the Wireless Works, as were other wireless pioneers such as Fred Paton who also completed his apprenticeship there.[38] Paton later went into business producing *Palec* branded electrical test instruments. Lance Duly and Wally Hansford met each other doing their time at Maritime Wireless before starting *Duly and Hansford*. They ran this business successfully for forty-eight years producing automotive valves, axles and bearings until it was sold to *TRW Automotive* in 1968.[39] Archibald writes to Superior General Meyer,

> *The company is looked upon by the Archbishop and priests of the Diocese as a Catholic Engineering College where the young men can be taught the sciences on their leaving [school].*[40]

Archibald was forever enthusiastic about the potential of the Wireless Works. He was unceasingly positive and this positivity rubbed off on his associates. His correspondence of the period shows he found it difficult to see the downside in almost *any* undertaking. In some ways he was like a *Pied Piper* – always looking forward toward the next 'big-thing' and manifesting the charisma to inspire his associates to follow along and do the same and, importantly, for his investors to part with their money and support his plans.

The next-big thing was coming fast. It was the establishment of a government-initiated network of nineteen wireless stations that were to be spaced around the perimeter of Australia. This was to be Australia's first Coastal Wireless Service. The stations would facilitate ship to shore communication for naval and merchant wireless traffic, and also provide a reliable means of linking Australia to the rest of the world. The wireless service offered an alternative to the congested submarine cables that had been carrying Morse signals from Australia to foreign lands since 1872.[41]

Whichever company won the Coastal Wireless contracts from the Australian Government would do exceedingly well financially. Archibald saw profit from this venture as another way to reduce mission debt and provide continuing funding for mission activities. However, he may have underestimated the initial investment required to make it happen. He was determined to submit the successful tender, largely on the basis that his operation was wholly Australian-owned and operated, unlike his competition. He was helped along by the election of Andrew Fisher's Labor Government which favoured government contracts being drawn up with Australian manufacturers.

Sometime after March, 1911,[42] in the months following the formation of the Maritime Wireless Telegraph Company, Edward Kirkby and his sons parted ways with Archibald. By 1912 Kirkby had set-up an independent business which was run from various locations in the city. He continued with the sale of his fire alarms and associated systems. In June, 1912, Kirkby had won a large tender to install automatic fire alarms in the new Sydney Parcels Office,[43] amongst other contracts. He may have still been using some of the engineering facilities at Randwick to continue with his manufacture. Kirkby's business continued to operate until his premature death in 1913 but his association with the Wireless Works at Randwick did not extend beyond 1911.

The Wireless Works won the contracts for the remaining Coastal Wireless Stations after the construction of the first two stations had been completed by the foreign interests of the German Telefunken company. The *Telefunken* company is still in business today and operates under the same name which literally means *using a spark to instantly travel.* To fulfil the contracts for the remaining new coastal stations the Wireless Works needed more men and machines to make the plant and provide the labour for their installation in remote locations all around Australia. During this expansion phase it is likely that the entire space of the Randwick site beind *Ascot*, was needed. Archibald had made clear the arrangement about Kirkby's workshop,

> *The men were informed that at any day whatever, we might need the land and they are quite willing to rent the shop under these conditions...* [44]

Perhaps that day had arrived.

Brian Kirkby, great-grandson of Edward Kirkby, suggests an alternate explanation.[45] At this time Edward's wife was quite sick and, having recently moved from Melbourne to Sydney, she may have required a period of care from her husband in the time before he set-up as E. H. Kirkby in Sydney. Perhaps because of these personal circumstances he was simply unable to keep his business at the Randwick site operating. Or, he may have simply been making a decent living from his fire alarms and thought that an ongoing association with an even bigger Wireless Works was inappropriate for the direction of his own business.

In the following months, the Wireless Works underwent an intense period of recapitalisation and growth.

XI

An Extraordinary Year

The year of 1911 was the busiest year in Archibald Shaw's life. As the Wireless Works entered a period of intense activity and growth, Fred W. Marks was appointed managing director[1]. Archibald acted as chairman for the small factory and, with his natural creative and entrepreneurial flair, sought out various opportunities to promote the activities of the works to obtain more production contracts.

Safety at sea remained a pressing concern for the government and political tensions in Europe, which eventually lead to the outbreak of World War I, gave Australian leaders good reason to consider improvements to the local defence position. By 1909 the government committed funding toward the first two coastal wireless stations operating under the Wireless Telegraphy Act (1905). One was located in Fremantle, Western Australia, and the other was established at Pennant Hills near Sydney, New South Wales. The Deakin Government had previously approved the installation of German Telefunken wireless sets in both stations and they were supplied by the *Australasian Wireless Company*, which, despite the name, was effectively a front-company for German interests.[2] The musicality of the transmitted signal and a cost significantly lower than their competitors were the reasons the Telefunken system was favoured. These two stations alone were woefully inadequate in providing a proper service for shipping around the vast Australian coastline.

Besides Telefunken, the other significant wireless manufacturer was the English Marconi Company. The two had been fighting patent disputes between themselves through the courts and were shocked when Archibald's relatively unknown Maritime Wireless Company was awarded the contracts by the new Labor Government for the remaining seventeen stations of the Commonwealth Wireless Service.

In these contracts Maritime Wireless was under instructions to produce wireless sets based not on Archibald's design but on a patent created by an Australian-born wireless engineer, John Graeme Balsillie, who had been recalled from England as the Australian Government's 'wireless expert'. Archibald and his engineers worked closely with Balsillie at Randwick. It was the Australian ownership and manufacturing capability of Archibald's factory, rather than any intellectual property or inventions held by Maritime Wireless itself, that sealed the deal for the award of the large government Coastal Wireless Service contracts.

Balsillie had previously invented a wireless system used by the *British Radio-Telegraph and Telephone Company* over which he was fighting Marconi in a patent dispute. Fortunately for Archibald, any potential patent dispute between Marconi and the Maritime Wireless Telegraph Company was academic because the Australian Government agreed to indemnify the Wireless Works and cover the cost of any Marconi patent challenge, win or lose, against the Balsillie system that Archibald was manufacturing at Randwick,

> *One can imagine the wrath of the great Marconi Co, at being turned down in favour of an unknown Australian inventor. They immediately brought an action against the Commonwealth in the High Court for infringement of the patent rights...*[3]

Despite this challenge being unsuccessful, the Marconi Company still managed to extract a pay-out from the government.[4] Sometime later when the patent disputes between the litigious Marconi and the Australian Wireless Company were resolved, both companies joined forces to form the powerful *Amalgamated Wireless Company of Australasia*, known since 1913 as AWA. Together they became a formidable force and actively competed against Archibald's Maritime Wireless,

All along they had hated and feared these works, and the opportunity to strike a blow at them came with the coming into office of the First National War Government...[5]

To the north of Australia, an unusual drama of a completely different kind was unfolding.

In December 1910, Miles Staniforth Smith, the Deputy Administrator of the Territory of Papua New Guinea, embarked on a three-week inland expedition over the rugged and mountainous ranges of the interior, exploring, mapping, and looking for mining and agricultural opportunities. His party started out from Goaribari Island, nearly three-hundred kilometres north west of the MSC mission on Yule Island and headed up the Kikori River. It consisted of a large group of seventy-five men: five whites, twenty armed native police and fifty native carriers. They carried enough supplies for three weeks.

Staniforth Smith's intention was to travel by boat as far up the Kikori as was possible, then track by land north to Mt Murray and follow the mountain ridges in a westerly direction, then return to Goaribari via a tributary of the Fly River. The inhospitable country and inability to see beyond the jungle to take proper bearings; the lack of edible food and fresh water; the loss of food, tents and navigation instruments in rafting accidents; the stress of travelling down rapids for hundreds of miles on flimsily-bound timbers, all combined to make for an ill-fated expedition. The three-week undertaking became fifteen. Throughout the course of the expedition eleven members died, mostly through rafting disasters.

A swashbuckling account of the expedition is retold by Staniforth Smith himself in a lecture made the following year in London to the Royal Geographic Society where he was fêted as an explorer. His 1912 report makes compelling reading.[6] A rescue attempt was mounted and Archibald, not one to waste a crisis, was in an ideal position to take advantage of the situation. He had an intimate knowledge of the conditions in New Guinea from his missionary days and saw the serendipitous timing of the disaster as a means to demonstrate to an international audience the contribution that wireless produced in *his* factory would make in coordinating the rescue mission and bringing the survivors back to civilisation.

Before the Staniforth Smith incident Archibald was already preparing to travel to Thursday Island and then onto Port Moresby to construct two government contracted wireless stations in the north. He had previously won the contract from these competitors: the *Anglo-German Wireless Syndicate Ltd*, *Australasian Wireless Ltd*, *Marconi's Wireless Telegraph Company* and the *Société Française Radio-Électrique.*[7]

And so the adventure began.

♦ ♦ ♦

In an already busy year, a relatively uneventful trip to deliver and install wireless plant in the far-north became a daring rescue mission into a dark land of cannibals and head-hunters. It was led by Archibald, accompanied by volunteer-staff from the Wireless Works, which set out on the Burns Philp owned *Mataram* from Circular Quay on Friday, February 24, 1911. Miles Staniforth Smith was also personally known to Archibald.[8] They first met when Archibald worked on the Yule Island mission.

Archibald gave an impromptu speech at the Wireless Works to recruit five members of his operating staff for the rescue mission. The event is recorded in the *Daily Telegraph*,

> *Then Father Shaw, who is a born preacher, turned loose the powers of his oratory. He told them how the Administrator of New Guinea and... other white men were lost in the wilds of New Guinea...*[9]

Archibald's speech is reported seriously enough by the journalist but it could not have been better scripted. It is easy to see him playing with the press. The overly dramatic account made to the young impressionable wireless operators is clearly for the benefit of the newspaper's readership. Nevertheless, it provides a glimpse into his capacity to inspire and create something positive out of a challenging and potentially dangerous situation,

Some of the operators and fitters around the base of the steel antenna tower at Maritime Wireless in a press photograph before departing for New Guinea on the Staniforth Smith rescue mission. Joseph Guis is shown bottom left. Above him is Archibald. To the right of Archibald is Edward Kirkby. *Credit: Daily Telegraph, February 25, 1911*

"Lost among cannibals", he told them; "lost among men who are simply hungering to eat them. Hemmed in by scrub and jungle, through which they have to cut their way. Sometimes barely able to make half a mile of progress in a day. Perhaps stricken down with fever and lying in torrents of rain, the drops from which sting you as they strike on you. Tormented with leeches. Hands and feet work with the spikes of sage palms and thorny bushes. Perhaps starving"...

The journalist continues,

It made one feel proud to be an Australian to see the unhesitating way those five men said with one voice, "We're ready to go at once".[10]

Notwithstanding the lyrical scene crafted by Archibald, the remote jungle environment is accurately described and almost identical in detail to the one recounted by Staniforth Smith himself in the report tendered to the Royal Geographical Society upon his return.[11]

The Staniforth Smith expedition rescue mission was funded by Archibald[12] with a part contribution from the Federal Government.[13] The undertaking offered Maritime Wireless extensive press exposure

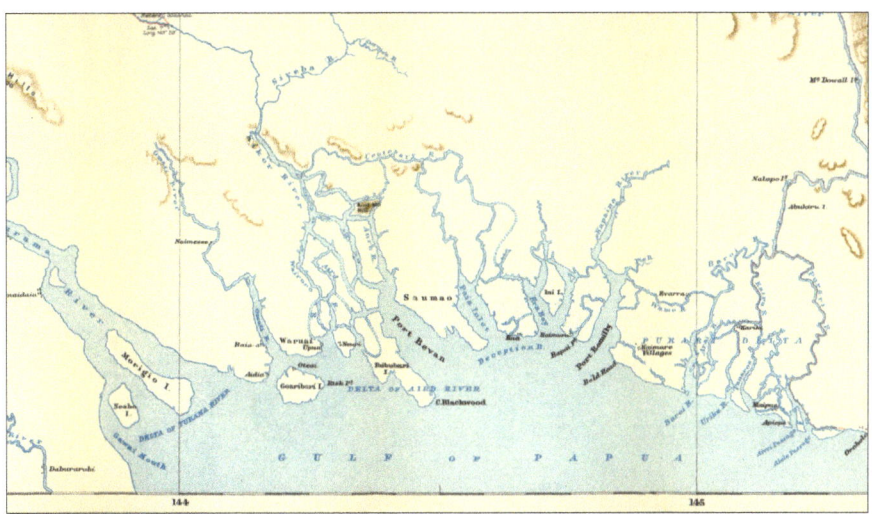

Detail from the map drawn by Miles Staniforth Smith after his ill-fated expedition. It shows the Deception Bay area and a myriad of rivers entering the Gulf of Papua from the highlands where it is easy to become lost. *Credit: Royal Geographica Society*[11]

and was covered in the newspapers for many weeks. Archibald's friend, Fernand Arnoult, himself having several years' experience in the Papuan missions, was one of the first to volunteer.[14] Other members of the group included Marion Mulrony as the chief wireless operator; Messrs G. Byrn, G. Scott and A. Sparks (operators); engineers Messrs D. Mitchell and Sam Mitchell; carpenters Messrs H. Harris and E. Woodhouse; Mr M. Thury (electrician); and Mr G. Scott, an additional operator, who had been given special leave from the navy to accompany the rescue mission.[15] Edward Kirkby was chief engineer at the Randwick Wireless Station during this period.

The Burns Philp owned steamship, Mataram. The steamer regularly travelled from Sydney to New Guinea and was used by Archibald for the Staniforth Smith rescue mission.
Credit: Mitchell Library, NSW

Wireless sets that had been hastily constructed and tested in Randwick were loaded aboard the *Mataram* berthed at Circular Quay in a remarkable ten hours. One was set-up on the deck to keep updated with news of the expedition as it was reported back to Sydney. The additional sets carried would be installed on smaller boats engaged in the search which were to sail from the Deception Bay area in the Gulf of Papua, up various rivers and tributaries around the Kikori and Fly Rivers where the expedition was expected to be found. The boats would report via wireless and be coordinated from the Australian rescue base temporarily set up on Thursday Island immediately north of Cape York. A Royal Australian Artillery garrison stationed on Thursday Island assisted in setting up the base station antenna mast. The station was operated by Archibald.

Amongst the hundreds of admirers and well-wishers farewelling the ship was Lieutenant George Taylor who toasted the success of the crew and his friend Archibald on the *Mataram* before it sailed,

> *Australia should be proud that we have with us such sterling spirits who, without hesitation at the call from the wild, stepped to the front; and proud that... the cry for help could bring into instant action six powerful, complete Australian-made wireless outfits.*
>
> *The Commonwealth Government should have no fear that the material and men under offer will not fulfil the most sanguine anticipation for success... As to the men, I have had the pleasure of many visits to Randwick wireless station and can vouch for the high scientific standard reached by Father Shaw and his brother workers...*[16]

During the celebratory mood at Circular Quay on the day of the *Mataram's* departure, a *Daily Telegraph* reporter hints at a Rasputin-like attraction Archibald held for women,

> *Off went his hat, thrown carelessly onto the wharf; coat and celluloid [collar] followed in rapid succession, and then was witnessed this energetic man in shirt sleeves, helping his companions to lift the heavy electric generators onto the deck. But the feminine hero-worshippers were not to be baulked. A dozen rushed to pick up the hat he had discarded. It formed a bone of contention, and in a moment, it looked as if the headgear would be distributed as souvenirs, but one fair maiden managed to escape with it out of the ruck. His coat was also held by tender feminine hands. Meanwhile the object of their interest was working harder than a union wharf labourer, and then by a strategic move, dashed into the smoke-room, which was sanctuary from the ladies...*

> *... as the vessel moved away... men waved hats and shouted; ladies waved handkerchiefs, and a few almost cried in their emotion...*[17]

The ship set off for New Guinea but first called into Brisbane to purchase further supplies which included a small engine for a generator.[18] The expeditioners were armed but Archibald was confident from his own New Guinea experience and mastery of the local dialect that the use of guns would be unnecessary. However, he took an unusual precaution in safeguarding the boat,

> *He... protect(ed) the boat by a wire screen which may be charged with electricity in an instant. Should any natives attempt to board the boat, they will be instantaneously electrocuted, and this, Father Shaw thinks, will have the effect of causing the natives to retreat.*[19]

In Port Moresby, popular opinion had all but sealed the fate of the Staniforth Smith expedition. Captain Goedhuis from the Dutch

Australian artillery soldiers assist hoisting the wooden antenna mast on Thursday Island for the Staniforth Smith rescue mission. Archibald Shaw far left.   *Credit: Arnoult Family*

steamer *Van Waerwyck* spoke his thoughts freely which were those of the majority of white settlers in New Guinea,

> *They are lost – yes… they are lost… Slaughtered by the natives. There seems to be no doubt about it up there, and from what I know of the place I consider the whole of the party has been massacred.*[20]

Finally, two months after the ill-fated group was supposed to return to civilisation, the survivors of the Staniforth Smith expedition wearily emerged from the New Guinea jungle unassisted and made their way to Goaribiri Island at the mouth of the Kikori River. When the news was received by wireless on Thursday Island, Archibald relayed it down to Kirkby in Sydney. He remained on Thursday Island with a small team to finalise the installation of what would later become the first wireless station of his Commonwealth Wireless Service contract. After that, he installed a temporary station on Paga Hill near Port Moresby which achieved wireless communication as far south as Sydney and as far north to warships located near Singapore.[21]

The Esplanade on Thursday Island, 1913, from where the wireless station masts can be seen. *Credit: C. Price Conigrave, Mitchell Library, NSW*

It didn't matter that the rescue mission organised by Archibald had nothing to do with Staniforth Smith making it back to civilisation – although it would have been the best reward for Archibald's team if they *had* found the lost expedition, especially after all the effort that had been made. But in proposing the rescue mission in the first place, offering to pay for it without hesitation, and carrying it out at speed, Archibald garnered much publicity and the Maritime Wireless Telegraph Company had become a household name.

Almost single-handedly Archibald created sustained press coverage which lasted for months. He had cemented his position as a well-known and popular figure in Australia. He had mastered the art of dealing with the media, he had the confidence of a seasoned entrepreneur and, most unusually, he was a priest. He was riding the crest of a wave.

The leadership of the Missionaries of the Sacred Heart were concerned about all this and the Assistant General, Fr. John Field wrote to Joseph Guis the procurator and Archibald's immediate superior, seeking detailed information on the circumstances of his involvement with the wireless company and how it all began. This correspondence, which I have drawn on earlier, holds the only record of the early period of the Wireless Works.

Both Guis and Archibald replied to Field in separate letters providing an historical account of the company's beginnings and justifying the MSC involvement in the company to Field's satisfaction. Archibald continued to have the support of the MSC leadership, if not all the rank and file from the congregation.

Since the later part of 1910, Archibald's station at Randwick was required by the Wireless Telegraphy Act to be licensed by the Postmaster-General's Department (PMG). The PMG already had jurisdiction over land-telegraphy and this was now extended into wireless. Not only were experimenters required to be licensed, they also had certain restrictions placed on their transmissions, such as the amount of power they were able to use in order that interference to other stations be limited. Power restrictions limited the range of a transmitter to a working distance of about five hundred miles.

Archibald's own license had the callsign *XPO* and was issued on October 11, 1910. It was the sixth wireless license issued in the Australian Commonwealth. Today there are tens of thousands of radio licenses active in Australia.

In all the excitement of conducting the Staniforth Smith rescue mission, the detail of the licence condition relating to the power used was conveniently ignored and Edward Kirkby, identified as the Chief Engineer of the Randwick wireless plant at the time of the rescue mission, faced a visit and an investigation from the PMG's Wireless Inspector on March 17, 1911. Newspaper accounts reported that the distances obtained by the Randwick station, and therefore the power that was used by the plant, were *greatly in excess of what the license provides for.*[22] The wireless inspector writes,

> *The maximum range of signalling with the licensees' own appliances shall be approximately 500 miles, whereas in the Newspaper clipping it is stated that the licensee has been operating up to a range of 2,400 miles...*
>
> *I recommend that the matter be brought under the notice of the Chief Office so that whatever action it is considered necessary may be taken to restrict the licensee, the Rev. A. Shaw, to the terms of the license.*[23]

Archibald was still up north during the wireless inspector's investigation and returned to Sydney on the *Mataram* a month later on Friday, April 21, 1911.[24] He had been away almost two months.

No record survives of the action taken against the Wireless Works for operating in breach of their license condition. In the weeks following, the temporary station on Thursday Island remained in regular contact with Sydney. Perhaps an extenuating circumstances argument was put to the PMG and Archibald successfully had his license condition temporarily amended in view of its use during the rescue mission. In the months following the Staniforth Smith adventure the excitement continued as the company took on another 'big thing'.

The Maritime Wireless Telegraph Company was one of several approached by Douglas Mawson's South Pole Expedition to supply equipment intended to keep the expedition in wireless contact with the mainland. Archibald explains to Fr Field, the MSC Assistant General, who happens to be visiting Randwick around this time,

> *I have been approached by the South Pole expedition to loan my wireless instruments to them.*
>
> *On the other hand, I have been approached by Capitalists saying that if I can make my instruments work publicly from Tasmania to the chief echelon of the expedition, which is 1800 miles, they would buy my wireless system for £2000 cash and give me £20 cash out of every £100 they make in selling my instruments...* [25]

Archibald is more eager to pursue the second option and by the end of his letter requests permission from Fr Field to set-up a wireless plant in Tasmania to take advantage of the opportunity, claiming with characteristic enthusiasm,

> *... if I do not accept, some other wireless system will get [the] same offer, as this will mean a profit of at least £40,000 [about $4m today] to us within the next two years, and as out instruments are already working 2000 miles every night, there is no possibility of failure to work the 1800 miles asked* [26]

The MSC Assistant General, Fr Field, who was visiting from Rome responded from Randwick presbytery the next day,

> *I am glad to hear of the offer made to you for the purchase of your wireless system, and sincerely congratulate you on the success of your labours.*
>
> *I feel certain I only interpret Fr. General's intentions when I say that you are free to accept, and as far as I can see, it is the best thing to do...* [27]

He added a timely and cautionary reminder that Archibald's duties as assistant procurator and his chaplaincy commitments to the Little Sisters of the Poor should not be made to suffer on account of his pursuit of wireless.

Contact with the Mawson expedition was scheduled to take place around the January of 1912 which gave Archibald plenty of time to plan and prepare. As with many of his undertakings there were multiple layers of purpose. It wasn't just about Mawson. A station was already planned to be built on King Island in Tasmania anyway; first as an experimental station to contact Mawson, then as a station registered to send public telegrams on behalf of the Postmaster-General's Department. Archibald's wireless station was the first to promise a communications link between King Island and mainland Australia. King Island had been bypassed by the submarine cable network from Victoria to mainland Tasmania and the inhabitants of the island were overjoyed to be finally connected with the rest of the Commonwealth.[28]

It was certainly no coincidence that Archibald had a lengthy friendship with the senator who represented Tasmania between 1910 and 1918: James Long. His son Leslie was apprenticed at the Wireless Works. It was Senator Long who pressed Archibald to bring King Island into the twentieth century. Long will feature significantly in the Shaw story later. Archibald's visit to King Island may have also precipitated an ongoing MSC presence in the village of Currie. Fr Aubrey Goodman was appointed the parish priest there from October 1912. He established the first Catholic Church on the island on what is still known today as *Shaw Street;* the road that led to the wireless station.

Upon returning to Sydney, Archibald had other pressing matters needing attention. The *Maritime Wireless Telegraph Company* was to be liquidated and recreated as a new company on the Randwick site with new directors and a significantly greater capital investment. It was reborn as the *Maritime Wireless Company (Shaw System)*.

Since its inception and continuing until the business was sold in its entirety in 1916 to the Department of Navy, Maritime Wireless had two separate income streams. It offered wireless manufacture, (Maritime Wireless), and it offered an engineering works, (Shaw Engineering), which wound electric motors, made generator sets[29] and produced all manner of mechanical and electro-mechanical devices. The finances of the two businesses were kept separate,[30] though Archibald claims with his usual positive spin that later the engineering side of the business was more profitable than the wireless,

> *Even if we never did any more wireless, the Company is so strongly organised and other electrical work pays better than wireless.*[31]

The objectives of the newly formed company were,

> *To acquire laboratory, workshops, apparatus etc., at present at Avoca Street Randwick, and the benefit of certain applications for Australian provisional protection for improvements to wireless telegraph apparatus etc.*[32]

Subscribers to the Memorandum of Association of the new company were: Randwick bookmaker and church parishioner Michael J. Moloney; Swiss engineer Mark Thury; secretary to the National Society of Amalgamated Brassworkers, W. J. Davis; M. D. Roach; assistant manager of the British Australian Cotton Association, E. R. Minell and businessman C. A. Humphreys. Each person held one share each.[33]

Applications for Australian provisional protection, mentioned in the objectives of the new company refer to the registration of certain patents which gave the company more value by making it the owner of intellectual property, instead of just machine plant, stock, property and manufacturing contracts.

Months before the registration of the new company, Archibald, in an already busy year, had successfully lodged three patents which were used in the manufacture of his own wireless sets. Hence the reason for *Shaw System* in brackets following the newly registered company name to distinguish it from the Balsillie System or any other system.

The company was registered on July 3, 1911, and the patents representing the *Shaw System* of wireless transmission and reception were recorded as Australian patent numbers 1683/11, 1684/11 and 1685/11. They were lodged through Archibald's patent attorney, Wilfred Spruson, mentioned before as one of the founding members and first treasurer of George Taylor's *Institute of Wireless Telegraphy*. Spruson had been a politician and was also an engineer with strong ties to the Catholic Church. Other inventors at the Wireless Works, such as Marion Mulrony, later registered patents for their own innovations through Spruson as well.

Patent 1685/11, called *Improvements in wireless telegraph receivers*, presented a simple but novel method for using two perpendicularly-opposed coils, or inductors, to improve the quality of a received wireless telegraphic signal. The state-of-the-art of wireless at the time was primitive - certainly by today's standards. Archibald's receiver was typical of the era. It had only six components – an aerial, a variable condenser, a crystal detector (a chunk of the mineral galena for example), headphones or an earpiece, and the two-coil inductor arrangement which was unique to his patent. With these few components inquisitive school boys could construct their own receivers.

The two other patents, 1683/11 and 1684/11, were more important and concerned with improvements to the spark-gap transmitter itself, increasing the efficiency of the system and therefore the range of the Morse code signals radiated by the aerial.

The former patent showed the invention of a novel rotating spark gap with a 'gas-quenching' system. This gave a musical note to the transmitted signal, making it somewhat easier to hear through the atmospheric noise and interference generated by other transmitters. The system of *quenching* the spark every time the transmitting key was depressed made for *dots* and *dashes* with a sharp decay time. This allowed them to be easily distinguishable in the noise and improved the accuracy of the received message. It also meant operators could transmit at a higher word-per-minute rate if they were capable. The system was popularly described as producing as *singing spark.*[34]

The final patent proposed a workable system of *electrostatically connecting the radiating and the exciting circuits through a common condenser*. According to Archibald's explanation, this method of transmission had been proposed earlier but, until now, had not been developed practically.

Together the three patents made up the *Shaw System* of wireless manufactured at the Wireless Works. However, the Coastal Wireless Service installations required the manufacture of wireless plant according to another system: the *Balsillie System* for which John Graeme Balsillie held the patents.

Like many wireless devotees of the period, Balsillie was an interesting character. He later made claims that Archibald had infringed his own wireless patents. However, a legal challenge became irrelevant and was not pursued because, in subesequent years, the interference prone, broadband spark-gap technology was superseded by electric valve wireless which had the capability of transmitting voice and music over a narrow bandwidth. Spark-gap wireless would soon be on the road to redundancy.

Having an interest in a variety of sciences and a certain degree of eccentricity well-acknowledged by his competitors, Balsillie went on unsuccessfully, after wireless, to pursue rainmaking experiments at Bookaloo in the desert of South Australia between Port Augusta and Woomera. This was done under the ebullient banner of *The Balsillie Rain Stimulation and Procuration Plant.*

Eccentricity was ubiquitous in early wireless and a familiar commodity at the Wireless Works as well. There is necessarily a certain degree of eccentricity required for an inventor to be successful. They need to solve problems by taking a point of view that is completely novel. The *wireless crank,* to use the colloquial term, went one-step further. They tried to improve the science in new and obscure ways, frequently under a veil of secrecy and from a peculiarly obsessive perspective.

Ray Allsop, apprenticed at the Wireless Works under Archibald, was later to become a brilliant electrical engineer in his own right. Yet he was probably regarded as a crank when he gave an account of his discovery of an *electric ray* which could destroy quarter-inch thick steel plate from a distance of two feet.[35] He thought he would soon be able to perform the same feat at a distance of two miles and use the device to destroy enemy aeroplanes, power stations or sink attacking battleships! Allsop never revealed the details of his experiments. No one else appears to have seen them conducted and no one has since been able repeat them.

With the formation of the Maritime Wireless Company (Shaw System) and the injection of fresh investor capital, the intellectual property of the patents, publicity from the Staniforth Smith mission and the Coastal Wireless Service contracts, the Randwick Wireless

Works became a very successful operation. A car was purchased which is referred to in historic photographs[36] as *Fr. Shaw's car*. This was a rare luxury in those days but seen as a necessity for the conduct of efficient business.

Later it became apparent that 'spare' cash earned by the business around this time was being diverted into various mining interests – a large coal mining company near Swansea on the Central Coast and a molybdenite mine near Deepwater, NSW. Archibald's interest in these businesses was not made known to his religious superiors.

The year was not yet over and the continuing success of the Maritime Wireless Telegraph Company was all but assured if radio contact with Mawson's South Pole Expedition could be established from King Island.

Fr. Shaw's car driven by Basil Low, Dutruc Street, Randwick, 1913.   *Credit: Low Family*

XII

Adventure on King Island

If someone living in 1911 found themselves the director of a wireless manufacturing company and simultaneously the owner of a newspaper, it would be a surety that they would back Douglas Mawson's *South Pole Expedition* in money or in kind. The businessman Hugh Denison found himself in just this position.

As a director of the *Australasian Wireless Company*, the Australian agents for the German Telefunken brand, he supplied Mawson with two Telefunken transmitters under contract. One was installed on Macquarie Island half-way between Tasmania and Commonwealth Bay in Antarctica, and the other was set-up in Mawson's Hut, the expedition base on mainland Antarctica. Denison also donated £1,000, (about $100,000 today), toward the expedition.[1]

> *Two complete sets of Telefunken wireless apparatus were purchased from the Australasian Wireless Company. The motors and dynamos were got from Buzzacott, Sydney, and the masts were built by Saxton and Binns, Sydney.*[2]

With Denison's position and financial clout the Mawson expedition was used to promote the Telefunken brand of transmitter. Wireless signals could typically be received on any crystal receiver within range, regardless of manufacturer.

The Telefunken wireless equipment supplied to Mawson did not come cheap,

> *In October 1911 Mawson purchased from the Australian*

> *Wireless Company, on a buy back agreement, two 2-kilowatt long-wave Telefunken wireless sets, costing £650 each (over $65,000 in today's dollars).*[3]

Denison founded *The Sun* newspaper a year before the expedition but his donation did not grant him exclusive rights to publish news from the Mawson expedition. There were many sponsors and the total cost of the expedition including goods and services received amounted to more than £56,000.[4] Though significant, Denison's donation was only a small fraction of the total cost.

Nevertheless, in acknowledgement of the support he provided, Mawson named a protrusion of land into Commonwealth Bay, near to where his hut was set up, *Cape Denison*.

Archibald would have appreciated the logic of Denison's sponsorship but aimed for a greater financial prize – the promise of on-going lucrative contracts for the Shaw system of wireless should he be able to establish contact with the Mawson expedition in Antarctica from Australia.

Archibald arrived at King Island, Tasmania, on July 16, 1911,[5] with the indefatigable Fernand Arnoult, eleven men and thirty tons of equipment to set up the station. Staying at *Parer's Hotel* in Currie with his party, they were well-received by the islanders. At a function held on the following Monday evening many toasts and ovations were made to Archibald and his team. In one toast, a Mr Palmer said,

> *He would regard Sunday July 16, as one of the happiest days of his life. For some considerable time he had followed every path that gave the slightest promise of the island securing electrical communications with the outside world. One of those paths led to their guest Fr. Shaw, who was then installing a wireless station on Thursday Island.*[6]

Within a couple of days of his arrival, a site was chosen for the wireless station and his team set about constructing it, starting with the erection of two impressive two-hundred and fifty-foot wooden antenna poles. The cost of the whole station was fully borne by Archibald's company, Maritime Wireless. The *Melbourne Advocate* reports that,

The good news sped along the various roadways and tracks of the island with a most electrical rapidity, and in a few hours' time great excitement prevailed, which was intensified by the wholly unpreparedness of the populace for such startling good news. During the day Fr. Shaw... examined several promising localities upon which to erect his station, and finally decided upon a site adjoining the Agricultural Show grounds, near Camp Creek...[7]

By September, 1911, Archibald's team had completed installing the wireless station at Currie and, not being one to waste an opportunity, duplicate telegrams were sent to the Prime Minister, the Minister for Home Affairs, and Australia's Postmaster-General proudly announcing the accomplishment,

Greetings by wireless. Pleased to inform you that King Island station is now complete and working.[8]

The government controlled PMG had been quite slow to connect remote parts of Australia wirelessly and the initiative of private operators like Archibald caused them some public embarrassment,

The newly built King Island Wireless Station completed by Archibald, Fernand Arnoult and the Maritime Wireless crew in September, 1911.   *Credit: King Island Museum*

Erection of one of two King Island Wireless masts for VZE.   *Credit: King Island Museum*

> *While the postal Department has been floundering with schemes for the erection and equipment of stations on the mainland – and incidentally discouraging private enterprise from taking a share in the work – private inventors have been determinedly equipping stations and sending and receiving messages.*[9]

Starting as an experimental station with the callsign *VZE*, a license was soon granted for the new Shaw station to send public messages and private telegrams which the government levied a tax on. The station also contributed to safety at sea by communicating with Bass Strait shipping.[10] Whilst a rebuilt *Parer's Hotel* stands on its original site in Currie today, the wireless station has been long since disassembled. However, *Shaw Street*, leading to the old wireless station site, keeps in mind the remarkable company behind the events of more than a century ago.

Following the construction of the King Island station, Archibald visited the Tasmanian mainland to explore the possibility of setting up another station at Low Head on the mouth of the Tamar River with the support of and for the benefit of the Launceston Marine Board.[11] Low Head was already the landing point of the submarine telegraph cable linking the Australian mainland with Tasmania which bypassed King Island. A wireless station here was never developed. It was deemed superfluous to the other stations that were planned for the Coastal Wireless Service.

Archibald gave little thought to who would manage the King Island Wireless Station during the much anticipated contact with the Mawson expedition which was expected to occur around the beginning of 1912. He selected his trusted old colleague and friend Fernand Arnoult[12] who had accompanied him and set-up the station in the first place. Arnoult was fêted by the King Islanders and returned to Tasmania in the middle of January of 1912 to manage the Mawson contact.

In fact, Arnoult, who held Australian citizenship since 1911, was drawn to the island so much he bought property there - a house near the butter factory and was gifted a farm of five hundred acres to the east of Currie. He later donated the farm to the Tumut RSS & AILA[13] sub-branch, the forerunner of the Returned Services League (RSL). It became the prize in a raffle to raise funds which were used to build Tumut's first club-house for returned war-veterans. Arnoult retired to Tumut in his later years – not far from the town of Archibald's childhood.

The chief wireless operator in Antarctica was Walter Hannam. He learned wireless science at *Sydney Technical College* and, a year before, was the wireless operator with Edward Kirkby and George Taylor during their Heathcote military wireless demonstration. Hannam's assistant operator, Sidney Jeffryes, was largely written out of the Mawson story because sadly, *his mental illness during and after the expedition saw him institutionalised and marginalised from Australian Antarctic exploration history.*[14] Arnoult and Hannam had prior acquaintance with each other, having met earlier at the Randwick Wireless Works.

The Mawson expedition was supplied with Denison's Telefunken wireless apparatus and their transmissions were received by a station set up for the purpose on Macquarie Island, about sixteen-hundred kilometres away (one-thousand miles) from Mawson's Hut in Antarctica. Archibald's King Island station was nearly twice this distance away, at three-thousand kilometres (or about one-thousand eight-hundred and seventy miles). Surprisingly, Archibald's team could not receive any transmissions at all from Macquarie Island.[15] The distance was certainly within the range attainable by Archibald's equipment when operated from Sydney but something else was at play which prevented wireless contact. Conditions so far south and so close to the pole proved surprisingly difficult for reliable communication.

Antarctica presented its own peculiar challenges to radio men and in 1912, no one knew anything about the problems associated with wireless propagation near the earth's magnetic poles. Aside from the loud ambient noise outside the wireless hut caused by extreme katabatic winds, making Commonwealth Bay the windiest places on earth,[16] conditions conspired to make even the setting-up of a decent antenna near impossible. Daily ice deposits and snow drifts caused the antenna to short to earth, thwarting all attempts at successful transmissions.

Furthermore, the continuous daylight reduced the effective range of communication.

Even if the equipment could be made to work reliably, the deafening noise of howling wind and barking husky dogs made listening to weak Morse signals near impossible.

Back in Tasmania, despite the best efforts of Maritime Wireless under the reliable supervision of Arnoult, the King Island wireless station had no success at all in contacting either Macquarie Island or Mawson's Hut in Antarctica. If the station on Macquarie Island could barely hear the Mawson expedition themselves there was little possibility a station twice as distant would be successful. Contact was attempted using the Shaw system under the callsign VZE. This was later changed to VIK when the Balsillie system was installed at the station and it began operating as part of the Coastal Wireless Service.

It is now known that atmospheric static and auroral activity[17] can severely impede radio wave propagation. Compounded with the physical challenges of conducting science in Antarctica, these factors conspired to prevent communication between the Mawson expedition and King Island. Needless to say, the promise of lucrative *capitalists' contracts* which were held before Archibald's Maritime Wireless as a prize for a successful Antarctic contact, and presented earlier as a certainty by Archibald to his religious superiors, evaporated. In fact, so challenging were conditions in Antarctica, that reliable wireless communication from Cape Denison to Macquarie Island was not successful until the following year, in February, 1913.[18][19]

If Maritime Wireless had been successful in making wireless contact with the expedition, not only would Archibald and his mission procurate have no further financial concerns, he would have likely had an Antarctic landmark named after him as well, just like Mawson's benefactor, Hugh Denison.

I don't think Archibald would ever have seen the failure of the Mawson contact as a failure of Maritime Wireless, just as he never saw the unexpected reappearance of the Staniforth Smith expedition as a failure of his own carefully planned rescue mission. He didn't think like that. Archibald's constant positivity held a blindspot for the negative. Business success in the mystical field of wireless was as much about public profile and public perception as it was about science. In a short space of time Maritime Wireless had become master of both.

By any measure, Maritime Wireless' accomplishments and ambitions under the guidance of Archibald were extraordinary. By October, 1911, there were only twenty-five experimental wireless stations operating in Australia; two in Victoria, one on King Island and twenty-two in New South Wales. Many of the early experimenters had some association with either Archibald or the Wireless Works too, often living in adjacent suburbs.

By December, 1911, Maritime Wireless was awarded the tender for the planned additional Coastal Wireless Stations to be erected in Hobart, Melbourne, Port Moresby, and Cooktown or Thursday Island. The Postmaster-General, Charles Frazer, claimed each station would cost about £575 for materials and £1,000 for installation, compared to £4,600 for the higher-powered Telefunken stations.[20]

Based on these figures the income from wireless for Archibald's company would barely cover expenses unless Maritime Wireless was also able to supply merchant and naval ships and other operators with wireless plant. This is highly likely but unfortunately there are no surviving records to validate the claim. Without them we can only assume that income from services provided by *Shaw Engineering*, operating from the same Randwick site, made up the shortfall.

By March, 1912, the government had approved expenses of £1,660 for Archibald to erect a permanent station on Thursday Island.[21]

A month later, a tragic shipping disaster in the middle of the Atlantic Ocean served as a timely warning for Australia to fast-track its Coastal Wireless Service. On April 15, 1912, with its sixteen watertight compartments, the 'unsinkable' *Titanic* struck an iceberg on its maiden voyage from Southampton to New York City. Over the next two-and-a-half hours it sank with some fifteen hundred lives lost. This was, and still remains, the deadliest peacetime maritime disaster in history. Wireless contact between the Titanic and the nearest ship capable of offering assistance, the *SS Californian*, was unsuccessful because the Californian's wireless operator had turned off his wireless and gone to bed.[22] The Californian was only five miles away.

The sinking of the *Titanic* jolted governments and naval

authorities all over the world into action. Australia followed the British by invoking the *Navigation Act of 1912*. This Act of Parliament made it an offence for shipping companies to take more than fifty people to sea without a wireless set and enough operators to monitor it twenty-four-hours a day. The *Titanic* tragedy forced the government to waste no time in completing Australia's Coastal Wireless Service.

The 1912 Navigation Act promised sizeable financial returns for wireless manufacturers well-positioned in the market.

At this time the Fisher Labor Government was in power which had been supportive of Australian manufacturing. In fact Archibald had the ear of the government through good friend and Labor senator, James Long, even having his son apprenticed at the Wireless Works.

By the end of 1912 there were eight stations operating in the Coastal Wireless Service and Archibald's Maritime Wireless had manufactured and installed six of them.[23] Expensive Telefunken plant had been installed at Pennant Hills in Sydney and on Wireless Hill near Fremantle, Western Australia, from the earlier contract with Australasian Wireless. Archibald's equipment, using the Balsillie system, filled the other stations and was installed by Maritime Wireless in Hobart, (in lieu of the station earlier proposed at Low Head near Launceston), Melbourne, Brisbane, Adelaide, Thursday Island and Port Moresby. Maritime Wireless was an efficient operation. In fact Archibald's stations in Melbourne and Hobart were commissioned before the Telefunken stations in Sydney and Fremantle, even though they had been ordered afterward.

The manufacture of wireless plant at Randwick was done under a strict ten-year secrecy order whereby neither Archibald nor any shop-workers were permitted to divulge details of the components or circuits used.[24] Setting up the stations was no small undertaking. Each required an enormous wooden antenna mast and large heavy engines belted to generators which were capable of delivering significant power to the transmitting apparatus. The delivery of the plant also required the deployment of significant manpower and funds.

In September, 1912, an accident at the government-run Pennant Hills Wireless Station using Australian Wireless's Telefunken equipment, brought the station off-air for an extended period. A pulley driving the generator had broken. Archibald's station at Randwick was charged with conducting all the wireless business from Sydney during the time of the outage.[25] An *Electric Telegraphic Code* book recently located in the Missionaries of the Sacred Heart library dating from this period was likely used by operators of the Randwick Wireless Station to facilitate official PMG communications during this time.[26]

Occasionally, like many growing businesses, the Wireless Works would encounter cash-flow problems. With no local oversight of the mission accounts, Archibald decided to make up any temporary shortfall of cash by creating a revolving line-of-credit between mission funds and the accounts of Maritime Wireless which the MSC leadership in Rome would have been naturally opposed to, had they known. The procure superior, Joseph Guis, was quite sick by the end of 1912 and, though still officially in the role of procurator, Archibald writes that he was more-or-less doing Guis' job himself at this time. In all likelihood Guis may not have been aware of Archibald's floating credit arrangement either.

Both Guis and Archibald continued to be overseen from the MSC General House in far off Rome. Without an immediate superior, the short-term lending of money from a mission account to a wireless account would have seemed a prudent thing to do as long as it didn't affect the operation of either enterprise. Suspicions were immediately triggered in Rome when the procure was unable to meet particular mission needs for which money had been allocated from Europe.

Despite Maritime Wireless being profitable, cash-flow problems increasingly became a recurrent theme of business operations over the next twelve months and were compounded by poor record-keeping for which Archibald had developed a reputation. Eventually, the situation necessitated another recapitalisation of the company. 1913 was destined to be the biggest year yet for the Wireless Works, given that Maritime Wireless had won the contracts for the remaining eleven Coastal Wireless Stations that needed to be built, delivered and installed *post-haste* to assure the nation that a tragedy the scale of the *Titanic* disaster would not befall Australia. Given the success of the company thus far investors were not difficult to find.

It is possible, though without records difficult to verify, that

Archibald received payments-in-kind for the supply of other services provided by the Wireless Works, or diverted cash profits into illiquid shares held in other businesses. This may explain the shares he held in the Bulga Saw Mill Company and some high-value shares held in mining companies at the time of his death. Accepting shares as payment in lieu of cash would have compounded cash-flow problems.

The partnership between the tolerant Joseph Guis and the free-thinking Archibald who together ran the mission procure adjacent to the Maritime Wireless Works began to strain. Guis, whose first language was French, made the mistake of allowing Archibald to look after accounts and deal with the bank. Guis made these observations to Superior General Eugène Meyer in May, 1912:

> *Do not think that there is anything fishy in the affairs of the procure.... Thank God, no. As far as my conscience and my poor skill allow me to know, everything is "on a straight line".*
>
> *The only fault, a huge one, it is true, is that all the bills and almost all the bills and letters from merchants and bankers are addressed to Shaw, who in Sydney is the big Manitou for everything that concerns missions. He alone has been known for many years. The bills therefore arrive at his house, and that's it; they accumulate and get lost, mixed up in a sheaf of paperwork. Only he himself can make sense of it. It's a pandemonium unlike any other.*
>
> *When he gets money, he pays for everything and there is some order for a while. During his frequent absences, I take possession of all the letters myself, and I also do it when he is here and he is not the first to meet the postman. But very often the postman arrives when I'm not here. In short, there are always some bills that do not reach me on time. Not that they are not lost, but I only learn about them by going to discover his cheque books, & by collating them.*[27]

Meyer first became aware of financial anomalies at the procure when materials ordered for the New Guinea mission were not dispatched. Now, he was aware of the disarrayed state of the procure accounts and some alarm would have been raised in Rome.

Nevertheless, financial discrepancies in the MSC mission accounts did not stop the company celebrating its significant accomplishments and milestones at the first Maritime Wireless annual dinner in December, 1912. It was held at *Sargent's Market Street Café* in Sydney[28] complete with musical items provided by the staff of the works.

Archibald was not present that evening but a toast was made to *our absent chief.* The general manager, Marion Mulrony, celebrated the uniqueness of Archibald's enterprise at Randwick and proudly made this point in a speech during the evening,

> *It was the only workshop in Australia where wireless instruments were made, and the wish of Father Shaw was that it would always be the premiere works.*[29]

By the close of 1912 there were about one hundred employees working at Maritime Wireless.[30]

Heads of departments at the Maritime Wireless Company in 1913. Marion Mulroney, the chief engineer and general manager, is seated middle row left of centre. William Fieldgate, works manager, is seated middle row centre.   *Credit: MSC Archives*

XIII

Prosperous Years

Further expansion of the Wireless Works took place in 1913 before the bulk of the Coastal Wireless Service stations were manufactured and installed. Stations at Mount Gambier (South Australia), Geraldton, Broome and Esperance (Western Australia), Rockhampton, Townsville and Cooktown (Queensland), Darwin (Northern Territory), Flinders Island (Tasmania) were each commissioned in 1913. The final stations at Roebourne (Western Australia) and Wyndham (Victoria) were commissioned the following year.

To increase the manufacturing efficiency and to meet the stringent delivery deadlines required by the Coastal Wireless Service contracts another round of recapitalisation was necessary. A significant investor was found in Sir Rupert Clarke, pastoralist, horse-breeder, entrepreneur and politician. Archibald knew Clarke from his days in New Guinea. He may have also been a silent partner in the Bulga Saw Mill Company.

Clarke held extensive plantations in New Guinea and later mounted an expedition from the Gulf of New Guinea in 1914, heading up the various rivers that Staniforth Smith planned to explore during his ill-fated expedition of 1911. Clarke self-funded this expedition on his own yatch, *Kismet,* and took Staniforth Smith aboard as a guest.[1]

By the June of 1913 wireless was finally starting to make its presence felt in some of the remote MSC Pacific missions too, as was Archibald's original dream. A French-born Missionary of the Sacred Heart priest, Maximilian Branger, the son of a tile-maker and machinist,[2] was one such experimenter and operator. He was working on a remote mission located at Inawi (or Mekeo) on mainland New Guinea about thirty-five kilometres north of Yule Island. He applied for an experimenters' license and for permission to erect an antenna from the Australian Department of External Affairs who then oversaw British New Guinea, and the Postmaster-General's Department who oversaw wireless installations.[3]

Unfortunately, no record survives of the station details. However, it would be reasonable to assume Branger's equipment was made at the Maritime Wireless Works and shipped to him from the procure in Randwick. Similarly, an experimental wireless telegraph license was issued to Brother Osmond in 1911,[4] who was the director of St. Mary's School run by the Marist Brothers in Darlinghurst.[5] Various Catholic teaching and missionary orders, like the Marist Brothers, showed a keen interest in the work being done at Randwick.

Branger's New Guinea station was the first established for the sole purpose of linking the MSC missions by wireless – one of the reasons Archibald became involved in wireless in the first place. If atmospheric conditions were favourable, contact would be made directly with the Randwick station, otherwise messages were relayed via intermediate stations.

Whilst Archibald was in contact with Branger in New Guinea a film crew had invaded the Randwick Wireless Works. A silent movie, titled *Australia Calls*,[6] was being made by Raymond Longford and featured Australia's first film-star, Lottie Lyell. It included scenes filmed at the Shaw Wireless Works. The film, sadly now lost, told the story of the imminent invasion of Australia by an unspecified Asian nation.

It was the first film in Australia to feature scale-model photography and included dramatic scenes depicting the bombing of Sydney from the air and the burning of several buildings and landmarks. Longford himself claimed it was also the first film in the world to feature wireless. It depicted the capture of the Pennant Hills Wireless Station by a mysterious oriental invading force but the scenes were actually filmed at the Wireless Station in Randwick.[7] The film reflected anti-Asian racial and cultural stereotypes typical of the time.

Archibald Shaw, c. 1913

Credit: MSC Archive

By July of 1913 the major recapitalisation of the Wireless Works was complete with an injection of funds from Sir Rupert Clarke. Additional workers were employed and the purchase of more efficient machinery from America was undertaken. The company operated under the same name, the *Maritime Wireless Company of Australia (Shaw System)*, and it still had its two divisions: the wireless and the engineering. The capital of the company was increased to £50,000, about $5m in today's money, through the creation of 20,000 shares at £1 each.[8]

Wireless manufacture was at its peak during this time but the engineering side of the business was pulling its weight also and generating more income than the wireless.[9]

The Wireless Works now had the capital to expand further and the business was able to purchase *Archina*, another large home built in 1907 at 49 Avoca Street, directly west of *Ascot* and adjacent to the Wireless Works. The purchase included the surrounding land and was registered in the names of both priests, Joseph Guis and Archibald Shaw.[10] The total land area of the Maritime Wireless site was now a little over two acres.

The large steel antenna tower, visible for miles in every direction, was set equidistant between *Archina* and *Ascot,* and the workshops housing the various departments of the works were located at the base of the antenna and to the west, with entrances from the three street frontages of Frenchman's Road, Dutruc Street and Avoca Street. Archibald continued to live adjacent to the works in *Ascot*, with Joseph Guis, in the procurate. *Ascot* was large enough to house visiting missionaries in convalescence from the islands and offered rooms to some senior employees of the Wireless Works as well.

Archibald continued to have his critics from within the MSC society but he also enjoyed financial support from some surprising sources,

> *The Cardinal gave me his approval and offered the use of his purse, the priests of the diocese did the same... as you know the priests have £7,000 in the Company, the Vicar General £1,500, Mgr O'Haran £1,500...* [11]

Archibald became the company figurehead, *le grand Manitou*[12] of Maritime Wireless, and his name was inextricably attached to the success of the venture. However, he was no longer the sole decision maker. He was answerable to a committee and finds himself at times in a difficult position. There is pressure on him to comply with decisions made at the company board level for the benefit of shareholders. He states,

> *I could not go against the company when they decided to put profits into more plant and machinery... seeing everything succeeding and the shares getting more valuable, it was prudent of me to secure as many shares as I could by letting my interests increase with theirs.*
>
> *The company is now capitalized [sic] to £50,000 and the assets are £72,000. The Very Reverend Father Linckens, understands this: that the shares have nearly doubled their value as the assets stand so high, £22,000 over the share capital.*[13]

On how his own income from Shaw Wireless was used, Archibald comments,

> *The Company voted me a salary of £600 per year which I am letting stand in to secure more shares. The company have still confidence in me and have asked me to supervise the erection of their big timber concessions*[14] *for which services they gave me more shares.*
>
> *Between the timber and the wireless I now hold shares to the value of nearly £12,000 which, when dividends are paid, ought to bring in between three to four thousand pounds per year - at the very lowest £2,000. I consider that with this revenue to be able to free the procure from debt and also not to charge the Missions for their staying at the procure.*[15]

The timber concessions likely refer to the Wireless Works' large share-holdings in the Bulga Saw Mill Company. By 1913 the Wireless Works were at their zenith and Archibald their flag-bearer.

The MSC saw that Archibald's involvement in the enterprise was becoming too extreme for a humble missionary priest. He was given instructions as early as July of 1913 to sever his connection with the Wireless Works and to return as a regular priest under the direction of the Australian Province.[16] From Archibald's perspective, and for the Wireless Works, this was not a good time. Much good-will would be lost by his immediate departure as would a significant loss of value for shareholders in the company. He was able to convince his superiors to postpone their orders and encouraged them to remain patient.

In defence of his position, Archibald claimed a turn-over of £150,000 for the company in 1912, ($15m today), with a workforce now extending to one-hundred and seventy-one men in the workshops. The business was not yet paying dividends; preferring to reinvest profits. This was not his decision – he no longer had sole control – but one made by the company board.

However, Maritime Wireless was maintaining the interest payments on the procure debts which gave Archibald some kudos in Rome. This was done in lieu of paying rent for the land surrounding the procure where the workshops were built. The unusual nature of a Catholic priest in the position of capitalist businessman continued to remain anathema to some in the MSC,

> *I stand well with the Commonwealth Government and cannot help it when Ministers ask me to dine and consult with them - this displeased certain ones of our order and I am a black sheep.*[17]

Archibald's ventures were like nothing an Australian priest had ever undertaken. Tensions between Archibald and more traditional members of the order had always been simmering and were a constant source of personal discouragement,

> *My intention is still the same, i.e. to free the procure from debt and create funds and I ask you to have patience a little longer; I have done what I set out to do. I will have a revenue for the procure, and not withstanding all criticism, I am still in the order and will stay there…*[18]

In reality Archibald was slowly losing control of the business and the business was beginning to control Archibald. He had become a slave to its demands. The operation was as large as it would ever become - with nearly two-hundred employees and it held serious financial obligations of its own, as well as being under increasing pressure from competitors such as the new Telefunken and Marconi partnership. The business had become an unwieldy colossus and far from the simple affair that first began in collaboration with Edward Kirkby a few years before.

A recurrent theme in Archibald's letters around this time is his request to remain under the governance of the Superior General in Rome rather than under supervision from the local Australian Province with whom he was living and working. He had, thus far, an excellent relationship with the General, Fr Eugène Meyer, though his relationships with some of the local administrators were faltering.

His reasons for maintaining this arrangement are valid, as he writes below, but it is difficult not to think he was arguing for continuance of his business' financial autonomy and wanted to preserve the freedom from scrutiny that the current arrangement provided him,

> *...one favour I ask, I was under the direct orders of the General and I wish to remain there; if this cannot be I would like to be considered a New Guinean Missioner; the Province as it is constituted has no time for me.*[19]

For the last few years Joseph Guis fell victim to the mounting stress of trying to keep the procure running smoothly,

> *It was physically impossible for me to do the accounts, because of many bills that I could not discover. How many times I asked Father Shaw for them. Each time it was a formal promise that it would be done. Then the wireless got him back into gear &... that was the end of the procurement accounts. When I received your letter the other day, I read to him everything that could concern him. He recognized the work immediately. He set about it... I'm saying it, he started, after an hour or two, then blah, blah, blah... the telephone... the Commonwealth Minister wants to speak to him, then it's*

the Postmaster General, then it's the Minister of War, then it's the Premier… Result: Shaw absolutely and immediately must leave & I am no further ahead than before.[20]

By September 1913, Archibald was paying the procure a £150 allowance from his salary of £600 and left the balance in the company as shares. Following the last recapitalisation of the company and a management overhaul, he now has more time for procure duties,

I am now freed from a lot of my [Company] work and will attend the procure duties till I am otherwise advised by you… the work of the procure is not heavy… as regards the real work of the procure, that is attending the shipping orders, I did it and in my absence the shipping clerk saw to it, and was paid by the company.[21]

Whilst Joseph Guis' role was procurator, he was also tending to the pastoral needs of the inmates at the *Little Sisters' Home for the Aged Poor* nearby and saying masses in their chapel, but Guis' health was failing. He fell seriously ill in 1913. His duties of procurator and chaplain to the Little Sisters were then taken up completely by Archibald. The continuing pastoral work for the residents of the Little Sisters home was seen as an *almost impossibility*[22] for the procure priests. Archibald petitioned for someone else to take on the job.

Regular priestly duties had not been part of his routine for some time. It was this growing inattention to his fundamental calling that brought an increasing ire from some within the MSC congregation and put him on the outer.

By the end of 1913 the company had not paid a dividend and was still unable to pay down the procure debt which was some £2,700 in October of 1913,[23] but the company had managed to keep up interest payments. Around this time Archibald arranged for photographs to be taken of the various departments at the Wireless Works. He sent copies to the MSC General Council in Rome in support of his argument that the place was flourishing and that they must remain patient. This gave the MSC administrators in Rome an accurate idea of the size of the operation. It is likely Archibald took the photographs himself, developed the negatives and made prints in a laboratory at the works.

WANTED, first-class Tool Makers, and Die Makers do not apply unless you are a high-grade man and hustler, experimenters keep away.
FIELDGATE,
Shaw Wireless, Ltd.,
Randwick.

WANTED, 30 Carpenters. The Maritime Wireless Telegraph Works, Avoca-st., Randwick.

WANTED, 20 Carpenters. The Maritime Wireless Telegraph Works, Avoca-st., Randwick.

WANTED, TOOL and DIE MAKERS, only mechanics of the highest class and men who can produce results considered, excellent working conditions, and latest American machine tools provided.
Apply FIELDGATE,
Maritime Wireless Works, Randwick.

WANTED, TOOL and DIE MAKERS. Only highest grade men considered. American mechanics preferred. Apply
W. FIELDGATE, Works Manager,
Maritime Wireless Co. (Shaw System), Ltd.,
Avoca-street, Randwick.

WANTED, 3 strong, experienced STONE CHOPPERS. Call on WORKS MANAGER, Maritime Wireless Telegraph Works, Randwick.

WANTED, an American Trained Milling Machinist. Only a specialist in this line need apply.
Fieldgate, Maritime Wireless, Randwick.

WANTED, first-class Iron Turner, who can work to micrometer measurements, American trained men preferred. Fieldgate, Maritime Wireless, Randwick

A sample of Maritime Wireless job advertisements placed by William Fieldgate, works manager from late 1912 to 1914, hinting at the variety of work available.
Credit: Sydney Morning Herald, Jan 24, 1913, 31; Daily Telegraph. April 22, 1912,3; Sydney Morning Herald, April 22, 1912, 15 & June 9, 1913, 12 & May 14, 1913, 23 & May 29, 1913, 29. Following page: Sydney Morning Herald, Aug 1, 1913, 13

> **WANTED**, qualified Bookkeeper, who is thoroughly conversant with card cost system, for electrical and mechanical work, must have mechanical knowledge, to be entirely conversant with our manufactures. Apply W. FIELDGATE, Maritime Wireless Company, Randwick.
>
> **WANTED**, a STOREMAN, who has had first-class experience in electrical and mechanical stores, and familiar with card system, only an energetic man considered. Apply, FIELDGATE MARITIME WIRELESS CO., Randwick.

Copies of the surviving photos show the only surviving glimpse inside the operations of the Randwick Wireless Works. They confirm a clean, spacious and well-organised factory organised into various departments with machinery that was state of-the-art for the time. That this place had grown from virtually nothing in the space of a few years to be the only wireless manufacturing facility in Australia was remarkable.

Complicating matters further, in 1913, there were separate ongoing patent disputes between *Maritime Wireless* and *Telefunken*, and *Maritime Wireless* and the *Marconi Company*. Remember that Maritime Wireless was manufacturing equipment for the Coastal Service according to specifications drawn up by Balsillie. Now before coming to Australia, Balsillie had lost a patent dispute to Marconi in England and under normal circumstances Maritime Wireless may have still been liable for the infringements as the manufacturer of the Balsillie system.

Fortunately, the Australian Government provided Maritime Wireless with a written indemnity insulating them from loss in the event of a successful patent challenge but this would not protect them from the potential fall-off in business if the cases were lost. Archibald, with characteristic optimism, again found it near impossible to see any downside,

> *If the Government win the case our shares will just double their value and I will try to realise for cash my own shares.*
>
> *If the Government lose our shares we will still have their pound value as we are at present making up lots of dynamos for the railways and are getting all kinds of Government work...*[24]

In the middle of all this, after a short stay in St Vincent's Hospital, Joseph Guis, Archibald's immediate superior in the procure and companion for many years, died on the morning of September 14, 1913. He was just forty-four years old; a year older than Archibald. He was very well respected in the Randwick community. He suffered from a complication of disorders almost certainly initiated from his time in the tropical missions. In Archibald's letter notifying Meyer, he variously identifies the cause of his death,

> *I hardly know what to say was the real cause of his death; his nerves were always giving him trouble, also the kidneys - he did have very black moments. I think his nervous state affected his stomach as he had severe vomiting a few weeks before his death. The Doctors were inclined to put it down as ulcerated stomach and general break up of his system...*[25]

Guis' death certificate was more succinct, citing the cause as *Addison's disease*. Besides being a missionary and procurator, Guis was remembered as a writer and musician, composing various pieces of music and *for some years conducting an orchestra in Randwick.*[26] His funeral filled the church at Randwick and he was buried in Randwick Cemetery, then known as Long Bay Cemetery - the first MSC priest interred there. His body lay next to two missionary brothers in a small plot on a rise in the north-east of the cemetery.

From Guis' grave the steel tower of the Wireless Works could be seen adjacent to his old home, *Ascot*, a few kilometres to the north. No one would have thought then that three years later Archibald would be buried next to him.

It was Joseph Guis who was ultimately responsible for procure finances. He was under significant pressure trying to juggle the monies between the procure and the Wireless Works – not wanting to see either fail. His illness may have precluded any knowledge of Archibald borrowing mission funds to cover short-term wireless debts, or it may have been induced further by Archibald's lack of attention to bookwork and the untimely payments of bills.

Both Guis and Archibald were supportive of each other in their many years of working together and Guis' gentle nature made it unlikely that the stress caused by Archibald would have been made known to anyone else, aside from him mentioning it in a few letters to the Superior General. It was Guis who first suggested selling the entire operation, including the houses, *Ascot* and *Archina* and the workshops at Randwick when word was given to Archibald to divest his interest back in July.[27]

Archibald continued in Guis' job after his death and sent the missions' financial reports to Rome. Amongst the MSC leadership there was a good deal of discussion about who would be the new procurator. Archibald promoted himself for the position but given his history, was unlikely to be appointed. There was even more pressure now to have him come directly under local authority. Fr Armand Pagès was appointed procurator but resigned soon after due to ill health. As a consequence, the financial oversight Archibald so badly needed was still not forthcoming.

In 1913 the General Council appointed Father Tréand, a much-beloved parish priest of Randwick, to investigate the state of finances at the procure and send a report to Rome.[28] According to a single sentence in a letter written some years later from Linckens to Archbishop Cerretti, the first Apostolic Delegate in Australia,[29] Archibald was less than cooperative during the Tréand investigation,

> *Father A. Shaw refused to execute the order he received from Father General to hand over to Father Tréand the financial administration of the [mission] house and of the mission money.*[30]

This rang alarm bells in Rome. As the drums of war started to beat throughout Europe, events were set in motion to have the procure, and indeed the entire Australian Province, properly examined by an official from the General Council of the MSC.

The workload on Archibald was significant in the wake of Guis' death, though his role within Maritime Wireless, especially with order from his superiors to get-out of the business, was changing,

> *During the last two years I have had the heavy work of organising these [Wireless] Works and the seventeen Government Wireless Stations, but now I have, as you see, a very good staff of assistants and I reserve for myself the position of Technical Advisor and the Government have their own staff now...*
>
> *If you wished me to permanently take charge of the procure I am perfectly free to do so as my work in the wireless is now only as scientific and technical advisor... the work of the procure would not... overload me as I have had to do it all along practically.*[31]

Archibald might have occasionally thought of and perhaps envied the comparatively simple life of his long-time friend, Fernand Arnoult. Archibald installed him as manager of the Bulga Timber Mill located in the forests northwest of Taree. Once a missionary brother, Arnoult had long since left the order and was about to marry a local Wingham girl, Ruby Thompson.

Some employees of the Wireless Works were given residence by Archibald in either *Ascot* or *Archina,* and for a period of time, *Archina* was also home to Amy Kennedy, Archibald's niece. She was an accomplished musician educated at the *Convent of Mercy*, Redfern. She taught music for a time at the nearby *Brigidine College*. Amy's sister Catherine attended *St Scholastica's College*, Glebe, and was caring for her mother whilst living with her at Petersham around this time.

It was Archibald who found the money to pay his nieces' fees during their school years after the incapacitating medical problems of their mother, Mary Kennedy, became apparent. Mary died on June 21, 1913, and was buried by Archibald in Waverley cemetery.[32]

Her daughter, Catherine, later worked as a governess in a house called *Woolerbilla* which still stands in Higgs Street, another high-point of Randwick – then part of Melody Street. She ended up marrying into the family that lived there in 1917. Six years later, just across the road, the first antenna and studio of the then commercial radio station 2SB, later known as 2BL, was built behind the house where Ray Allsop lived. Occasionally mistaken for Archibald's wireless station by following generations, 2BL existed on this site until its relocation in 1939.

The Shaw Wireless Works spent considerable energy trying to generate business as the Coastal Wireless Service contracts came to an end. The factory had a presence in Victoria in the latter part of 1913. Representatives set-up an impressive exhibit at the *All-Australian Exhibition* which ran for two months from the middle of September to the middle of November, 1913. It was held at the Exhibition Building in Melbourne.[33]

The display served as a marketing opportunity and featured working models which showed-off various industrial processes from a host of manufacturers. The manufacturing capacity and engineering capabilities of the Wireless Works were on public display here and it is evident from the extensive newspaper coverage that wireless manufacture was in fact only a small part of the operation. A tongueless buckle for rifle slings or tramway cash bags was made on the Wireless Works site at one time,[34] as were electric motors and air compressors.[35]

The display from Maritime Wireless was reported as one of the best in the exhibition. Other items included telegraph and electrical instruments, wooden casting patterns and metal punchings; brass castings; terminals and relays; sounders and transmitting keys; magnetic detectors; condensers; a time computer; armatures and brushes; laminators; a petrol motor and generator; aluminium castings; Leyden-jars coated in copper by a completely new process; induction coils, x-ray machines and equipment for photography.[36]

Meanwhile, back at *Ascot* on October 20, 1913, during an otherwise uneventful day, the then Australian MSC Provincial, Fr Edward Nouyoux, blustered into the procure-house unannounced, speaking to Archibald and whoever else was present. He proclaimed that, on the authority of the Father General, Archibald was to now hand over the running of the procure to a Father John Lee, the second Australian-born MSC priest, who would be taking over in a day or two.

Archibald was compliant to a degree but Nouyoux's order conflicted with previous correspondence that he had received from the Father General in Rome. Archibald produced the Meyer letter written only a month before which effectively gave him permission to maintain temporary charge of the procure until a decision was made about who would take over permanently following Guis' death.

Archibald asked Nouyoux if his instructions post-dated these letters. He reports a surprising response in the next day's mail to his superior, Meyer, in Rome,

> ...*your two letters to me dated 14 and 17 September came to hand and I immediately went to Kensington to show the Provincial...*
>
> *I asked him if his instructions from you were dated [after this] and he was much confused and admitted that he had no instructions from you at all.*
>
> *I told him that I was therefore compelled to act on your instructions and I would look after the procure duties till further instructions by your good self and Councillors.*[37]

Archibald saw through Nouyoux's clumsy approach. It was clear the local leadership wanted him out of the procure without delay. Archibald wrote to Meyer and the MSC General Council in his deferential way and finished with his usual request,

> *Thank you for entrusting me with looking after things as it shows you still have confidence in me which is exceedingly gratifying to me.*
>
> *One favour I ask of you, that is not to be put under the direction of the Australian Province as it is now constituted but that I may depend direct from the General or the New Guinea Missions...*[38]

In a separate letter written on the same day to Eugène Meyer and the General Council, Archibald reaffirms his commitment to serving the missions and hints at the difficulties he endures from the local administration,

You know me as a rough man, but my intentions are always for the welfare of our Order.

I hate fighting and wrangling and wish to live at peace with all. As you know I am deeply interested in our procure and Missions and I would like to tell you again you can count on me for any work you wish to give me.[39]

But the writing was on wall for Archibald.

♦ ♦ ♦

It was not unusual to have a senior member of the congregation – a *Visitator* – personally investigate all sorts of matters in far flung provinces. There was now an urgency for the European MSC leadership to make an expeditious Australian visit which could not be deferred, despite the threat of looming war.

Meyer and the General Council dispatched Hubert Linckens – arguably the most tenacious man the order had - to investigate the state of affairs, not only at the Wireless Works, but throughout the entire MSC Australian Province. Lickens reported directly to the Superior General and had authority to promulgate local guidelines and bring regulation to the province wherever he saw fit. His apparent heavy handedness created friction with many of the local missionaries.

Had Linckens been born a few centuries earlier he would have made a formidable inquisitor. The Dutch-born German was forensic in his attention to detail and meticulous in setting rules and codes to be followed in matters where he thought that laxity had otherwise prevailed. He had previously been provincial of the German Province and was a member of the General Council. It was Linckens who founded *Mission House* at Hiltrup and established the museum there in 1897 with artefacts displayed from MSC missions across the Pacific. Fr Rascher's rifle, which was used by Tomari to initiate the New Britain Baining massacre of 1904, was on display at the museum.[40]

Linckens' Germanic leadership style made him extremely unpopular in the young Australian Province which had until now, because of its distance from Europe, evolved more fluidly in serving the spiritual needs of the local Catholic population.

It was just a matter of time before Hubert Linckens put the procure, Archibald himself and the business he had valiantly fostered and defended, under proper scrutiny.

Machine Shop, Maritime Wireless, 1913. *Credit: MSC Archive*

PROSPEROUS YEARS

Electrical Department, Maritime Wireless, 1913.   *Credit: MSC Archive*

Moulding and Casting Department, Maritime Wireless, 1913.   *Credit: MSC Archive*

Pattern Shop, Maritime Wireless, 1913. *Credit: MSC Archive*

Power Room, Maritime Wireless, 1913. *Credit: MSC Archive*

Punch Press Department, Maritime Wireless, 1913. *Credit: MSC Archive*

Tool Room, Maritime Wireless, 1913. *Credit: MSC Archive*

Winding Department, Maritime Wireless, 1913.   *Credit: MSC Archive*

Generator Assembly, Maritime Wireless, 1913.   *Credit: MSC Archive*

XIV

Hubert Linckens Comes to Town

In January of 1914 a fire engulfed one of the workshops at Maritime Wireless destroying a quantity of machinery and materials valued at about £3,000 ($300,000 today). It was promptly attended by officers from the Randwick Fire Brigade just a block away and assisted by the Waverley Fire Brigade who came from a neighbouring suburb. By the time the brigades arrived significant damage had already occurred. The fire was discovered by Archibald himself in one of the machine shops about ten o'clock, during his nightly rounds of the premises. Fortunately, the site was insured against such a calamity.[1]

The fire was not just an omen of things to come. It was a dress rehearsal for what ended-up being a tough and peculiar year. Archibald approached the fire and all that was to be thrown at him later with characteristic positivity,

> *'All these machines and parts gone', [one of the workers] exclaimed. 'All our work wasted.'*
> *'Never mind,' returned the head of the concern, 'it has been done before; it can be done again'.*[2]

On Saturday, June 27, 1914, Archibald with some of the MSC brothers set-off from Kensington toward the city in the Wireless Works' car to welcome Hubert Linckens who had just arrived in Australia, having departed from the port of Bremen in Germany a few weeks earlier.[3] This was Linckens' second visit to Australia. They drove him from the berth at Circular Quay[4] to Kensington monastery where he would be based.

The very next day, Austrian Archduke Francis Ferdinand was assassinated in Sarajevo. This resulted in a sequence of European hostilities that led directly to the commencement of the First World War. Now Linckens was a Dutch born German citizen and was prevented from going back to Europe for the duration of the war. In fact, he returned some seven years later in May, 1920,[5] for reasons that will become apparent later.

Linckens was *a gifted, fluent linguist, knowledgeable and widely travelled.*[6] This is how a young Australian priest, James Power, remembers him,

> *He was a model of regularity, punctuality and exact religious observance; in this, no deviation – all day, every day, at the appointed place or duty, whether the call were to prayer, work, recreation. So consistent was he that it could not pass unnoticed - this the comment often heard that 'one could set his watch by Fr Linckens'.*[7]

Hubert Linckens. *Credit: MSC Archive*

Linckens' regulatory methods and authoritative nature clashed with many priests in the Australian Province and the advent of World War I meant that he would be exercising his authority in Australia much longer than originally planned. In an attempt to limit his influence he was, at one time, denounced as a German spy in an anonymous telegram sent to the Ministry of Defence. The accusation, based on no evidence whatsoever, was probably sent by someone within the Tasmanian MSC community in the hope that he would be detained by the wartime government or at least have some restriction imposed on his travel. He was scheduled to visit Tasmania and, whoever the author was, clearly did not want him snooping around. The telegram read,

> *A German priest visiting Australia for a second time, his expenses paid by the German Government was about to visit Tasmania. Residence at present, Kensington College, Sydney. Believed to be a spy.*[8]

Naturally the government had an obligation to investigate the anonymous accusation. Linckens was able to clear himself through an embarrassing court process that involved responding to questions directly from the Minister for Defence. Thereafter, he spent considerable time vehemently seeking the identity of his unidentified accuser. Whilst he held various suspicions, his efforts at finding the perpetrator were ultimately unsuccessful.

Within days of arriving at Kensington, Linckens visited the procure at *Ascot* next to the Wireless Works and the true state of its financial affairs became immediately apparent. The Wireless Works were still not paying a dividend and without dividends it was impossible for Archibald to repay money he had borrowed from mission accounts to fund Maritime Wireless' cash shortfall. Yet it was Archibald's cavalier attitude to the accounts and invoices that surprised Linckens most,

> *A visit to the Wireless Works… revealed a great industry of men working in a factory attached to the residence of the procure. In this residence was the office of the procure and for the wireless works – but the office was an untidy mess and it meant that before any documents could be found, he*

himself had to spend two days putting the office in order.[9]

One wonders why Archibald made no attempt to make matters easier for himself by tidying the books and trying to bring some semblance of order before Linckens' arrival. Attention to detail at this level was not part of his character. He always had an eye on the bigger picture and overlooked detail. In fact, such was the mess at *Ascot* that the true level of debt owed by Archibald to the missions was only ever a best-estimate whenever it was calculated by Linckens.

Outstanding invoices were sent to the procure office on account of the Wireless Works' business. Linckens himself maintained it would be several months before the true state of affairs could be known.[10] In reality it turned out to be several years.

For Archibald the diversion of mission funds to cover short-term cash demands was a temporary solution but it proved to be a fatal error of judgement once discovered. Linckens saw no merit in a line-of-credit between procure and Wireless Works accounts and called-out Archibald's actions as *embezzlement* when reporting on his liberal behaviour back to Rome. Linckens had little time for a priest's involvement in worldly business pursuits.

Archibald saw the situation somewhat differently. For him, it became a *duty* to keep the business afloat in order to limit the risk of losing money that individuals: his friends, fellow priests and business associates, had already put into the company,

> *As you know I have an opportunity to pay [the procure debts] by the wireless, but in taking other peoples' money I have a double debt upon myself. To make matters short and clear, were you to order me to leave the procure I could not attend to the wireless and without me the company would break up and I would have it on my conscience - also the £20,000 that [the] gentlemen have put in my patents so I would be placed in a very awkward position.*[11]

Fr Linckens, acting on behalf of the MSC General, Fr Eugène Meyer and the MSC General Council, wrote years later to the Apostolic Delegate, the pope's representative in Australia, stating,

> *In 1910 Father A. Shaw began some experiments in the wireless branch. By 1912 the General Council of the Society prohibited expressly that Father A. Shaw take for that purpose or even have at his disposition any cash of the Society or of the missions...*
>
> *Since I am in Australia, I gave to Father A. Shaw all facility in order that he may repair his fault, but all his manifold attempts were without result.[12]*

By the early part of 1914 the final two Coastal Wireless Service stations had been installed at Roebourne and Wyndham in Western Australia and the big government contract was now concluded. Income from engineering activities continued. However, the glory days of the works were now past and business was actively being sought to sustain the operation. This was difficult in a climate of war. Furthermore, the Fisher Government which had whole-heartedly supported domestic manufacturing was replaced in June 1913 by the anti-Labor party of Joseph Cook which reverted the supply of wireless for various government departments, including the Navy, to Amalgamated Wireless Australasia (AWA), created from a partnership between the old competitors of Marconi and Telefunken.

Despite its name, AWA in those days was Australian only in name. The technology of wireless was also developing and moving on from spark-gap into what was called *continuous wave*. This was not pursued at the Wireless Works with the same enthusiasm. There was always the possibility as a last resort, that the engineering business of the Wireless Works could fulfil some government war materiel contracts like munitions or arms manufacture if they became available.

From this point Linckens officially ordered Archibald to sell the Wireless Works and divest himself of all financial interest in it. The process was not straight forward and it would eventually take two years for Archibald to extricate himself from the business. Fr Jozef Wemmers, a fellow countryman of Linckens and, like Linckens, previously a provincial of the Northern (German) Province was procurator during this period and Archibald, whilst still living at *Ascot* in Dutruc Street, Randwick, became engaged more or less full-time in the business of sustaining and eventually selling Maritime Wireless.

The pressure was certainly on Archibald. He had Linckens, his polar-opposite, overlooking every transaction; he had a business that was beginning to struggle in the war-time climate under the new Liberal Government, he had a large debt to repay, and he had the investors and employees to consider. One can only imagine the numerous difficult and uncomfortable meetings that took place between Linckens and Archibald. Fortunately, Linckens had other concerns in the Australian Province besides the financial affairs of the Wireless Works which gave Archibald an occasional reprieve.

For his own part, Archibald had other concerns too and began, not for the first time, to reconsider the direction his life was taking.

Once Linckens thought he understood the state of financial affairs he formalised an agreement between Archibald and the procure. Archibald was made to sign a declaration admitting that he owed the sum of £4,363/12s/1d to the *Catholic Mission of New Pomerania or New Britain*. With interest charges of 6% a year, the total sum owed and unpaid by September, 1915, was £4,960/16s/1d. Archibald was under an obligation to pay this debt as soon as possible and to maintain interest payments on the unpaid portions.[13] In today's money the debt is a significant sum - just shy of half-a-million dollars.

However, this finding was not the end of the matter. Linckens had just begun a long and frustrating journey of incremental discovery. Soon after, he discovered Archibald had also borrowed monies from other mission accounts,

> *According to the final statement signed by Father A. Shaw on September 30th, 1915, he owes £9,586 three shilling and eleven pence to our missions in New Guinea, New Britain and of the Gilbert Islands for cash taken without due permission for his purposes.*[14]

Whether Archibald had any clue as to what monies he had borrowed over time and from where, or whether he was intentionally feigning ignorance is unclear. Given what is known of his personality, it is more likely to be the former. His obliviousness to the financial state of affairs meant he had no alternative other than to put his trust in Linckens' accounting. As more borrowings came to light his debt to the mission accounts approached one million dollars in today's money.

The only possible way to repay this enormous sum was for the business to be sold. Linckens realised this even before the full extent of the debt was known and Archibald knew it too. Archibald continued with an unswerving loyalty to his investors and the workers by trying to exact a sale of the works which would honour the investment his shareholders had put up and ensure continuing employment of his workers. As had been the case now for some years, his priestly duties were long neglected and became the least of his concerns. This was very apparent to his superiors. Linckens writes,

> *What seems worse to me is that Father A. Shaw has no more any love for his religious and priestly duties, so that he has not ever the wish to exercise any ecclesiastical ministry, but he ventures continually upon new experiments, which all turn out to be fallacies.*[15]

Some of the 'fallacies' Linckens refers to were, in fact, novel, wide-ranging and creative ideas - despite them having no commercial value at the time. What Linckens does not mention is that, with the onset of war, experimental radio stations were ordered to be disassembled and remain unused by the government from August, 1914.[16] Wireless was only authorised for use by the PMG and the defence forces, to whom Maritime Wireless continued to supply components in competition with other suppliers.[17] But whilst the *wireless* side of the Wireless Works was in a forced pause, the engineering side of the business sustained operations at Randwick. This brought about some remarkable creativity from the factory staff.

Some of the experimental concepts developed at Randwick were a century ahead of their time and are widely used in various applications today considered to be 'cutting-edge'.

Marion Mulrony, then the long-serving manager of the works and previously an electrician in the United States Navy from back in 1907, had patented a tool for removing and tightening difficult to reach nuts. He was a quietly spoken man who 'lived radio'[18] and had been part of the Wireless Works since its inception. At the works he also patented[19] an ingenious dynamo capable of generating electricity using wind energy. His design was based on a double-vaned windmill. A working prototype was built at Randwick and set up in the grounds of the Wireless Works mounted atop its own tower. It remained operating there for several years.[20] It was capable of powering an electric fan and a string of incandescent electric lights, which themselves were a novelty and had only become available in the last seven years. Such a device was ideal for operating wireless sets or providing electric lighting in remote and windy locations where heavy generators would be prohibitive.

Mulrony also developed a portable high-voltage generator capable of powering short-distance wireless transmitters or for operating an x-ray tube in the field.[21] This device could be used to x-ray wounded soldiers in field hospitals on the Western Front. He had so much confidence in his patents that he eventually left the Wireless Works and set up the *Mulrony Electric Company*,[22] a partnership in Sydney, selling these items before he returned to the United States to begin building and managing the commercial radio station, KGU, in Honolulu.

A new kind of motor car[23] was also developed at the Randwick site. It was driven by an electric motor and operated similarly to the current crop of hybrid-electric cars on the market today. A small, two-cylinder petrol motor connected to a dynamo charged batteries which operated an electric drive motor. There were no gears. When the car went downhill the drive motor acted as a generator and charged the batteries. A hundred years later modern incarnations of these vehicles are common during the transition from fossil fuels to renewable energy. There was even talk of a remote-controlled submarine being developed at the Wireless Works using *an ingenious system of clocks [that] could be launched in Sydney Cove and directed out of the harbour to sink an enemy ship outside [Sydney] Heads.*[24]

Such was the capability of the factory that Shaw Wireless made an offer to the government in 1915 to manufacture aeroplane engines for the war effort.[25] The offer was never taken up.

In principle these ideas sound wonderful but what was missing was the commitment of investment in materials and labour for research, development and in the machinery to bring the projects to market. Besides, Archibald had his orders to sell and, realistically, there was no motivation to do anything else.

On December 8, 1914, under pressure from Linckens, Archibald offered the Wireless Works to the Postmaster-General's Department for £55,000. He claimed some £78,000 had been spent on the site and that the reduced sale price would offer good value to a prospective purchaser. The price included *the works, buildings, plant, land, and the Australian rights of the Shaw wireless patents.*[26] After several months of assessment from a wide-ranging committee of experts, including the PMG Chief Electrical Engineer, the manager of the Small Arms Factory at Lithgow, the Department of Defence and the Commonwealth Lighthouse Engineer, the offer was declined.

Seeing that hostilities in Europe were going to drag on, control of wireless in Australia was belatedly transferred by the government from the PMG to the Department of Navy on November 1, 1915. The Navy man in charge of wireless, the *Fleet Wireless Telegraphy Officer*, was Engineer-Lieutenant Frank G. Cresswell – not to be confused with William R. Creswell who conducted the first naval ship to shore wireless communication mentioned earlier aboard the *Gayundah*[27] back in April, 1903, in waters off Brisbane. Engineer Cresswell, who later became Commander, saw the necessity of the Australian Navy having its own workshops for the manufacture and repair of wireless sets.

The aforementioned, Captain William Creswell, who conducted the Brisbane wireless trials and for whom the Royal Australian Naval College at Jervis Bay is named, later went on to become a Rear Admiral and is regarded as founder of the Australian Navy. This Rear Admiral Creswell later recommended the purchase of the Shaw Wireless Works to the full board of the Navy when it was offered to them.[28]

As work dried up at the Wireless Works some talented employees began to leave and look for employment elsewhere – some starting businesses of their own. The intellectual capital of Archibald's enterprise, so important to its original growth, started to wane. One previous employee was Ewald Anthony Raves. He was, like Linckens, a German citizen stuck in Australia at the outbreak of war. He started a business called *Twentieth Century Engineering* in nearby Dolphin Street, Coogee, after leaving Maritime Wireless. His nationality brought him under immediate suspicion but his activities would have gone completely unremarked if he were not caught with a wireless set whilst Australia was on a war-footing,

> ... [he] had in his possession after he left those works a wireless apparatus which he subsequently was obliged to surrender. Some enquiries should be made with regard to this man and the nature of the business carried on by his company.[29]

In the months ahead further complications arose in Archibald's life which went a long way to explaining his apparent neglect-of-duties as a priest.

The following events only became publicly known during testimony given to a Royal Commission held to examine how the eventual sale price of the Wireless Works was arrived at and how the sale itself was conducted. The evidence and findings were first published in 1918, two years after Archibald's death.

In April or March, 1914, Archibald met Evie Providence Hoad.[30] Evie was the daughter of Walter and Olieve Hoad who managed the Yarrangobilly Caves and the associated accommodation known as Caves House. The caves are located in the vicinity of Tumut and Adelong, the town of Archibald's childhood. The Hoad family had a long association with Yarrangobilly Caves and it is likely that Archibald met Evie on a trip to the caves to visit her father.

Walter had known Archibald since his boyhood.[31] It is quite likely that the then newly married Walter and Olieve fostered the young Archibald for a time after the unexpected death of his mother, Catherine, in 1880. Whilst there is no direct record of this,[32] somehow or other a bond formed during Archibald's youth with the Hoad family that was strong enough for him to revisit them in later life.

Evie was born in 1887, the same year that Heinrich Hertz discovered the photoelectric effect and demonstrated the production and reception of radio waves. The missions and wireless were the two great loves of Archibald's life, and now there was a third: Evie, affectionately known to Archibald as just *'E'.*[33] She was twenty-seven years old when they first met, seventeen years younger than Archibald. Within a few months of their meeting Archibald had asked Evie to marry him and she accepted. Further proposals for a secret wedding were also made multiple times by Archibald,

> *He had asked me to marry him two years before he died, and he was just waiting until he got everything settled up...*
>
> *He said he would leave the church as soon as he could. As a matter of fact, he asked me several times to marry him secretly; but, of course, I would not do that...*
>
> *His idea was, as soon as the works were sold... to go off to America. Either that, or he would go first, and I and my sister should follow...*
>
> *He expected to make good at engineering over there... I was getting impatient. I was waiting two years for him to get his affairs settled up...*[34]

When in Sydney Evie stayed with her sister, Sylvia, at 31 Frenchman's Road, Randwick, only a minute's walk from *Ascot*, the procure office, in Dutruc Street.

The promise of marriage Archibald made to Evie in 1914 remained secret and was only known to a small circle of Evie's friends. Remarkably, the content of Evie's testimony did not diminish the esteem the public held for Archibald and the contemporary newspaper reporting of the Royal Commission evidence later gave little hint of a sensationalist or scandalous coverage – unlike accounts of the story that were published some sixty years later when journalists retold it focussing on certain salacious details for a different audience. The post-war matter-of-fact press coverage of the affair between Archibald and Evie remained quietly unsensational, possibly because it was only a minor detail in more important issues under investigation by the commission.

The distraction of Evie in Archibald's life from 1914 may explain his cavalier attitude toward the procure accounts and toward the orders Linckens gave him to sell the works and repay the debt owed. Evie's presence would certainly have contributed to his lack of interest in conducting priestly duties.

We do know from the Royal Commission evidence that Archibald confided in Evie, as would be expected in any close relationship, about the proposed selling of the Wireless Works. He confided in many people. However, Evie's own concerns were about their future life together rather than matters relating to Wireless Works' business,

> *I do not know why he talked his business to me at all; but the fact remains he did tell me of his business matters, and I told him I did not understand anything about it.*[35]

As has always been characteristic, Archibald was looking beyond the present to the next 'big thing'. This no longer just included divestment of the business and returning to life as a regular MSC missionary. His life was about to undergo a profound redirection. It was rapidly and unexpectedly evolving along a completely new path in a new country, with an uncertain future, and no longer as a priest.

However, in 1914 the plans he shared with Evie had to remain secret or else the sale of the business, for its best possible price – difficult enough in the war years - would be scuttled.

This was because Archibald's name was intrinsically linked to the good-will of the Wireless Works. The patents were in his name, increasing the monetary value of the business by providing intellectual property. The investors he lined-up were backing Archibald himself as much as the business he created. All the creditors had to be paid-out upon the sale of the works, as did the debt he owed to the missions. Not only that, but Archibald was fighting off convoluted patent challenges from Marconi, Telefunken and now, most recently, a new one from Graeme Balsillie, the man behind the design of the Coastal Wireless Service. He accused Archibald of stealing his designs and claimed that the *Shaw System* was actually his own.

In fact, by 1916, a separate Royal Commission was anticipated to determine whether it was Archibald or Balsillie who had actually invented the wireless system that was in place throughout Australian Coastal Wireless Service.[36]

Given all that was going on in Archibald's world, it is a fallacy to think he lived a peaceful life. Perhaps he could not recognise the stress he was under, living by the maxim he gave to the reporter earlier in the year when interviewed after the destructive fire at the Wireless Works:

Never mind… it has been done before; it can be done again.[37]

XV

Crossroads: Meeting Evie

The course of Archibald's life changed completely after he fell in love with Evie Hoad. Outwardly, however, nothing much appeared to change at all. Linckens was fruitlessly chasing him for mission money and furtive attempts to sell the Wireless Works in accord with Linckens' instructions, at a price sufficient to cover his debts, had thus far been unsuccessful. Archibald had large and small investors with a stake in the business, including some his own confreres. He continued to hold a personal responsibility for their investment and tried to ensure the ongoing employment of Maritime Wireless workers as business continued to wane through the war years.

For quite a while Archibald had showed little interest in the duties typical of a priest. There are no records of marriages, baptisms or funerals conducted by him during this time.

The affair with Evie and his multiple promises of marriage was completely incompatible with his role as an ordained Roman Catholic priest. He was not the first priest to tread this path and wouldn't be the last. The church had rules in place for such eventualities. Under more ordinary circumstances he would have, *post haste*, applied for a dispensation of his vows from his congregational superiors – a relatively simple process – and then applied to one of the departments of the Roman Curia – the *Sacred Congregation of Religious* - for 'laicisation'. Unfortunately, his position and history with Maritime Wireless, if only as figurehead, precluded this as he remained intrinsically tied up with its good-will and monetary value.

Evie Providence Hoad, c. 1915 — *Credit: Colin Hoad*

He and Evie were forced by circumstance then to conduct their relationship with the utmost secrecy. They had a protracted engagement - mostly because Archibald saw a forced delay of his application for laicisation as the only viable path for a profitable sale of the works.

Were the relationship to be discovered, there would be grounds for immediate action from Archibald's superiors in accordance with the advice set out in decrees from the Roman authorities. These were officially published in the *Analecta ecclesiastica* – a collection of documents concerning the administration of all sorts of legal matters within the Catholic Church and its membership. We will see later that Archibald's relationship with Evie was indeed discovered and made known to Linckens in the months before his death. Consequently, Linckens had no option but to invoke the rules for dismissal presented in the *Analecta,* but fate was to intervene, as it frequently did in the Shaw story, and changed the expected course of events.

Wireless technology continued to make advances. However, Maritime Wireless did not pursue the manufacture of transmitters using the latest modulated continuous-wave technology which relied on the new glass-valve technology.

Point-to-point communication was made more efficient in these years too by radical developments in antenna design, specifically with the implementation of *beam antennae*. These shaped wireless signals to propagate waves in a particular direction in contrast to earlier omni-directional wire-caged designs which wasted a lot of energy. Beam antennas became ubiquitous over the next decade or so. The drain of technically competent individuals from the works, such as Mulrony, made keeping up with contemporary advances in wireless impossible. Eventually, the application of the Fleming diode valve and later, the triode valve in wireless, which allowed voice messages and music to be carried over a narrow bandwidth, signalled obsolescence for the electro-mechanical spark-gap sets that the Wireless Works had built its reputation on.

The new wireless technology was rapidly adopted by a host of competitors including the recently formed Amalgamated Wireless (Australasia) Company, familiarly known as AWA, formed by the partnership of two earlier competitors, Marconi and Telefunken. AWA became the dominant force in the Australian wireless and electronics market – a position maintained for decades. Ernest Fisk, with wide ranging interests from spiritualism to metaphysics, became its first chairman. He once seriously suggested to the amusement of his employees that wireless would, one day, be used to contact the dead.[1] No progress was made in this endeavour. However, a few years later Fisk received, at his home in Wahroonga, the first wireless messages transmitted direct from the United Kingdom to Australia. These were sent by the Australian Prime Minister and Minister for Navy during a UK visit. The messages recognised Australia's commendable war effort.[2] At this time the England to Australia path was the longest distance wireless messages had ever been sent.

By December, 1915, only a small amount of electrical engineering work continued at the Wireless Works, together with the manufacture of motorcycle parts for the Postmaster-General's Department.[3] The glory days of wireless manufacture were over. Whilst awaiting a buyer for the works, Archibald made the necessary and reluctant decision to apply for a government munitions contract at Randwick to keep the place afloat and support Australia's war effort. The contract was for six months.

The patience of Evie Hoad was being sorely tested during this time according to her Royal Commission testimony,

> *He told me in December [1915] he was going to start munitions [manufacture] and he hoped to make good, but he has been going to make good so often that I did not think he would ever make good...*[4]

A new manager, Albert Cornwell, was installed by Archibald to oversee the munitions manufacture. He reluctantly came to Randwick with his family from the Lithgow Small Arms Factory. As a mechanical engineer he brought the necessary experience associated with munitions production. Cornwell was unenthusiastic about the job at first because he thought his employment would be temporary and would not continue after the contract for the shells had been completed. He had a wife and children to support. Under his watch the factory produced some forty-thousand eighteen-pounder shells[5] during its six-month contract with the government. Cornwell lived with his family in the adjacent building, *Archina,* in Avoca Street, Randwick.

The conversion of the factory from Wireless and engineering services to shell manufacture is best explained by Cornwell himself,

> *I got in touch with Shaw, or Shaw got in touch with me at... the end of May, 1915, and he put a proposition to me and said he wanted to take part in contracts given out by the New South Wales Government...*
>
> *He asked me later on at his works to give him an opinion as to whether he could efficiently manufacture shells in those works, and I gave him my opinion, and said that I thought his plant was not entirely suitable, and that personally I advised him not to engage in the manufacture of shells, but he persisted, and he eventually offered me employment and guaranteed me a year's salary in the event of the contract ceasing....*
>
> *I told him he would have to spend certain sums of money to augment his plant to make it suitable... and he told me he had plenty of money to do that...*
>
> *I found after I had been there a little while that he had very little money with which to erect machinery for the manufacture of shells.*[6]

The undertaking of Maritime Wireless to make war munitions became the greatest paradox in the Archibald Shaw story. Years earlier the Randwick Wireless Works were proudly touted as a Catholic Engineering Factory with a Catholic priest at its helm. Now it was an armaments factory producing shells designed to maim and kill an enemy on the Western Front – activities far-removed from genteel Christian values of tolerance, love and forgiveness. Furthermore, the Superior General's representative in Australia, closely monitoring the actions of Archibald, was Hubert Linckens, himself a German citizen. The munitions produced at Randwick were destined for Europe to kill Linckens' own countrymen! What a strange and improbable scenario Archibald, Linckens and the management of the Wireless Works found themselves in.

One can only imagine Linckens' seething frustration at the reluctant MSC participation in the whole enterprise. The ethical questions bandied around between the stake-holders of the works and the discussions across the dining tables of the Kensington monastery and other MSC houses, would have provided a tantalizing dilemma for the most gifted moral philosophers.

Militia forces guarded Maritime Wireless during the period of munitions manufacture but someone still managed to secrete out an eighteen-pounder shell into the largely residential neighbourhood. Randwick was a gentrified suburb and increasingly seen as an unsuitable location for a manufacturing factory – particularly armaments. The shell was found 'live', with its detonator cap in place. It was inadvertently dug-up from a garden, a few inches deep, at the home of the Houghton family living at 8 Stephen Street, Randwick, some twenty-four years later.[7] Stephen Street is a few blocks north-east of the Maritime Wireless site.

Albert Cornwell became good friends with Archibald Shaw[8] during his tenure as works manager and put aside the moral questions of munitions manufacture. After the war the *Daily Telegraph* recorded,

Mr Cornwell points out that most of the shells never reached England, being forwarded on two boats which were torpedoed on the way.[9]

The manufacture of wartime munitions at Maritime Wireless served to remind the government of the usefulness of small local factories and provided momentum for an improved sale price. But Archibald could not negotiate the sale alone. He had, years before, befriended James Joseph Long, the Tasmanian Labor Government senator. It was Senator Long who encouraged Archibald to set-up the initial King Island wireless station for the remotest members of his constituency.

When Archibald made known his intention to sell the works, Long offered to facilitate and negotiate the sale to the government. And so began a tedious back-and-forth, which lasted many months, between Archibald and Long; between Long and Jens Jensen, the Minister for Navy; and between Long and various government agencies and advisors.

When the works were sold most of the proceeds would be returned to the principal creditor, Sir Rupert Clarke, who was due for an agreed payment of £25,000. This was only a fraction of what he had put into the company. Clarke had covered debts to the London Bank for some £27,000 and had made a six-month rental agreement on the Wireless Works land with Archibald for which Clarke was to be paid £15,000 during the period of munitions manufacture. Clarke and his solicitor, Henry Whiting, a partner in the law firm *Whiting and Aitken,* effectively held a mortgage over the Wireless Works. There were also other issues at the works which limited manufacture during the time of the munitions contract. The government had commandeered some of the plant for their own purposes and the steel supplied by the Broken Hill Company had certain flaws in it, making it difficult to work.[10] Consequently, the company defaulted on rental payments.

After Clarke, the next creditor in line was Hubert Linckens with the large debt he was recovering on behalf of the MSC. It was just under £10,000. Discussions between Archibald and Linckens resulted in Linckens expecting that only one-third the amount owed to the MSC would actually be recovered.[11] Linckens was an unwilling creditor because of Archibald's unauthorised use of mission funds. Of course, Linckens would not have invested at all if circumstances were different but the peculiar situation that arose conspired to make him work the hardest of all creditors to recover the misappropriated money when the factory was finally sold.

The first half of 1916 saw Archibald under more duress. He had no idea what to do if a sale failed to materialise when the munitions contract ended. Evie Hoad describes his demeanour,

> *He seemed to be downhearted because the munitions were about to close, and I asked him what he would do, and he said he would sell the works...*[12]

On May 16, 1916, Archibald met with Mr Percy Cotes, another director of Maritime Wireless, and received approval to proceed with the sale of the works to the government. Cotes had replaced solicitor Henry Whiting as director when the latter went to war. Whiting was also a prominent share holder in the Wireless Works himself and his law firm represented the interests Sir Rupert Clarke, the principal creditor. Together their share-holding was about 21,000 of the 35,000 shares in the company.[13] Via a letter drafted by Senator Long, Archibald wrote to the Minister for Navy, Jens Augustus Jensen (known as Gus), offering for sale the entire plant, machinery, inventory, buildings and patents for £57,000 ($5.7 million today). The matter was considered by the Navy and in the meantime, Archibald prepared on June 9, 1916, a complete inventory of everything that was to be included in the sale. The inventory was valued at some £74,461/12s/4d. Surprisingly, this included an *appreciated* value of some older machinery, forty percent above its original purchase price.[14] This inflated valuation was sanctioned by Archibald himself.

Engineer-Lieutenant, later Radio-Commander Cresswell, who visited the works as a prospective purchaser on behalf of the Navy, saw the works' ownership in a wider context besides just the manufacture of wireless telegraphy equipment. The works was a versatile operation and capable of much more: manufacturing motor cycles, machines guns, gun sights and was ideal for a variety of light engineering jobs appropriate for defence purposes. It was the adaptability of the plant that made a Navy purchase so attractive. In later years Cresswell's foresight proved correct.

On June 29, 1916, the acting Prime Minister and Minister for Defence, George Pearce, was advised that Cabinet would accept the recommendation of the Minister for Navy for the purchase of the Wireless Works subject to a proper valuation of plant, machinery and stock.[15] This valuation was conducted by a Mr Herbert Ross of *Ross and Rowe*, Architects and Engineers, Sydney. There was a certain urgency to proceedings as the government wanted the matter concluded before the return of Prime Minister William Hughes from his visit to the United Kingdom.

Ross made his own valuation of the plant at £46,496 on July 12, 1916. This was significantly less that Archibald's calculation. When added to the Department of Home Affairs valuation for land (£3,680) and buildings (£10,560) this amounted to a total sum of £60,736. Ross noted that his valuation was based on the works being taken over as a going concern and that *a number of expensive patterns, dies and electrical apparatus were obsolete and can only be taken at the market value of raw materials,*[16] suggesting himself that a realistic valuation for purchase would be closer to £40,000.

The method of Ross' valuation was questioned years later at the Royal Commission but the end result was that the National Cabinet approved an expenditure of £55,000 for the purchase of the entirety of the Wireless Works on July 14, 1916. The following day, July 15, 1916, a formal offer was put to Archibald. To his inordinate relief the board accepted the offer a few days later on July 18, 1916. The great anxiety he held for the sale of the Wireless Works could finally be laid to rest.

Curiously, Rear Admiral Clarkson, the Engineering Member of the Naval Board who offered technical advice to Navy Minister Jensen, remained strongly opposed to the purchase of the Wireless Works. Jensen chose to ignore Clarkson's advice and overruled his opinion. This ensured the sale proceeded quickly, before Prime minister Billy Hughes returned from England.[17]

As well as the two houses, *Ascot* and *Archina*, an the surrounding land the Wireless Works comprised four workshops. *Shop No. 1* was the machine and fitting workshop. *Shop No. 2* was given over to machine, tool and press work. *Shop No. 3* was occupied by electrical instrument makers. *Shop No. 4* was part of the armature winding department. There was also a pattern shop, foundry, store, laboratory and power house. Part of *Archina* was also used for the laboratory and manager's residence.[18]

Various incidents on a personal level now compounded to further the complexity of Archibald's situation and it is important to have a look at them to get a comprehensive picture of the demands he was subject to.

In June of 1916, a long-term employee of the Wireless Works, also a resident of *Ascot*, was accused of theft and faced court action initiated by the company. This information comes to hand from letters reporting the matter that were written by Linckens to the Superior General, Eugène Meyer. Linckens' discretion does not mention the employee by name.[19] As an aside, Linckens' letters characteristically exhibit a remarkable methodology in the conduct of his own affairs and those of the MSC province. He numbered the paragraphs in each letter. As well, for each letter that he wrote, he must have kept a copy because, in subsequent letters, he was able to precisely refer back to points he had previously written about by their date and paragraph number.

The accused thief thought the matter serious enough to employ a lawyer who served a summons on Linckens to appear as a witness at a hearing. In the days preceding the court hearing the accused and his lawyer met with Linckens at Kensington monastery where they spelt out before Linckens various criticisms of Archibald's behaviour which Linckens recounted to Meyer in an obscure fashion,

> ... he came to see me yesterday and briefly explained his case, accusing Fr Shaw of a host of things... The lawyer of the accused wants to dodge the issue and attack the private conduct of Fr. Shaw – I don't see the connection between the offending act and what Fr Shaw has done... I don't understand why I should have to produce all the books, etc, concerning the administration of the procure...
>
> I will make enquiries about what to do, but if the matter turns out this way, you understand the consequences it will have. In any case I will put things right because I have nothing to fear in telling the truth.[20]

There was no connection between Archibald's 'private conduct' - whatever that might have been - and the act of theft on the part of the accused. The ploy of the accused and their lawyer was to have Linckens intervene so that the case would never go to court at all and thereby prevent some potentially embarrassing stories about Archibald, which were irrelevant to the case, coming to public attention. And that is exactly what happened.

Linckens exercises exceptional discretion in his letters to Meyer, preferring to omit most all details to the point where it is hard to even make out what the alleged accusations against Archibald are. This makes piecing together the case of the accused difficult. Whilst the letters are the only surviving record of the incident, there is some information contained in the Royal Commission evidence which correlates with this and can be used to help reconstruct events.

By June, 1916, it was apparent the sale of the Wireless Works was going to go ahead and Archibald proceeded to honour his proposal to Evie, first by making application to resign himself from the Missionaries of the Sacred Heart and then the priesthood.

However, it is likely that Archibald's hand was simultaneously forced by Linckens – probably triggered by the aforementioned indeterminate accusations that came to light during Linckens' mediation of the dispute between Archibald and the alleged thief.

Gatherings, soirées and parties, attended by Wireless Works staff and their families, were held occasionally around a grand piano in the library on the ground floor of the large house, *Archina*, during the tenure of Albert Cornwell,[21] and most certainly before this also, probably from when *Archina* was first purchased by Maritime Wireless at the commencement of 1913. The Royal Commission testimony of Albert Cornwell, in the Commission's Minutes of Evidence Report, under questioning from Senator Long, speaks of an interesting find,

> *I told you Father Shaw was very indiscreet in leaving letters about, even when he was in competition with the Marconi Company, when he was stopping at 'Archina' which was on the property. A subsequent search at 'Archina', in the library, revealed the fact that there were a lot of photographs there. There was a drawer full of photographs, and some of these photographs were of women in certain garb and lack of garb, and one of them was Father Shaw, in fact in the same condition, emphasizing his indiscretion in leaving these things about.[22]*

Were the above photographs of naked women with a naked Archibald, so casually placed, and accessed by someone such as an accused thief, they would have provided a surety that prosecution would not proceed. The content of the photographs, amongst the other accusations that were made known to Linckens became the spark that fired him into mediating between Archibald and the thief. Similarly, the content of the photographs may well have been the find that *forced*

Archibald to write his resignation. Linckens retains a certain dignity and discretion in all this, never committing any of the details in writing to either Meyer or the Apostolic Delegate, Archbishop Bonaventura Cerretti, the pope's representative in Australia. It is my speculation that the employee accused of theft was Marion Mulrony. This is based on comments made by Archibald to Cornwell in letters retained as Royal Commission evidence. The long-serving Mulrony had just been superseded as manager by Albert Cornwell as the direction of Maritime Wireless changed to arms manufacture.

The engineering and wireless work was not enough to sustain the business of which Mulrony was previously manager. He left the works in 1916 at the time of this incident and, in the following year, set-up his own partnership, *The Mulrony Electrical Company*, in the city. In June, 1917, Mulrony hurriedly left Australia, making an *Emergency Passport Application*[23] before moving to Honolulu. Furthermore, it appears the accusation of theft made by Maritime Wireless might at first be related to Archibald's patents which Mulrony claimed as his own.

Any prior friendship between Archibald and Mulrony had evaporated. In a letter to Cornwell, hand-written from Melbourne just before the sale of the works was concluded on Monday, July 3, 1916, Archibald makes an interesting reference which implicates Mulrony as blackmailer - the man who approached Linckens,

> *Dear Cornwell,*
> *... I was able to nail that blackmail, the Minister [Jensen] and Senator Long heard Mulrony declare himself that they were my patents. Anyway, his letter is waste paper now...*[24]

John Graeme Balsillie, the government wireless expert engaged to oversee the design and installation of Coastal Wireless Service plant manufactured at Maritime Wireless, would dispute this. Balsillie was to claim these inventions for himself. He maintained an ongoing dispute with Archibald about who actually invented the quenched spark-gap used in the system. In fact, it was anticipated that the ownership of this intellectual property would be resolved through its own Royal Commission conducted by a Justice Murray[25] which never eventuated.

When the works were finally sold, the Balsillie versus Shaw challenge petered out without resolution. Wireless technology had moved on from spark. One press account reports,

> *Involved in the purchase of the Shaw plant is the settlement of the wireless dispute between the Shaw Company and Mr. Balsillie, the Commonwealth radio-telegraph consulting engineer. There will probably be no need for the projected enquiry by Royal Commission into the merits of the respective systems to determine who really invented the Australian system.*[26]

◆   ◆   ◆

On June 8, 1916, Archibald presented Hubert Linckens with a brief one-line request written at *Archina*, Avoca Street, Randwick,

> *Very Rev'd Father Visitor,*
> *I ask you to obtain for me the remission of my vows for reasons known to yourself.*
> *Yours in J. C.,*
> *Archibald Shaw*[27]

The next day Linckens informed the Apostolic Delegate Cerretti by letter and provided him with an outline of Archibald's MSC career history and a summary of the reasons why his application for the remission of his vows should be accepted. This included details of his misuse of mission funds and a general failure to partake in religious and priestly duties. No other indiscretions are mentioned. There is no doubt Linckens would be glad to see the back of Archibald. Linckens had never supported any of his ventures nor had he the vision to see any potential benefit his undertakings might have had for the MSC missions.

Linckens did recognise in Archibald the same character traits that were identified by Fr Jean-Marie Vandel all those years ago when

Archibald was a seminarian at Kensington,

> *He is of a rough and capricious nature who starts off with great enthusiasm in the beginning and then runs out of steam, who lacks attention to detail… who makes fine plans – sincerely - but his nature cannot carry them through for long. We all know him for that.*[28]

The role of 'priest' in Linckens' eyes was clearly defined and Archibald had strayed well beyond its boundaries. Linckens finishes his letter to Cerretti,

> *Under the circumstances not only do I support his request for the remission of his vows of poverty and obedience, but ask further your excellency to give him a secularisation as complete and extensive as possible.*[29]

Linckens ordered Archibald to attend a meeting with the Apostolic Delegate, no doubt to formalise his application to renounce his vows and bring some finality to his priesthood – but he did not receive the summons. He had already left for Melbourne by train to facilitate the sale of the Wireless Works. On June 19, 1916, Linckens again wrote to Cerretti,

> *Wishing to tell Father A. Shaw he should call to your excellency [tomorrow], I am informed by a man of his office that Father Shaw left yesterday night for Melbourne without giving any particulars.*
>
> *As soon as I shall be informed of Father Shaw's return I shall instruct him to [call] to the apostolic delegation at a convenient time.*[30]

Archibald spent the next couple of months in Melbourne, which was then the seat of the Australian Government and the nation's capital, to finalise the sale of Maritime Wireless and maximise the price and conditions of the sale. He obtained continuing employment for his friend, the new munitions manager, Albert Cornwell, after the works were transferred to the Navy and he had some time to get his own life in order before beginning its next phase - a life with Evie and her sister in America.

His faithful old friend, Fernand Arnoult, the ex-missionary and who stood beside Archibald on many of his undertakings and adventures, was again with him during this tumultuous period, if only for a short time. Arnoult was about to enlist as thirty-seven-year-old engineer in the 1st Battalion Pioneers to fight in France, the country of his birth. Two years prior he married Ruby Thompson from Wingham whom he met whilst managing the Bulga Saw Mill that Archibald held a financial stake in. He chose to serve simultaneously his adopted country, Australia, and the country of his birth and took the opportunity to catch-up with Archibald by enlisting at Victoria Barracks in Sydney instead of closer to his home. He stayed with Archibald prior to enlistment, giving his address as *The Wireless Station, Randwick* on his attestation papers.[31]

Fernand Arnoult, June, 1917.
Credit: Arnoult Family

Linckens continued to juggle problems on several fronts: the wayward Archibald, a calculating thief and his lawyer, and hoping-upon-hope that the mission debt would soon be repaid. A week after Archibald applied for the remission of his vows, Linckens reports to Meyer on July 2, 1916, about a resolution in the case of the alleged Wireless Works' thief,

> *After long talks and various interviews in which I was involved, and the question of a doubtful trial, the two parties have left an explanation and retraction, following which the procedure was stopped. The scandal which would have resulted from it was therefore avoided.*[32]

Whilst Linckens minimises collateral damage by negotiating a truce between Archibald and the thief, the following cryptic passages to Meyer indicates the incident is not completely over and there could be matters arising that further need attention,

> *The reason for my silence is not that I am afraid to tell you the truth, but only that I have clear evidence that certain facts I have written about have been misused – facts that have absolutely nothing to do with war or politics, but only with certain people involved in this process to whom they have been revealed.*
>
> *As I draw from these facts not only correct but also inescapable conclusions for me and my office, I will see to addressing the complaints to whom they are due so the matter is finished. Despite the indirect threats, I will continue to fulfil my office according to my conscience.*[33]

Before proceeding on to other things in his letter, Linckens advises Meyer that he has consulted with Apostolic Delegate Cerretti on how to deal with Archibald's request to rescind his priesthood and they both resolved to wait until the Wireless Works sale was finalised,

> *Yesterday I saw the Apostolic Delegate at great length about the steps to be taken concerning Fr. Shaw; we have agreed to wait for the result of his present proceedings for which he [Archibald] feels that a fortnight will suffice.*[34]

After a long two-year wait, Linckens finally received the news he was waiting for on July 23, 1916. In a letter to Meyer he states,

> *This week Fr. Shaw announced by telegram that at last the sale of the Wireless Works has been finalised and that in about ten days or so I should have a cheque for the part owing to us – that is a proportion which will be a little more than a third of the sum that he has embezzled. I will believe it when I hold the cheque and say, 'better something than nothing'. Later then will come the question of Fr. Shaw himself.*[35]

Archibald's letter to Albert Cornwell announcing the sale and Cornwell's continuing employment was jubilant,

> *Dear Boy,*
> *She's gone.*
> *The Minister will wire you any day now to take charge. Your salary with residence will be at least £450 if not more. That has been agreed. I expect it will be a week or ten days before the Govt. take control.*
> *There will be no public announcement of [the sale] until the cheque is paid over… You are going to be left to organise as you like. Cresswell said he has a first class dynamo design for you.*
> *Your ever grateful old man,*
> *Shaw*[36]

Curiously, there was further mention of the Mulrony incident in Archibald's letter to Cornwell. It appears that the matter of theft spoken about earlier may have originally referred to Archibald's patents but it had escalated into the stealing of physical components from the prototype electrical vehicle that had been constructed at the works,

> *Re: Mul[rony]*
> *The wheels etc of that electric car was taken away and put on his Ford etc, we might have him there, also on the drawings etc. If Baldwin can make a statement? You were quite right in what you said re case!*[37]

Meanwhile, back at Kensington monastery, Linckens' joy that the Maritime Wireless matter was finalised was short-lived. Archibald never made it back to Sydney alive.

He died in Melbourne on Saturday, August 26, 1916, shortly after the sale of the Wireless Works, in circumstances that remain a mystery to this day.

XVI

Missing Money & Mysterious Death

When Fernand Arnoult and Archibald bid farewell at Randwick in July of 1916 it was in each man's mind that the person least likely to return alive was Arnoult. Archibald was only travelling by steam-train to Melbourne but Arnoult was travelling half a world away to serve as an engineer with the 1st Pioneers Battalion in the battlefields of France.

Archibald's unexpected demise in the weeks following became enigmatic and helped spawn the Royal Commission. Without the evidence preserved in the commission documents we would know much less about the operations of the Wireless Works, the character of Archibald himself and the circumstances of the sale. In fact, without the Royal Commission, the Shaw story would have faded into history and there would be no possibility of reassembling long-forgotten details. More about the Royal Commission later.

In his forty-sixth year Archibald was a large, robust man – somewhat overweight - with large worker-hands and a full-head of dark hair. He was not in good health. Like many of the missionaries, he suffered from the long-term effects of chronic tropical disease with symptoms that came and went over the years. Most of the missionaries were similarly afflicted. There are accounts in the letters of Joseph Guis that Archibald suffered from bouts of sciatica pain as well possibly caused by uneven weight distribution on his legs from the permanent limp he carried from his childhood ankle operation – or perhaps caused by chronic nephritis of the kidneys from which he suffered.[1] Guis writes,

> *Poor Fr Shaw. For sometimes he suffers terribly from the agonising pain of sciatica - he has a few days respite and then it takes him again worse than ever...*[2]

We glean from the testimony of Evie Hoad and from the early letters Archibald wrote to Eugène Meyer when their relationship was happier, that Archibald had his dark days too - possibly indicative of melancholia or mild depression.

This trait is in opposition to the Archibald the world saw. Publicly he showed extreme positivity and even displayed a propensity for some calculated and miscalculated risk-taking behaviour. For most of his life he carried a cavalier 'she'll be right' attitude. Often, he is unable to envisage the consequences of his risk-taking - but he never loses the ability to come up with a plan to solve a problem, no matter how far-fetched - even if his personal challenges were largely self-inflicted.

The reality of Archibald's life was one of struggle following his parents' early death until his own final days. His ability to see the positive allowed him not just to survive but to flourish. He capably used this vision to inspire others. It could be argued that his behaviour at times was symptomatic of what is identified as *bipolar disorder* today. Of course, in Archibald's day little was known of illnesses affecting the mind. Modern psychiatry was in its infancy, the mind remained a mystery and mental afflictions were not well understood. Curiously, Archibald's sister, Mary Kennedy, whose children he supported financially for a time, died in the middle of 1913 the result of 'weakness after an operation'. Her medical notes, as does her death certificate, record that she also suffered from 'acute delusional mania'.[3]

When Archibald arrived in Melbourne by train to finalise the sale of Maritime Wireless he was dressed *incognito;* in regular street clothes. He arranged accommodation at one of Melbourne's coffee palaces and registered as Mr Shaw[4] to retain some anonymity. Coffee palaces were a popular form of accommodation during the temperance era. They provided a pleasant alternative to hotels by providing accommodation without serving alcohol. In any case Archibald neither drank nor smoked. It was the *Melbourne Coffee Palace* that would be his base for a couple of months until the sale was completed. This was a five-story accommodation complex with restaurant and billiard rooms in the heart of the central business district at 216 Bourke Street. From here it was an easy walk between Parliament House, the Treasury Offices, the Railway Station, the Post Office, the Naval Radio Office in Collins House,[5] various lawyers' offices and the London Bank where he held accounts - all the places he needed to visit.

The Melbourne Coffee Palace in Bourke Street, Melbourne where Archibald stayed for several weeks to facilitate the sale of his Maritime Wireless Company. He became unconscious in his room here on August 21, 1916. *Credit: MSC Archive*

He was staying only a few doors down from the *Parer Brothers' Crystal Palace – Restaurant and Café* and directly next door to *Parer's Hotel*. Both these businesses were owned by the same family that ran *Parer's Hotel* on King Island where he and his team of eleven were accommodated during construction of the King Island Wireless Station. In those heady days, five years previous, Maritime Wireless would successfully complete projects bordering on the impossible.

The Maritime Wireless Company held business accounts

at the *London Bank of Australia* which had a Sydney branch in the Haymarket at 651 George Street that Archibald frequently visited. The original building still stands though it is no longer a bank. When he conducted business in Melbourne he attended the London Bank branch at 401 & 403 Collins Street West. These banking chambers were replaced after World War II.

Following now is a reconstruction of the events immediately before and after Archibald's death based on evidence from various primary sources.

After many weeks of negotiation and with the sale of the works finally concluded, Saturday, August 19, 1916, was a busy day for Archibald. He visited the Department of Treasury to pick up a cheque for £55,000 ($5.5 million today) made out for the complete purchase of the Maritime Wireless Company – buildings and workshops, plant and equipment, inventory and patents – the whole kit and caboodle. He could not have been happier. From there he walked to the London Bank in Collins Street the morning[6] of the same day and, upon entering, met with the manager Percy Strong,[7] who passed the cheque through to James Butchart, the bank inspector, who in turn gave it to

London Bank, Collins Street, Melbourne, c. 1905. *Credit: Patterson Bros.*

an unidentified cashier occupying cubicle ten of the banking chamber.[8]

Then he proceeded to write several cheques for different amounts according to a list he had brought with him from Sydney.[9] The first cheque for £25,000 was made out to *Whiting and Aitken*, solicitors who were acting for his principal creditor, Sir Rupert Clarke. This was the agreed amount Archibald would pay even though his debt to Clarke was significantly more. It is likely, when he left the bank, that he walked immediately two blocks west to the offices of Whiting and Aitken, at 101 King Street, Melbourne, and delivered the cheque in person.

A second cheque for £250 was passed to Whiting and Aitken at the same time. This was their share of eight months rent that was owed to them by Maritime Wireless.

A third cheque, numbered A417,663 was made payable to 'cash' for £5,300. Archibald cashed this himself in the chamber of the bank. Where this money went became the subject of intense scrutiny. It is a mystery that remains unresolved.

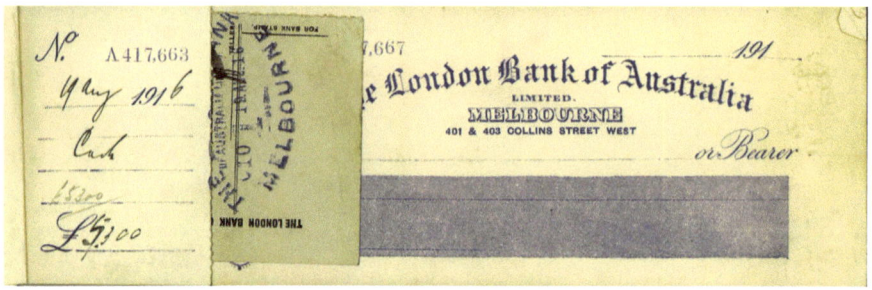

Archibald's chequebook showing the butt of the cashed £5,300 cheque. Where this money went became the focus of the Royal Commission enquiries.
Credit: NAA: CP661/10, NN,261988

The amount of £5,300 pounds represents about $530,000 today; an extraordinary sum for an unaccompanied person to be casually carrying around the streets of Melbourne in their trouser pocket.

Concerned about the large amount of cash Archibald was carrying, bank officer James Butchart recalled the following conversation he had with Archibald,

> *He came to my room as far as I can remember, with that money in his possession, and he told me he was leaving for Sydney, I think, the next day, or possibly the day after, so I said, 'Surely you are not going to Sydney with all that money in your possession. Let me give you our bank's cheque in exchange for the notes, as that will be much safer.' He put his hand on my shoulder and said, 'Mind your own business,' and smiled, and I think that is where our conversation ended.*[10]

Another cheque, for £7,000, was then made out to creditor Thomas Peters of *Lane and Peters*, a large civil construction firm that was responsible for constructing some of the big dams throughout NSW. Yet another cheque was written, for £17,000, and directed to Archibald's London Bank account at the Haymarket in Sydney. It was from this amount that Hubert Linckens and Archibald's Sydney creditors would be repaid when he returned to Sydney in a few days.

Because of his unexpected death it took many years and the cost of several lawyers for Linckens and the other creditors to retrieve the money they were owed. The £17,000 was added to the balance of Maritime Wireless' accounts. It became part of Archibald's estate and came under the control of his sister, Blanche Monday, who had promptly applied for and was granted letters of administration for all the property held in Archibald's name upon his death. She was somewhat difficult to deal with and, according to a claim put in by her brother Charles Fraser Shaw, left-out certain items from the estate and misvalued others. It was of no help to anyone that Archibald died without a will. According to Linckens who wrote to Meyer in Rome,

> *When I first came here [to Sydney], Father Shaw assured me he had made a will; since he could not find it, I insisted to him on many occasions that he make another one but I do not know if he did...*[11]

After Archibald wrote the cheques and before he left the London Bank in Collins Street he did something quite out of character. He offered a gratuity of £200 to the bank teller occupying cubicle ten, the person who assisted him cash his cheque. This was a person he had little more than a passing acquaintance with. It was a large sum in those days and about the equivalent of $20,000 in today's money – a sum close to what the bank teller would earn in an entire year. His unusual behaviour is consistent with someone exhibiting an episode of impulsive mania. From the testimony of Senator James Long at the Royal Commission who met with Archibald at Parliament House later in the day,

> *I wish to say that there is a gentleman whose name has not been mentioned hitherto, and who cannot by any stretch of imagination be connected in any improper way with the sale of these works, and that is the gentleman who was the cashier of the bank where the late Father Shaw cashed that cheque. I think I mentioned this to you, that Father Shaw that morning had drawn something out of the bank to pay a few debts, and he said that the cashier at the bank had been so kind that he insisted on him taking £200. The cashier said he refused to do it, but Father Shaw insisted on him taking the money...*
>
> *He, [Archibald], told me it was with much reluctance that this gentleman accepted it...* [12]

On the same day the cheques were drawn-up, Saturday, August 19, Archibald sent a three-word telegram from the Melbourne Post Office in Bourke Street to Cornwell who was managing the Wireless Works in Sydney,

> *Home Tuesday,*
> *Shaw* [13]

By late morning that same day, Archibald walked up to Parliament House in Spring Street and met with Senator Long in a room known as the Senate Club Room, now the dining room. According to Long's account which is disputed by others, this is what happened,

> *Father Shaw gave me one package of money, the one package of money only, which he took out of his right trouser pockets between 11.30 and 12 o'clock that morning, and no other money reached me [£1,290] in £100 notes, [a] £50 and two*

twenties, I think. [14]

He said to me, 'Thank God I have got the whole thing fixed up. Look, Jim, old man. I will never forget you for your kindness. I do not know what I owe you, but I think this will square us.' He handed me that money. I was sitting on the big chair and he half embraced me and left the club-room, and I never saw him afterward conscious. [15]

Long was forced to later concoct a discombobulated story explaining the money Archibald gave him. The Royal Commission was able to obtain copies of Long's bank statements but, of those implicated in receiving payments from Archibald, he was naively, the only suspect who made a large cash deposit into his account around this time. Shortly after meeting Archibald, Long banked a sum of £2,400, well in excess of what he claimed to have received in cash from him. He later claimed that this money was part gratuity and part repayment of debts. Long claims to have supported Archibald financially during the defence of his patent disputes with Balsillie.[16] He also said that he lent him a considerable amount, approaching some £300 over three years, for gambling at the races as well.

Furthermore, to make his defence even more unlikely, Long maintained his bank deposit was bolstered by significant horse racing wins for which he could neither remember the horses he bet on nor the bookmakers he placed bets with. The commission did not buy into the story and formed the opinion that the whole of the £2,400 deposited into his account two weeks later on September 4, came from the gratuity paid to him by Archibald for his efforts in smoothing the sale of Wireless Works to the government. If so, this left £2,900 from Archibald's cashed cheque unaccounted for.

Albert Cornwell provided further written evidence after the formal commission hearings ended. He spoke of a conversation he had with Senator Long back at the Wireless Works. The conversation was recorded secretly by a stenographer in an adjacent room. During the meeting Long admitted to receiving not one but four separate packets of money from Archibald at Parliament House. The others destined to receive money distributed by Long were Jensen and two other senators besides himself, believed to be Senators Russell and Gardiner,

> *He [Long] said that Shaw, on the Saturday morning, was bubbling over with excitement and approached him, I think, on the Senate steps and gave him four packages...*
>
> *He was certain of his own amount because that was the amount he was supposed to receive, and he assumed the others had received the correct amounts too...*[17]

Testimony from Evie Hoad and Archibald's secretary at *Shaw Engineering*, Joseph Lynch, followed. They were able to shed further light on the matter, identifying gratuities being paid as follows: Senator Long (£2,000); the Minister for Navy, Jens Jensen (£2,000); Commander Cresswell (£1,000). Lynch himself was evidently to be rewarded with a trip to America with Archibald which never eventuated following his death.[18] No evidence was found by the Royal Commission that either Jensen or Cresswell had received payments.

August Carroll, a salesman in the employ of the *Australian General Electric Company* became a friend and confidant of Archibald despite working for a firm that was in competition with him. He gave testimony that he too was to travel to America with Archibald. He stated that Archibald was prepared to pay Jensen significantly more than was previously suggested in the form of a bribe for political influence,[19]

> *... there is just one little matter that was given to me by Father Shaw. There is just the slightest doubt about it. I know the bait was put there. I said to Father Shaw, 'Do you think that Jensen is going to fail?' He said, 'It will be a big stake to win him over, but I am prepared to give anything from £5,000 to £10,000.' No... He said 'WE' all the time.*[20]

Much time and effort was fruitlessly spent by the Royal Commission trying to work out where the balance of the £5,300 withdrawn by Archibald ended up. With Long's payment subtracted, the commission could not account for the balance of £2,900.

In all likelihood the whole of the £5,300 was distributed during the Saturday to various people throughout Melbourne who helped facilitate the sale. The reasoning for this is that Archibald returned to the London Bank in Collins Street and cashed another cheque - a much smaller one - for £50 on the following Monday. He would not have done this if he was still carrying cash from the earlier withdrawal.

The Report of the Commission a couple of years later presented this summary,

> *The Commission has not been able to secure any positive evidence as to the disposition of the balance of the sum of £5,300 drawn on the Saturday morning, but as Father Shaw withdrew a further sum of £50 from his account on Monday morning, 21st August, 1916, and at the time of his death had only a very small sum in his possession, it is evident that the money in question had been disposed of by him in some undisclosed way between Saturday, the 19th, and Monday, the 21st August, 1916.*[21]

Archibald sent another telegram to Cornwell back at the Wireless Works on Monday, August 21, 1916, with a refinement of his travel plans,

> *Am returning by tomorrow night's express,*
> *Shaw*[22]

That was the last anyone heard from him, except for a letter he wrote to Evie which she received in Sydney on the Monday that he lost consciousness.[23] She could only recall its contents in part at the Royal Commission two years later because, at Archibald's direction, she had destroyed all their personal correspondence. She recalled Archibald telling her in his letter that there were *four* people who were to receive payments but she could only remember the names of Long and Jensen for amounts of about £2,000 each.[24]

Cornwell remained distrustful of Long and suspicious of his involvement in the sale of the works. In the weeks surrounding the Royal Commission interviews, after all the evidence was heard, his mistrust was such that he agreed for a stenographer to secretly record a conversation between himself and Long which was held in an adjacent office at the Wireless Works.[25] Cornwell was expecting Long to implicate both himself and Jensen in the ensuing discussion. The transcript of the conversation was passed on to the Royal Commission and remains in the evidence file. Long was wary enough to incriminate neither himself nor Jensen nor anyone else during the conversation; at least no more than he already had at the hearings in Melbourne. When pressed by Long, Cornwell puts forward another idea, albeit unlikely, to explain where the missing money may have gone,

> *Long: How do you explain the difference [i.e. the missing money]?*
>
> *Cornwell: Well, because the old man [Shaw] was having a loose leg in Melbourne. It is quite likely that he got through from £400 to £1,000.*[26]

Archibald planned that Monday night, August 21, 1916, would be his last in Melbourne. He intended to celebrate the sale of the works and met with an old friend by the name of Carter who lived in Melbourne. This man was 'quite hard-up financially' according to a police report that reconstructed Archibald's final movements. Carter and Archibald took two prostitutes into their company that evening.

The girls and Carter were in Archibald's room at the Coffee Palace when he took ill and became unconscious. This information is recorded in testimony during the 1918 Royal Commission and was based on a police report that was made available to the commission at the time but now cannot be located in the Victoria Police archives.[27]

Naturally, suspicion immediately fell on both Carter and the prostitutes for foul play in regard to both Archibald's collapse and the missing money. Police enquiries revealed that Carter had pawned his own watch[28] just days after Archibald's death. He was, therefore, an unlikely thief according to the police report. The *disreputable women*, as they were described in the police report, were identified as just that, and neither thieves nor murderers.

Later that evening Archibald's unconscious body was moved from his room in the Melbourne Coffee Palace in Bourke Street to Miss Garlick's Private Hospital, located about half a kilometre to the south-east in a building called *Lumea* at 108 Flinders Lane. The private hospital has long been demolished and replaced by a multi-story car park. The coffee palace where Archibald boarded in Melbourne is no longer there either, having been replaced with a bland shopping mall. It was probably Carter that arranged for Archibald's transport adn admission to the hospital.

Archibald briefly became conscious a couple of days later and then returned to his unconscious state.[29] Linckens writes to Meyer in Rome,

> *I have found out that the dean of the cathedral in Melbourne anointed him in his final hours, gave him the last anointing but Fr Shaw was unconscious.*[30]

Archibald died five days after his initial collapse at about 1 pm on August 26, 1916, in Miss Garlick's Private Hospital having lived a remarkable life of forty-five years and eight months.

Joseph Lynch, Archibald's secretary, travelled to Melbourne the following Sunday, August 27, to retrieve his body and personal effects. He visited the coffee palace where Archibald stayed and then proceeded to Miss Garlick's Hospital,

> *I came to bring his body back to Sydney; but it had returned that morning.*[31]

At the coffee palace he was given £26 which belonged to Archibald, a small bag and an overcoat. Inside the overcoat pocket was Archibald's cheque book, now held as part of the Royal Commission evidence in the National Archives of Australia.[32] These items came back to Sydney with Lynch. He testified at the commission that the cheque butts dated August 19 were each written in Archibald's hand but the pencil annotations on the butts were not.

The nurse at Miss Garlick's Hospital, likely Lucy Garlick herself, received instructions by telephone from Sir Rupert Clarke's solicitors, Whiting and Aitken, not to release any of Archibald's belongings.

Returning to Sydney in time to attend Archibald's funeral on the Tuesday, Lynch put the bag and overcoat he had retrieved from the Melbourne Coffee Palace in Archibald's room at his Dutruc Street home, *Ascot*. His sister Blanche came for them but did not take them away. They were passed onto Blanche's solicitors, Pigott and Stinson, who gave them to her at a later time.

Lynch returned to Melbourne again on Tuesday, August 29, by the night train under instructions from the Sacred Heart Mission Fathers – no doubt Linckens himself - who had by this time clarified who Joseph Lynch was to Whiting and Aitken. Lynch stayed at the coffee palace and went to the hospital with a priest from the St Patrick's Cathedral, Lonergan; the same one who had administered the last rites to Archibald. There Lynch retrieved a heavy Gladstone bag and a smaller case which was withheld from him on his first visit. He brought them back to Sydney without examining their contents and, on instructions from Linckens, passed them onto Linckens' solicitor, J. J. Carroll.

Blanche Amelia Monday, Archibald's sister and administratrix of his estate.   *Credit: B. Clark*

News of Archibald's unexpected death spread quickly, particularly through the papers. Nothing was mentioned of the specific circumstances. These details came to light, with little fanfare, through newspaper reports two years later when the Royal Commission proceedings were published.

Evie Hoad, who was waiting patiently in Sydney for Archibald's return, only learned of his death through a newspaper clipping passed on to her,

A friend of mine had sent me a notice in the paper of his death, and I was expecting him every day. I went on the Monday morning to see Mr Cornwell – of course, I did not know anybody [at the Wireless Works] – I had my two sisters there and some intimate friends, who knew that I was going to marry Father Shaw... I told him I did not know about Father Shaw's death until a friend of mine had sent a press clipping in the newspaper sympathising with me.[33]

Given the circumstances of the death it was unusual that no inquest or post-mortem autopsy was performed despite uncertainties held by the attending doctor. Dr Paul Farmer, who attended Archibald at the hospital and certified his death, records the cause as:

Chronic nephritis; cerebral haemorrhage; indefinite.[34]

On August 27, 1916, Linckens notified Meyer about Archibald's death,

Also yesterday a telegram announced the death of Fr. A. Shaw, who died in Melbourne, in a private hospital.... After a public announcement of the project, various attacks appeared in the press, which finally led to the announcement on August 18th that the Government had finally bought the whole thing. On August 21 the payment was made and Fr. Shaw was preparing to return to Sydney in the evening, when he was suddenly attacked by a stroke of apoplexy. A friend had him taken to hospital. On Wednesday, August 23, a Wireless employee went to see him, found him speechless, and returned with the hope that he would recover. Yesterday, Saturday, a telegram announced that he had died at one o'clock in the afternoon. May the good Lord have given him a favourable judgement! I don't know yet if he will be buried in Melbourne, or if he can be brought here.[35]

Archibald's body was returned to Randwick. Gordon Sleight, working for Melbourne undertaker Roy A. Sleight, arranged transport of his remains to Sydney.

A large funeral was held at the Randwick church he knew so

well, Our Lady of the Sacred Heart, on Tuesday, August 29, 1916. It was a big affair, presided over by the Sydney Archbishop, Michael Kelly. The many priests and deacons in attendance processed in from the rear of the church as was custom at this time. They were dressed in *cassock* and *surplice*, and sat in the front seats to one side. Included amongst the clergy was the then Australian MSC Provincial, Edward Nouyoux, and one of Archibald's original priest-investors, Monsignor O'Haran, secretary to Cardinal Moran and one of Archibald's original supporters[36] when the first company with Edward Kirkby was formed. One of the young deacons at the service was James Power whom Archibald vouched for on his application to join the MSC.

All of the Wireless Works employees attended, as did many of Archibald's business associates. A large number of Randwick parishioners to whom he was well known were present also, as were a large number of MSC priests, brothers, seminarians and members of his family. Archibald's brother, Charles Fraser Shaw, was absent. He had left Sydney only a week before and was a soldier on a transport ship heading to England. Evie Hoad, with her small entourage of sisters and friends was present and remained deeply affected by Archibald's death which was made all the more painful by her inability to share publicly their dreams of a future together.

Archibald was buried a priest because that is what he was when he died, despite it being a calling he no longer wanted. He had not seen himself as priest for years - certainly since his proposal to Evie and despite the pending question of his recent application for the remission of vows. As far as Hubert Linckens was concerned, Archibald was midway between being dismissed from the priesthood or undergoing a secularisation initiated by his own request, for which neither had been finalised.

After the funeral, a procession was held from the church to the cemetery a few kilometres away. All the attendees and the employees of the Wireless Works followed slowly behind the hearse. Archibald was buried in Randwick Cemetery, then known as Long Bay Cemetery, on a small rise in a plot of twelve graves[37] purchased in advance for deceased members of the MSC Society. His body was lowered into the ground[38] next to his old friend and work colleague Joseph Guis.

Guis had amiably supported all Archibald's dreams and endeavours from the beginning when Maritime Wireless was just a loosely-formed foggy idea in a wooden shed behind *Ascot*: an audacious attempt to make the procure debt free. Similar to the grave of his original business partner, Edward Kirkby who is buried in nearby Waverley Cemetery, there was an uninterrupted view from Archibald's resting place to the prominent steel antenna tower at the rear of Ascot, two-and-a-half kilometres away to the north west. Fr. Peter Tréand presided over the graveside prayers.

No one would have been more frustrated and confused by Archibald's death than Linckens. One can almost hear his brain ticking over during the burial service. Archibald did him no favour dying unexpectedly. Linckens recalls a conversation he had with Cerretti, the Apostolic Delegate, who read of Archibald's death in the newspaper. Cerretti exclaimed,

> *'The finger of God is here!', but I explained to him that unfortunately the matter was not finished and that it was going to cause me a lot of trouble.*[39]

Linckens could not have been more correct. Had Archibald lived, Linckens would have received payment for the MSC debt owed on the day he returned to Sydney and the matter would be concluded. Now, settlement of Archibald's affairs dragged on for another five years.

From Archibald's confreres there is an abundance of silence on his life. No judgement was ever voiced, even from Linckens. However, he does take the liberty to report a comment made by Fr Lonergan of the Melbourne Cathedral who anointed Archibald before death,

> *The dean of the Cathedral who gave the last anointing to Fr Shaw... adds some remarks on the big mistake of allowing religious to busy themselves with matters outside their vocation and who wear lay dress and are called Mister instead of Father.*[40]

Privately, Linckens attempted to justify his own actions against Archibald, looking for the reasons the society allowed him to run so free for so long without accountability. He placed a fair amount of blame for this on Monsignor Louis Couppé,

> *Mgr Couppé encouraged Fr Shaw in his illicit enterprises. Fr Dicks assures me that in 1912 Mgr Couppé wrote along these lines to [the office of] Propaganda; Fr Wemmers assures me that last year too Mgr Couppé spoke favourably to him of his ventures and I too that in 1915 after his stay at Ascot. Mgr Couppé opposed my acting against Fr Shaw who encouraged him while for my part I believed it my rigorous duty to blame him and put a stop to his ventures* [41]

The circumstances of Archibald's death, the missing money, the presence of disreputable women in his room and the fact that no autopsy was held, led some to believe he was murdered and that the murder was subsequently covered up. The idea of foul play was postulated by Senator Long during the Royal Commission hearings. It was similarly put forward privately in a conversation John Lonergan, the Administrator of St. Patrick's Cathedral who saw his body near death, had with another Melbourne priest, Fr Jack McNamara,

> *'I will tell you something... A priest by the name of Father Shaw, a Sacred Heart Father, was killed during the war in 1916'. He wasn't actually killed – the word he used was 'he was murdered' and the cause of his murder was his contact [with] and his inventing of wireless, particularly commercial radio. He related this without ambiguity.*[42]

Archibald did not invent wireless nor did he invent commercial radio. Lonergan is trying to infer a motive for murder over some sort of commercial rivalry. He is basing his conclusion on the *appearance* of Shaw when he administered the last rites. If so, it is likely Archibald's body presented a badly bruised head-wound. This was the evidence used by Farmer, the attending doctor, who without a proper autopsy, inferred that a cerebral haemorrhage contributed to his death. What remains unclear to the researcher today is whether Shaw had a cerebral bleed first, causing him to collapse and *then* received an external headwound after he fell, or if he was first struck sharply on the head, or fell, or was pushed, which then caused a cerebral bleed *the result of his head wound.*

The lost Victoria Police report referred to in the Royal Commission evidence suggests there was nothing suspicious about the death and, because of this, no murder investigation was conducted. This conflicts with the attending doctor who records *'indefinite'* on the death certificate. J. F. McMahon, the first Shaw researcher, writing in NSW during the early 1980s when police corruption stories were making the news, intimates the possibility of a police cover-up. There may indeed be something to this, especially as the original police report referred to at the Royal Commission has disappeared. There is another possibility too: if a cover-up was undertaken, it may not necessarily have been of a murder. It might have been undertaken to protect the integrity of Archibald himself who was a well-known public figure, or to prevent a scandal within the Catholic Church. No one was to know then that a Royal Commission would open the matter up for detailed examination. The police report *was* available at the time of the Royal Commission and may have been surreptitiously removed afterward by someone sympathetic to protecting the church's reputation.

Three years after his death and a year after the Royal Commission report was released, the Member for Melbourne, Mr Maloney, resurrected the idea that Archibald died from violence, *or some[thing] other than natural causes,*[43] and that his body should be exhumed for examination.

An exhumation did occur but not for the reason proposed by Maloney. Thirty-one years after his death, on June 27, 1947, Archibald's remains together with those of the other MSC priests and brothers who were buried in the Randwick Cemetery plot, were exhumed and re-interred at the MSC cemetery adjacent to the monastery at Douglas Park in the south-west of Sydney. During this period the Missionaries of the Sacred Heart were consolidating the remains of their Sydney deceased members into a single cemetery.

Within the space of a week, both the Maritime Wireless Company and its creator were no more. Immediately after the sale Maritime Wireless became a government-owned operation. It was known henceforth as the *Royal Australian Navy Wireless Works* and supported Australia's defence forces under the continuing capable management of Albert Cornwell.

A rare photograph survives of the 1917 Naval Wireless Works picnic held for workers and their families at Correy's Gardens, a popular picnic and entertainment venue adjacent to Cabarita Park on the Parramatta River in Sydney. A ferry, operated by the Gardens, carried picnickers from Circular Quay to Cabarita. The employees were all men. The department heads wore a metal badge on a ribbon. The badge bore a pair wings bisected with an image of an electric spark. This was the logo of the newly formed Naval Wireless Works. Many of the employees shown in the photograph had worked at the factory during the preceding years when the business was operating as The Maritime Wireless Telegraph Company.[44]

Archibald was the first Australian-born priest of Missionary of the Sacred Heart order and now he had achieved another albeit unwelcome first. He was the first Australian-born missionary of the society to die.

MISSING MONEY & MYSTERIOUS DEATH

Royal Australia Navy Wireless Works 1917 family picnic day at Correy's Gardens, Cabarita. Most of the staff shown here were employed when the business was Maritime Wireless five months prior.   *Credit: Mitchell Library, NSW*

XVII

Blackmail, Fraud and a Royal Commission

When the sale of the Wireless Works to the Department of Navy was publicly announced, the amount which the government paid for the business was initially withheld. *The Sun* newspaper, under the editorial direction of owner, Hugh Denison, published the price and a critical assessment of the government's valuation of the works[1] before it was publicly declared. Denison was also chairman of Amalgamated Wireless Ltd. (AWA), Maritime Wireless' chief competitor.

Amalgamated Wireless had the support of the incumbent Hughes Government and was determined to see its foothold grow in Australian wireless manufacture especially as public broadcasting was just around the corner and every household would soon be purchasing a wireless receiver. AWA attempted to diminish the monetary and practical value of the government purchase. As is typical in conflicts of any sort, truth is the first casualty. The story published by *The Sun* contained a number of factual errors and exaggerations which were countered by the Minister for Navy, Jens August Jensen, in response to a letter from Treasury. For example, *The Sun* claimed,

> ...the Amalgamated Wireless Co. has contracts to supply all the ships on the Australian register for the next 10 years. So that if a Commonwealth factory were established it could not make plants for these ships...[2]

Minister Jensen countered,

> *This statement is incorrect... a number of ships on the*

Australian Register are under an agreement to a Company, but on the other hand, a very large number have not yet installed wireless. This large number of the Australian owned ships have refused to accept the conditions laid down by the persons who wished to provide wireless and have therefore done without same.[3]

Amalgamated Wireless continued unabated with its assault on the Maritime Wireless purchase through subsequent articles in *The Sun* and was ever-critical of the price paid by Navy Minister Jensen. AWA went so far as to value the Randwick machinery and plant themselves at only £2,000 which was less than one twentieth of what the government had paid.[4]

Their arguments were repeatedly countered and contradicted by Jensen to the Department of Treasury but doubt about whether the purchase was good value had been sown in the mind of the taxpayer through *The Sun's* vociferous stories.

Back at Kensington monastery Hubert Linckens was still trying to sort through Archibald's financial affairs following his death. There was also the suspended question of applying one of the decrees[5] from the Rome-based *Sacred Congregation of Religious* which he and Archbishop Cerretti, the Apostolic Delegate, were still mulling over. This would effectively revoke Archibald's priesthood. Now that Archibald was deceased, the issue was academic but it was a discussion he and Cerretti nevertheless pursued.[6]

Linckens wrote a curious few lines to Fr. Meyer in Rome in the months following Archibald's death telling him that he had an unexpected visit from a woman making overtures for money in connection with Archibald. He intimates to Meyer that the woman is holding something over him for which she is attempting extortion. Linckens, again, typically exercises the utmost discretion in his correspondence. He does not name the woman and goes into limited detail about what he interprets as a blackmail attempt. But it's not too hard to join the dots and work out what is going on. On October 29, 1916, Linckens wrote to Meyer,

In addition, in an interview that I had with a certain person

(female) who came to see me, everything I indicated in my [previous correspondence] is confirmed to me beyond my suspicions.[7]

In a second letter of December 10, 1916, Linckens provides more detail,

... the person of whom I spoke to you in my letter of October 29... has tried to extort a promise of money from me to keep silent on this matter; all her attempts are futile as far as I am concerned; she won't get a penny from me.[8]

And again, in a third letter, Linckens provides a further update to Meyer on January 7, 1917,

The ... affair here which I spoke to you about on October 29 is aggravated in the sense that I have had new proofs of a similar situation with another person in Melbourne. I was suspicious of this situation but I have had proof this week. I hope that all this will remain hidden. I asked for the destruction of the proofs that were shown to me but I cannot be sure that this was done.[9]

What can made of this?

Based on his correspondence, Linckens is a blunt, legalistic, fair-minded person who is somewhat Manichean in his thinking. When he first identified the mess the Wireless Works accounts were in, he wasted no time accusing Archibald of embezzlement. Technically, he was correct - even though Archibald did not take the money for his own personal use. However, Archibald saw his own actions very differently from Linckens' accusation of *embezzlement*. Archibald saw a temporary accounting anomaly that was necessary to keep everything afloat. His ability to see the positive fostered a misplaced belief that, in time, all would be made right and the books would balance again. Archibald saw the grey where Linckens saw only black and white.

It is likely the woman who came to see Linckens was Evie Hoad[10] and in a similar manner to his assessment of Archibald as an *embezzler*, Linckens identified the approach made by Evie as *extortion*

- probably within moments of the meeting beginning. She saw her approach to Linckens differently despite the absence of detail in the historical record. Evie must have felt entitled to at least *something* from Archibald's estate, given that they were engaged for two years and she had been waiting patiently all that time living on the strength of Archibald's promises.

All Evie had was her story, and perhaps some compromising photographs to hold over Linckens if need be. But there was little to be gained from this approach. The threat of blackmail, no matter how subtle, incensed Linckens and further strengthened his resolve to withhold from her any money from the estate or from MSC funds. Linckens would have realised she would be embarrassing herself in the act of making her story or any photographs public and Evie would have known this too. In any case, Linckens now had no control over Archibald's estate - though Evie may not have understood this at the time.

The *destruction of proofs* mentioned in Linckens' January letter likely refers to the photographic prints of Archibald with women in various states of undress found in the library drawer at *Archina*. These are probably the same photographs that Albert Cornwell refers to in his testimony at the Royal Commission.[11] Linckens was correct in stating earlier that he could not be sure that they were destroyed. It appears they were not. Stories referring to the photographs have come up infrequently in historical features about Archibald in recent decades. The compromising photographs were discussed two years later at the Royal Commission and appear to have survived right up until the 1980s if press accounts from this period can be believed.[12]

Linckens had, by now, considerable experience in averting scandal and he had successfully averted another one by refusing to entertain a payment of money for silence. In his quieter moments he must have asked himself: *what could possibly come next?* He didn't have to wait long to find out. There was a growing feeling within the wider community that something was not right with the Shaw Wireless Works transaction. The press coverage of the sale, particularly through the caustic stories pumped out in Hugh Denison's *Sun* newspaper, prompted the government to initiate an enquiry which brought into the light of day and made public many things that had been hidden from scrutiny. Denison set out to destroy any remaining value in the Shaw enterprise so that *Amalgamated Wireless (Australasia) Ltd*, AWA, could exercise a virtual monopoly on the future of wireless in Australia.

Circumstances necessitated that a full-scale enquiry should be held into the war-time procurement practices of the government – particularly in respect of the Shaw Wireless Works and, to a lesser extent, the purchase of two ships, the steamships *Emerald* and *Togo* which the Navy had bought around the same time. All these purchases took place under the administration of Minister Jens Jensen. Aside from the high price paid by the government, the Shaw Wireless Works naturally warranted particular investigation after the discovery of Archibald's large cash withdrawal from the London Bank in Melbourne that could not be accounted for after his death. The enquiry was done in the form of a Royal Commission.

The Wireless Works enquiry was not the first probe into Naval and Defence issues in recent years. There was a prior enquiry that made a Royal Commission into the Maritime Wireless purchase inevitable.

Between 1914 and 1916 a *monumental* financial fraud was perpetrated on the Australian Defence Forces by a single officer resulting in subsequent sensitivities to government procurement practices that had even the remotest whiff of corruption. It was this grand-theft that initiated a Royal Commission into Navy and Defence Administration in the first place – the enquiry into the Wireless Works sale was an addendum. Historian Eric Andrews summarises the circumstances of the earlier fraud,

> *Lt David C. W. Howell-Price was on the administrative and instructional staff at Victoria Barracks, Sydney, in 1914. As Adjutant of the 9th Light Horse, he had begun by forging forage contracts, then in 1915 went on to paysheets for the unit's non-existent time in camp, cashing the resultant cheques himself. In the end he defrauded the department of £67,374 - his salary at the time being £275 a year. Only his laziness led to his discovery: he neglected to forge acquittance slips, and*

a new Pay Officer became suspicious. Yet after all this, he was merely charged on two counts of forgery and sentenced in March 1917 to four years' imprisonment. Further possible charges were abandoned the following May, despite the Board of Inquiry strongly urging they be pursued. With good conduct and armistice remissions he was released in 1919 and only £19,756 was ever recovered.[13]

Compared to this fraud, which amounted to some $67 million in today's money, the graft-money from the Wireless Works sale, some $530,000 today, was small change. However, the investigation was not just about money. Importantly, the enquiry was designed to preserve the integrity of taxpayer funded undertakings and root out corruption of government officials or anyone else who was nefariously involved in government transactions, regardless of scale.

Hearings for the Royal Commission dealing with the sale of the Wireless Works were conducted in private[14] over six days commencing on Tuesday, November 12, 1918, which was an unexpected and hastily announced public holiday held the day after Armistice Day. The hearings were scheduled to extend until the following Tuesday, November 18, 1918.

To the layman, wireless remained a novelty in the years before public broadcasting commenced in Australia. Ten weeks before the commission hearings began, with considerable public interest, AWA's director, Ernest Fisk received the first of two wireless messages at his own home in Wahroonga in the northern suburbs of Sydney. He brashly, (and inaccurately),[15] touted these were the first ever direct messages received from the UK, (Carnarvon in Wales), to Australia. One message was from the Prime Minister, Billy Hughes, and the other from Joseph Cook, the Minister for Navy who would go on to replace Jensen after he was later sacked. Both politicians were visiting England at the time and Fisk was using an Australian designed receiver made by AWA engineers employing new valve technology for the contact which significantly increased sensitivity.

In Melbourne the Royal Commission hearings were conducted in a small court-room located at the rear of the Law Library in the quadrangle of the old Law Courts building on the corner of Lonsdale and William Streets. The room was known as the Court of Marine Enquiry[16] and it also doubled as the Licensing Court. Signage extant from this period survives on the outside of the library showing the location of the room. Today it has been re-purposed. The hearings were not open to the public and the findings and testimony were only released when published in their entirety by the commission on December 2, 1918. Witness testimonies were frequently published *verbatim* in the press when released.

Melbourne Law Courts, c. 1915. The Royal Commission was held in the Court of Marine Enquiry within this building. *Credit: City Collection, City of Melbourne*

The lengthy official report of the Royal Commission was then summarised in the press and it publicly blazoned the unknown private lives of Archibald Shaw and Eve Hoad which would have remained forever hidden if no inquiry were held. It is through testimonies given during at the Royal Commission that we know so much about the operations of the works and indeed anything at all of the relationship between Evie and Archibald. Without it the story would be barely a footnote in the history of Australian manufacturing.

The findings of the Royal Commission came as no surprise to Linckens. He was privately grateful they remained focussed on the actions of government and less on the personal life of Archibald. The Chairman of Royal Commission, William McBeath, neatly summarised its purpose,

> *What is troubling the Commission is this: Father Shaw drew a cheque for £5,300 from the bank, and we cannot trace where that money has gone.*[17]

When Linckens wrote to Meyer on February 3, 1919, passing on updates about the settlement of Archibald's financial affairs, he made the following comment,

> *Since I last wrote I got myself a copy of the report of the Royal Commission of more than 100 pages of small print. I find it is the confirmation of matters I already knew... my suspicions were far from being rash judgements. Fortunately, attention was restricted to the principal matter, i.e. political influence without descending too much in personal affairs which were far from edifying...*[18]

The scandal he worked so hard to contain was now permanently etched in the public record. Yet Linckens remained sanguine. The remarkable and surprising thing is that nobody seemed particularly outraged by the matter-of-fact reporting of the story in the press as details came to hand and the published record of the enquiry was analysed and digested.[19] Archibald had always been publicly well respected, possibly due to the extensive and very positive press coverage from his earlier undertakings. Perhaps it was the end-of-war climate that distracted attention from the story. The fact that Archibald allegedly orchestrated illegal payments for the services of various politicians, or the salacious overtones of his private behaviour which left little to the imagination, did not diminish the respect the public held for his memory. No doubt if he had been alive to defend himself the commission would have run a different course.

Evie Hoad was a soft target for the commission's chief inquisitor, Hayden Starke, a barrister acting on behalf of the Crown

Solicitor. He attempted to portray her as a harlot in the saga and interpreted her relationship with Archibald, and their planned one-way trip to America, as reason enough to explain the missing money.

Christened *Eva Providence*, she was always known as Evie, or Eve in later life, and to Archibald was known as just 'E'. *Providence* was a family name passed down from prior generations. Curiously, the record of the Royal Commission, whose stenographers exercised a rare exactitude, recorded her middle name as *Prudence* during the hearings. There is not a single misprint or spelling error in the finely printed report of the Royal Commission – even with the confusingly similar names of the two witnesses *Creswell* and *Cresswell*.

Used as a noun, *providence* derives from the Latin *providere*, to provide, and is frequently used in a religious context meaning *being provided for God* or *coming under the protective care of God*. In secular terms providence could be interpreted as *getting something for nothing* or *for no real work*.

Evie may have thought that her name alone might suggest to the commissioners that she was the recipient of the missing money and it was better, or more prudent, for her to use a name with which it was frequently confused with. The name Evie *Prudence* Hoad was duly recorded in the official 1918 report and it is reasonable to conclude that this was the name provided by Evie herself to the commission. It would not be the only time Evie exercised a fluidity with names.

Thirty-one-year-old, Evie, had just started working as a manageress at Jenolan Caves, several hours travel to the west of Sydney, in the weeks before the hearings began. She took the stand as the seventh witness on the fourth day, Monday, November 15, 1918. She had travelled to Melbourne for the hearing by steam train the day before. Starke, the Crown Solicitor, attempted to rattle her during questioning, using a kind of misguided logic and an aggressive and antagonising line of interrogation,

> *Your relations were of the utmost intimacy were they not?*
> *- What do you mean by that?*
> *Sexual intercourse took place between you?*
> *- No*

Never?
>   *- No*

Do you swear that?
>   *- Yes. I went to see him many times at his house.*

Do you swear that sexual intercourse never took place between you and Fr Shaw?
>   *- Yes; I do.*

You used to visit him at his house?
>   *- Yes; very often.*

Alone?
>   *- Sometimes alone and sometimes with my sister.*[20]

Evie held her ground. The repetitive innuendo was irrelevant to locating the missing cash. It was a hounding attempt to destroy her character. She denied receiving any money except for a small amount given as a birthday present and explained to the commission she understood her relationship with Archibald was that of an engaged couple, albeit in secret. She told the court that Archibald had asked her several times to marry him, even suggesting a secret marriage, which she refused. She had waited two years for the sale of the Wireless Works and for him to leave the priesthood so they could move to America and her patience was being tested. Her frustration was clear during the testimony.[21] However, the question of how Archibald and Evie's new life in America would be funded was a valid consideration for the commissioners and reason enough to bring some suspicion on Evie.

Colin Hoad, Evie's nephew, knew her well in the last thirty years of her life and loved her as his *favourite aunt* when I interviewed him in 2021. He said he knew her as an exceptional, creative, flamboyant and a unique individual who loved life and lived it to the fullest. He remembered her proudly driving around in a big, black, head-turning, convertible Graham-Paige car. He maintains she would not have hesitated to have had an affair with someone like Archibald and her personality was such that she would have read with delight the press coverage of her own testimony[22] without a hint of embarrassment. Nevertheless, the personal cost to Evie was significant and became evident later in her life.

Of course Evie was not the only target in the commission's sights. Senator James Long, who seemed to lack the ability to keep his mouth shut, presented an unfamiliar naivety for a politician. He disembogued a convoluted story where he openly admitted receiving a gratuity from Archibald mixed in with the repayment of some gambling debts and other monies. He had no option but to express a degree of honesty since there was a record of a large cash deposit into his bank account - £2,400 - the largest personal deposit of his life. It was made a couple of weeks after meeting Archibald at Parliament House.[23] Long's story became further complicated as he wrote verbose explanations to the Prime Minister in an effort to exonerate himself well after the commission hearings concluded.

However, the wily Jens "Gus" Jensen, Minister for Navy, was not so forth coming. He was, incidentally, the only person at the enquiry represented by legal counsel. This was offered to every witness but only taken up by Jensen.[24] He admitted doing no wrong whatsoever in the purchase of the Wireless Works, nor in any other defence purchase he oversaw, not least of all the receiving of graft-money for greasing the wheels of government. Yet, Commander Cresswell, the Navy Department's wireless expert, had previously valued the purchase at £40,000 and, after an interview with Jensen, inexplicably changed his mind and considered Archibald's offer of £57,000, the one presented to Cabinet in an altered report, to be reasonable.[25]

Jensen never told Cabinet of Cresswell's dramatic change of mind regarding the valuation which irritated the commissioners.[26] The offer made by the government and accepted by Archibald was £55,000. Independent testimony from Evie Hoad, Joseph Lynch, Albert Cornwell and August Carroll,[27] whom Archibald had known as an employee of the General Electric Company some twelve months earlier, suggested that Jensen was to receive at least £2,000 from the transaction. No evidence was found by the commission that suggested Cresswell received anything.

What is interesting in all this is the relationship between Long and Jensen. It was not at all cordial. Once friends, their association had been strained for years. Yet, if Archibald did give the whole of the missing money to Long in four separate packages destined for four individuals, as recorded in the testimony of works' manager Albert Cornwell, it is difficult to understand why Long never snitched on Jensen, given he held a fundamental dislike for him and despite the fact that he was fighting to save his own political career. In fact, the last time he was recalled as a witness Long agreed that *he absolutely absolved Mr Jensen from any connection of having received any money at all from Father Shaw.*[28]

By the same token, Cornwell, the continuing manager of the works under Defence ownership, distrusted Long to such a degree that a stenographer was arranged to record a private conversation between the two back in Sydney days after they both had given evidence. One newspaper reported that this was an arrangement made between the Royal Commissioners and Cornwell in the hope that the loose-lipped Long would implicate himself and finally put the matter of the missing money to rest.[29] However, the transcript of the conversation was supplied to the commission by Leo Cussen,[30] then legal counsel for Jensen – so the secret recording may have been orchestrated by Jensen himself. Long implicated no one and the whereabouts of the money, aside from the deposit in Long's account, remains unknown.

During the recorded conversation with Long, Cornwell repeats some of his testimony probably in the hope that Long would let slip some information he had not yet revealed,

> *Shaw asked me to value the place in April or May 1916. I told him it was a big job and that I should require help in the form of previous valuations if such existed.*
>
> *I valued the place and told Shaw that I had no hope of reaching £63,000 for him unless I inflated values. This was done. For instance, the machinery was taken at its cost price, although most of it had been in service for three years, and to its original value 40% was added. In other words, it was really second-hand machinery largely appreciated over its original cost.*
>
> *I am supposed to have £13,000 odd worth of machinery and as a matter of fact what I had is worth about £7,000.*[31]

It was ultimately Jensen's decision to purchase the Wireless Works for the price it was offered. Nevertheless, both Long and Jensen lost their jobs as a result of the commission's findings. Forced out of politics, Long moved into business and bought a couple of hotels.[32] Jensen was made to resign from his ministerial portfolio but remained a politician until 1934.[33] Members from both sides of politics continued to argue for a judicial enquiry following the Royal Commission – an enquiry with the power to prosecute - but the government refused.[34] Long himself was amongst those calling for a judicial enquiry.[35] The feeling was that the commissioners, who were a group of businessmen,[36] did not represent the best means of finding an answer to the question of where the missing money had gone.[37]

The threat of continuing legal action from the government toward Long for the recovery of monies he admitted receiving ceased by mid-1919.

There is a fascinating post-script to Jensen's involvement in the story coming from an unlikely source.[38] It dates to 1936, many years after the Royal Commission concluded. A Melbourne priest called Jack McNamara was posted to Elsternwick Parish and recalls being notified by a third party that one of his parishioners, an ageing Gus Jensen, was now blind and suffering from diabetes. He was living in a weatherboard home in Downshire Road which still stands today and he was close to death. His house was surrounded by barbed-wire entanglements which made getting to the front door very difficult,

> *I made several attempts without success but finally I did get in and was extremely well received by Mr Jensen who knew himself that he was not far from death and made his last confession...*[39]

The barbed wire surrounding the Jensen home served another purpose which became apparent when McNamara visited on another occasion accompanying a nurse, Sister Greening, who attended Jensen in his final days. In addition to having a wife and two children, Jensen also had a child with his cousin, Miss Maggie Jane Gilbert, and been living in a de facto relationship with her at the Elsternwick home. They had been in this relationship for some thirty-seven years,[40]

... so I went with her and I met the supposed Mrs Jensen who indicated to me then that all the reason for the barbed wire entanglements which prevented me getting an entry into the house on Downshire Road; it was because of the money she was holding for or of Mr Jensen which was buried in the backyard; she was paying out money in cash to the people she owed it to – the nurse, the doctor, the undertaker, the trades-people.[41]

◆ ◆ ◆

As happens at the end of all Royal Commissions various recommendations are made and how they are acted upon depends on the whim of the government of the day. In its report of 1918, the commission recommended that the Wireless Works at Randwick be removed from the control of the Melbourne-based *Naval Radio Office* and placed under the supervision of the General Manager of the Naval Dockyards at Garden Island in Sydney Harbour.[42] This was duly done.

It also recommended that the plant and machinery at Randwick be moved to workshops on Garden Island and the land and buildings on the Randwick site be sold for residential purposes. The latter part of this recommendation was acted upon the best part of a century later. In the years following the 1918 Royal Commission the Maritime Wireless site continued at various times to be an interesting mix of workshops, laboratory, a training school for returned soldiers, an Army Reserve base and a suburban naval storage depot.

The large steel tower behind Ascot had been more than a local landmark. It was a symbol of the experimental daring and manufacturing prowess of the first wireless manufacturing factory in Australia - powered by the extraordinary vision of an unusual Catholic priest who was recognised as *one of the cleverest men in wireless in the world.*[43]

The tower had been erected by Archibald, Edward Kirkby and his employees all those years before when their business was little more than a dream. It had proudly borne the experimental aerials of Maritime Wireless Works and, at one time, transmitted the most powerful radio signals in the country. Without fanfare the tower was disassembled and disappeared from the Sydney skyline sometime in the 1930s. The story of Archibald and the Wireless Works then began to dim. The government sold the site to a residential developer some eighty years later.

Archibald's tower was replaced by another. In 1937, Ernest Fisk, whose company purchased the ageing Coastal Wireless Service stations[44] for reorganisation and refurbishment with continuous wave equipment, started construction of the landmark AWA building and its now famous tower, in York Street, Sydney. The enormous steel antenna on top of a brand new fifteen-story building was inspired by Gustav Eiffel's creation in Paris. Until the 1960s it was the tallest structure in Sydney - apart from the Harbour Bridge. The tower which has been refurbished in recent decades still sits atop the AWA building.

Whilst the York Street tower had a practical function as a wireless aerial, it also powerfully symbolised AWA's ascendancy in the industry just as the tower at Randwick had done for the Maritime Wireless Telegraph Company more than two decades before. With the advent of broadcasting and commercial radio in the 1920s, the dominance of AWA was several orders of magnitude greater than Maritime Wireless ever achieved at its peak.

Were the political climate, financial management and other circumstances different, the building on York Street might well have become the headquarters of the *Maritime Wireless Telegraph Company* instead of *Amalgamated Wireless*.

Ernest Fisk's AWA building and tower at 45-47 York Street, Sydney, completed in 1938.
Credit: M. Ryan

XVIII

Settling Matters

As business deals go, the price realised for the sale of the Wireless Works was exceptional. Aside from lingering moral questions over the way the sale was conducted or whether its purchase was the best use of taxpayers' money, the sale exemplified what Archibald was good at – selling an idea and working with people.

The settlement of his estate was a completely different matter and proved as messy as his accounting practices. Settlement became a drawn-out affair, a source of great frustration to creditors, and a financial windfall for the eloquence of lawyers working on behalf of the interested parties.

Hubert Linckens writes to the MSC Father General, Eugène Meyer, in October, 1916,

> *I'm renewing my efforts in the Shaw case. The reply has been given that 'it will take a long time' in view of the mixed-up state of things. No one can tell me whether it will be a matter of weeks or months...*[1]

It was a complicated and convoluted process that ended up taking *years* to resolve, with a significant amount of compromise and negotiation between solicitors for the chief claimants. Probate was granted on February 16, 1917, but the matter proceeded for another three years in various court actions. Resolution of the settlement was punctuated because of legal action taken by Archibald's brother, Charles William Fraser Shaw, on January 21, 1918,[2] against his sister

Blanche Amelia Monday who was executrix. Charles claimed that she had mis-valued some of the assets and sold them undervalued. She wasted little time claiming administration of the estate after Archibald died whilst her brother was away in Europe on war service. There was the question too of whether Archibald's assets would even cover his debts - with the very real possibility of bankruptcy. There was another significant problem too; just *finding* all of his assets.

Linckens previously made an agreement with Archibald that the Missionaries of the Sacred Heart be repaid some £3,700 from the sale of the Wireless Works – *better something than nothing,* as he once wrote to Meyer.[3] This was only about a third of what Archibald owed the society. It was revealed by accountants looking into Archibald's assets that, in the first half of 1914, Archibald had deposited some £17,000 *into* the mission accounts via several instalments.[4] Following Archibald's death, Linckens placed a claim for the full amount owed, some £10,113/16s/11d, realising that he would probably only get a pro-rata payment on this amount if Archibald's assets, assembled by Blanche, were insufficient to cover the amounts owed to the other creditors.

Linckens had repeatedly requested a list of Archibald's assets and liabilities since proceedings began and by July, 1918, his request was finally granted. Altogether there were about one hundred and sixty creditors[5] and,

> *... many of them doubtful – that is, not well established in my opinion and could not produce their rights...*[6]

The assets and creditors list provides a fascinating glimpse into Archibald's life.[7] It is a window into the largest debts owed to Sir Rupert Clarke and Hubert Linckens down to the minutiae of his daily activities. Amounts are specified owing to bookshops, to a dentist, to the *Coogee Laundry* in Avoca Street, to the local garage servicing his car, to Nurse Garlick who ran the Melbourne hospital where he subsequently died, to the doctor that witnessed his body after death and completed his death certificate, and even to the supplier of his paints and canvasses used for his artwork. There is an amount owing to a coking coal supplier (Warburton & Sons), a material from which "suction gas" was derived. This confirmed that the generator at the Wireless Works was powered by gas produced onsite as described in one press article.[8]

The Captain of the schooner *Pearl*, an MSC owned boat which was destroyed back in 1904 in a storm off New Ireland the very day the Baining massacre occurred, briefly re-enters the Shaw story again. He continues with the old claim, made through his solicitor, for the outstanding £400 in lost wages he believes he is still owed.

On the assets list also is a twenty horse-power engine in Mildura lent to Reg Wilkinson and a surprisingly large number of shares held in the Wallarah North Colliery. Representatives from the Wallarah North company had attended Archibald's funeral.[9] His share-holdings in this business made him a principal partner. The New South Wales mine was located about one hundred metres west of the main road into Swansea,[10] a mile south of the township. It is not to be confused with a nearby mine of similar name, the Wallarah Colliery at Catherine Hill Bay. Archibald wrote from Melbourne to Albert Cornwell at Randwick during the sale of the Wireless Works about moving a new engine to 'a mine' when the works are sold.[11] This was probably Wallarah North. It seems that Archibald had plans to make a significant profit from developing and selling the mine to overseas interests.

August Carroll recalls in Royal Commission testimony given on Tuesday, May 14, 1918,

> *I did not know Father Shaw more than twelve months before he died. I was with the General Electric Company. He had a coal-mining scheme. People were coming out of the States – two millionaires. The General Electric Company wrote [to] Father Shaw saying they were sending speculators out.*[12]

Albert Cornwell, manager at the Works and Archibald's confidant adds,

> *I know the old man [Archibald] was interested. He said he hoped to bring off a much bigger thing than he did with the works. Those were his own words...*[13]

The speculative deal with the coal mine at Wallarah North

involved investors from General Electric and could have been the means that Archibald planned to support Evie and himself when they set up in America.

Archibald's assets list, compiled by executrix Blanche Monday, show the value of his Wallarah North holding. Surprisingly, his 5,000 shares were realised at £1 each which represents some $500,000 in today's money. There was some consideration too that these shares had been undervalued.[14]

In the following year, 1917, another surprise was discovered in a previously unknown mining asset. It was found that Archibald owned a half-share in a molybdenite mine near Deepwater, NSW. When Blanche originally collated Archibald's assets and liabilities she was unaware of the Deepwater mine.[15] Linckens and the Missionaries of the Sacred Heart were also in the dark about this investment,

> *In these last weeks I have found out that the deceased was engaged in another business which fortunately increases a little our assets. With good will and honesty there would be some way of making good the losses he has caused us – at least for the most part but I don't want to build up my hopes.*[16]

It certainly appears Linckens' was kept ignorant about any assets which were not held on the Wireless Works site. It is difficult to believe this is just an oversight on Archibald's part. Remember, that within days of his arrival in Australia, Linckens was at *Ascot* trying to bring some order to the Maritime Wireless accounts. One of the first things he must have sought from Archibald was a statement of assets and liabilities.

It is surprising too, given his attention to detail, that Linckens agreed to a settlement sum without knowing the full extent of Archibald's assets, unless he was intentionally misled. A sceptical reader might think Archibald's accounting dishevelment was a ruse to actually hide assets and this may explain why he made no effort to get the books in order before the arrival of Linckens in 1914.

After one conference with solicitors representing various stakeholders who were making claims on the estate, Linckens writes to Meyer,

> *At this meeting I learned many more details which prove once again that a religious, who has a conscience, does well not to interfere in the affairs of this world.*[17]

Molybdenum, tungsten and bismuth are minerals frequently found in the ground together. Tungsten was used extensively for filament production in the newly popular and widely-used incandescent lamp. Molybdenum, refined from molybdenite, is a metal alloyed with steel to improve its quality for industrial applications. They have been mined in the Deepwater area since 1905. Archibald's half-share was in the *Allies Mine,* registered in the name of E. A. Baker. The mine still operates today when prices are high and sits on private land to the south-east of Deepwater township. Cornwell notes,

> *Baker was his partner in a mine at Deepwater. He was practically financed by Shaw.*[18]

There is a fascinating aside to this mining partnership which indicates a long-standing connection between the Shaw and Baker families. Archibald's mining partner was Ernest Arthur Baker. He had interests in the nearby Bow Creek Mine as well and several other mines in the district, extending into gold and arsenic which were also mined in the area. In 1913 Baker lived at 'Ten Mile' in the Deepwater district, and also lived at various addresses in the Sydney suburbs of Coogee and Randwick in later years with none of them being very far from the Wireless Works.[19] He was a mining engineer and inventor, having been granted several mining-related patents and one specifically for the development of a machine for molybdenite separation in water.[20] His patent attorney was none other than Wilfred Spruson whom Archibald used for his inventions and Archibald's associate in the Bulga Sawmill Company, 'Gunyah' Green, also used.

Now the father of Ernest Baker shared the same initials as his son. The father was Ezekiel Alexander Baker. He was at various times a mineralogist, newspaper publisher and mine proprietor. He had twice been the Minister of Mines and was elected a member of the Legislative Assembly for Goldfields South – which included Adelong

– Archibald's hometown, during the time of the Henry Parkes' Government. In fact, Ezekiel Baker was known to Archibald's parents because he held constituent meetings at Shaw's Hotel in Adelong[21] when Archibald was just a small boy.

In a case of history repeating itself, there is an astounding parallel between the elder Baker's story some thirty-five years earlier and the findings of the more recent 1918 Royal Commission into the government's Maritime Wireless Works purchase.

In uncannily similar circumstances, Ezekiel Baker, associate of Archibald's parents in Adelong, just like Minister Jensen, lost his job as Minister of Mines because of the findings of a Royal Commission which was held during the Parkes' era. The elder Baker was found guilty of misappropriating funds in a financial scandal known as the *Milburn Creek Affair* where some £4,710 of public money could not be accounted for. It was suspected of being used to bribe elected officials.[22]

Archibald's brother, Charles, knew about his half share in the mine at Deepwater and complained to the court that Blanche, who had left it out of his assets, was not performing her duties properly as executrix. He was granted permission to return early from war service to deal with the matter and attempted to have her removed from the job.[23] Once made aware of Archibald's share in the mine, Blanche realised his share for cash shortly thereafter, which she was legally entitled to do, and sold it for £1,800 or about $180,000 today. According to Charles this grossly undervalued the asset.

Charles Shaw challenged her valuation in court, further delaying settlement. He wanted the court to take over administration of the estate and sought to recoup losses from Blanche. (At the same time he challenged the amount Linckens was claiming). Charles had a universally unpopular solicitor who was characteristically delaying proceedings as well. Linckens, in his inimitable style, considered that ongoing procrastinations with the settlement were nothing less than *deceptions* by the lawyers and wrote as much to Meyer,

Once more deceived… I heard indirectly that the solicitor of

(Archibald's) brother is a quarrelsome type – hated by his own and even by the court judges...[24]

Charles was ultimately unsuccessful in his court action and Blanche remained executrix.

Archibald's mining interests support contemporary newspaper accounts that there was a laboratory for mineral analysis and treatment[25] at the Randwick Wireless Works. Archibald had some association with respected priest-geologist Milne Curran[26] who spent years in the Central West of NSW and lectured in geology and mineralogy at Sydney Technical College. Archibald's father, Charles, had early interests in gold mining at Adelong[27] before moving into hotels when Archibald was a boy. His mother continued to hold shares in a large gold mine at the time of her death.

By the end of 1918, with Archibald's estate still not finalised, Linckens received a letter from Eugène Meyer recalling him to Rome to plan for a leadership meeting of the Missionaries of Sacred Heart Society which was held every six years, known as a *General Chapter.*

Fr Wemmers can look after the Shaw case – your presence is needed in Rome to prepare for the Chapter.[28]

Jozef Wemmers, at various times the provincial of the Northern Province in Europe, an Assistant General and a novice master,[29] was a Dutch-born missionary priest who was acting as mission procurator in Sydney at the time of Archibald's death. He was,

... the only real friend he [Linckens] could relate to being a fellow Dutch countryman... [Linckens] had given Fr Wemmers power of attorney in the Shaw case in order that he would be able to manage any further matters that may arise...[30]

Linckens left Australia aboard the *Orsova* on May 29, 1920, after a prolonged six-year stay in Australia because of the outbreak of World War I and complications arising from the settlement of Archibald's estate. He must have walked aboard the ship with a huge sense of liberation. The Australian Missionaries of the Sacred Heart he farewelled also breathed a deep sigh of relief at his departure. He had all but finalised reclaiming money from Maritime Wireless for the missions, he had brought rules and organisation where he thought they were required in the Australian Province, and he brought order where he thought there was chaos.[31]

What remained of Archibald's estate after the creditors were paid out was very little. Some £212[32] was divided by Blanche amongst her brother Charles William Fraser Shaw, herself and five nieces and nephews who were the children of Archibald's sister, Mary Kennedy, who had predeceased him: William, Catherine, Amy, Edward and Charles Kennedy.

Linckens' diligent and patient efforts resulted in the recovery of the bulk of the £10,113/16s/11d Archibald had borrowed from mission funds to prop up Maritime Wireless. I cannot find a record of the costs of Linckens' solicitor which would have been significant because the matter took four years to finalise. Still, he was able to recoup much more than the £3,700 agreed to before Archibald headed to Melbourne to facilitate the sale. Throughout his investigation Linckens was never aware of the full extent of Archibald's assets.

Despite a lack of attention to detail particularly in regard to the finer points of book-keeping, Archibald was always planning ahead, always readying for the next *big thing*. It is fascinating to speculate how he planned to support himself and Evie in America and how things might have played out if he had returned to Sydney as planned on the overnight *Sydney Express* train of Tuesday, August 21, 1916. He would not have embarked on a completely new direction trusting solely on providence. It is likely Evie knew more about his intentions than she revealed at the Royal Commission. She just wasn't asked the questions that a judicial enquiry would likely have pursued.

The most probable scenario for a stable financial future was tied up with his upcoming deal involving the *General Electric* speculators from the United States who were to look over the mine at Wallarah North. This may have provided a windfall even after his full debt to the mission accounts was repaid. Archibald might have even secured employment with *General Electric* in America as part of the deal.

Despite the largess of money Archibald redirected over time, or *embezzled* as Linckens would say, there is no evidence Archibald was a thief in the ordinary sense. Had he lived, there might well have been a Royal Commission but there would have been full accountability and little mystery if the commission was able to bring him back from America to testify.

A circumstantial argument could be made that Archibald was outright dishonest and the dishevelment of his accounts was a ploy to disguise, cover-up and divert attention from various assets he might make use of in America with Evie. On balance, I think this conclusion is unfair. Certainly, Archibald's priorities changed dramatically from the days when he had committed all his energy and abilities to being a missionary. He had developed some extraordinary skills in wireless, in manufacturing and business, and most importantly, in dealing with and inspiring people. He was a visionary but was handicapped by his own lack of attention to detail and by his limited interest in book-keeping and financial management despite having the experience of many years as mission procurator.

It all started out quite innocently with Edward Kirkby and Joseph Guis in the backyard of *Ascot*. Archibald, the talented and driven man, just wanted to develop a mechanism to provide ongoing funds for the missions and keep them out of debt. In the end he could not control the business he created – in fact the opposite occurred, it began to control him. His priesthood was already secondary and, after meeting Evie, his life changed course completely following his private commitment to her. His ongoing obligation to the business, to repaying the Missionaries of the Sacred Heart, and to preserving the jobs of his employees, forced him to live concurrently in parallel worlds with great difficulty. His situation induced extreme stresses which he kept to himself.

The perceptive Fr Jules Vandel, his one-time seminary teacher, foretold something of this back in 1902 when he wrote,

> *I don't think the missions will ever be satisfying to Fr Shaw…*[33]

How right he was.

♦ ♦ ♦

SETTLING MATTERS

The Archibald Shaw story reads like a Greek tragedy. Archibald becomes the tragic hero through his own actions. He doesn't live a life of malice or malevolence, but the consequences he faces seem greater than what he deserves – ending ultimately in his death. In the end he finds himself trapped in institutional religious life but has the honour to stay until his debt is repaid. He may have been a prisoner of his own greatness, a casualty of hubris, a victim of circumstance or a combination of all three.

He became many people over the course of his life: born as John Archibald and becoming Archibald John, then orphaned, then Archie as a youth in the Telegraph Office. He then became Brother Placid the Passionist and later a Sacred Heart Missionary in New Guinea. He became Father Shaw when ordained a priest and then turned into an experimenter and industrialist, an entrepreneur and businessman. With the simple goal of uniting the remote missions by wireless and making a few pounds to keep them economically viable, he ended up building Australia's first wireless factory. His company united the whole of Australia through the manufacture and installation of the first Coastal Wireless Service. There is no denying his business was an extraordinary force in the early days of Australian industry.

Like the archetype flawed heroes of antiquity, Archibald's story plays out his strengths and his dark side in full view. This makes his character so fascinating. But *all* the people in this tale are absorbing and any one of them could be any one of us.

In their unconventional lives flawed heroes lead the way and this story has no shortage of them.

Whilst reckless at times, Archibald and Evie show patience and persistence and display a natural courage in the face of some existential questions about what it is to be human and about finding a purposeful direction in life.

The casual visitor to the cemetery at Douglas Park will remain unaware of inaccuracies on Archibald's headstone. They serve to memorialise the confusing nature of the man. Subtle efforts might have been made to erase Archibald's schemes from the historical record in the decades following his death but even in life he remained bewildering to many.

Now, all but forgotten, the Maritime Wireless Telegraph Company was proudly the first wireless manufacturing factory in the early days of Australian industry. It was renowned as a nursery for novel scientific and industrial ideas and became the *Silicon Valley* of its era, attracting talented and eccentric people, drawn there to work under the mantle of the enigmatic Archibald Shaw.

In 1947 the remains of Archibald were moved from Randwick cemetery and interred in the MSC community cemetery at Douglas Park monastery. The date of his death is recorded correctly; not so the other dates. He was born Dec. 16, 1870, was first-professed on Sept. 24, 1896, made his perpetual profession on Sept. 27, 1899 and was ordained on June 5, 1900.

Credit: M. Ryan

IXX

Epilogue

The small village of Issoudun in central France, where Jules Chevalier founded the Missionaries of the Sacred Heart in 1854, is today the main transmitter site of France's overseas short-wave radio service, *Radio France Internationale*. Nine one-hundred kilowatt transmitters and twenty-five hundred kilowatt transmitters and their antennae are located in the fields immediately south-west of the village.

Joseph Slattery, the priest-scientist and teacher at St Stanislaus' College, is recognised as a pioneer of x-ray and wireless in Australia. Archibald met him in 1905 during a month-long trip to Bathurst. He was transferred from his beloved teaching job at the beginning of 1911 and moved into parish work in Ashfield, thence to Eastwood. Then he worked in seminaries at Springwood and Manly, and later served as Vice Rector of St. John's College in the University of Sydney. He died on March 31, 1931.[1] He did not pursue further work in x-ray or wireless after he left Bathurst in 1911. A biographer writes,

> *[He] was less persuaded than anyone else of the value of the aid he had given to the development of medical and surgical science in Australia and to the technology connected with wireless telegraphy.*[2]

Slattery's laboratory at St Stanislaus' College holds his original equipment and is preserved as a small museum.

Marion Mulrony started an electrical manufacturing business in the city of Sydney after leaving the Wireless Works. He was a partner in *The Mulrony Electrical Company* which sold his instruments including the dual-vaned windmill generator he patented at Randwick. The business was short-lived. He moved to Honolulu and established another electrical business. There he constructed the first broadcast radio station on Oahu in 1922, with the callsign KGU, when only a handful of receivers were available for listening to voice and music transmissions. The station was formed in partnership with the *Honolulu Advertiser* newspaper and a seventy-foot tower was mounted atop the Advertiser building with studios on the third floor. It officially commenced broadcasting on April 1, 1922. Mulrony remained the station manager until his retirement in 1952 after which he moved back to the mainland USA with his wife.[3]

When smoke was seen billowing from the direction of Pearl Harbour shortly after lunch on December 7, 1941, Mulrony climbed the KGU antenna on top of the Advertiser building to get a better view of the harbour several blocks away.[4] Whilst up the tower, a concrete wall at the rear of the building[5] was destroyed by an exploding shell causing Mulrony to immediately descend. He saw that the noise and smoke from Pearl Harbour was no accident. It was later revealed that Japanese pilots used transmissions from the Mulrony designed KGU transmitter and another station, KGMB, as a beacon to give them a bearing to Oahu and their target, the American fleet at Pearl Harbour. This marked the Japanese entry in to World War II. Mulrony died in Tacoma, Washington, on July 6, 1960.

Amalgamated Wireless (Australasia) Ltd continued to grow from strength to strength. By 1927 it had established a beam telegraph service to Britain which undercut the price of submarine cable services. The business evolved into large scale valve and radio manufacturing for the consumer and commercial markets. It also became involved in niche marine telecommunications and radar production, defence electronics and aviation electronics (avionics), often in partnership with the Australian Government funded research organisation, CSIRO. AWA provided equipment for the first colour television broadcasts in Australia and mass-produced consumer television sets. It became involved in the computer service business and in power transmission after exiting the consumer electronics market when cheaper imports became available. The building in York Street served as the AWA Headquarters until the early 1990s.

In 2014, after a century in business, AWA went into administration and, somewhat paradoxically – given that the founders, Denison and Fisk, had fervently tried to destroy the viability of Maritime Wireless in its early years – the remains of the company were bought out by Cabrini Health Limited, a Catholic healthcare provider engaged in the provision of biomedical engineering services, computer services and equipment commissioning, maintenance and servicing.

Shortly after Hubert Linckens was recalled to Rome he was diagnosed with cancer. He died two years later on October 5, 1922, and was buried at Hiltrup, just south of Münster, adjacent to the Provincial House of the German Province and the Mission Museum that he established. The museum was one of several started by various congregations throughout Europe and it occupied several floors at Hiltrup. Many artefacts, animal and plant collections and even human remains collected by the missionaries from the Pacific Island Missions were put on display there. Some contributors, like Matthäus Rascher, were renowned ethnologists and anthropologists in their own right. The museum collection once included Rascher's gun and ammunition pouch; the one used by Tomari to initiate the 1904 Baining massacre. Its whereabouts are now unknown. In 1941 the Nazi regime took control of the Hiltrup Mission House and the museum forcing the MSCs to move entirely from the Rhineland area during the war. The museum material was dispersed, mostly to the Ethnographical Museum in Berlin and, after the war, some objects were eventually returned to the MSCs and other collections were sold.[6]

The Gazelle Peninsula in New Guinea was scene to other brutal massacres during World War II. In February, 1942, around one hundred and sixty Australian prisoners of war were shot or bayoneted by the Japanese Army after the capture of Rabaul. In a separate incident, Japanese soldiers machined gunned Baining and Tolai tribes-people and buried them in a mass grave during reprisal attacks for an American raid on a Japanese base in the closing months of the Pacific war.[7]

The Missionaries of the Sacred Heart Society continue to work today in schools, parishes and various missions around the world. Whilst Archibald Shaw has gone from living memory in the current generation of missionary priests and brothers, the congregation never held him in judgement and neither celebrated nor scorned his memory. Despite being on the verge of leaving the society he was treated like any other member at his death and respectfully buried as a priest. In 1947 his remains were re-interred at the community cemetery at Douglas Park having been moved from their original burial site in Randwick (Long Bay) Cemetery. He is remembered annually in the society's *Necrologium* which recalls deceased members of the society on the anniversary of their death.

The Wallarah North mine just south of Swansea, in which Archibald was a significant share-holder, saw bitter and long-winded strike action from miners during the late 1930s and throughout the war years. It was the site of the first "stay-in" strike in New South Wales industrial history. Miners, protesting against industrialisation, entrenched themselves underground and electrified surrounding fences.[8] The mine, depleted of coal over the ensuing decades, has since closed and is now all but unrecognisable having been reclaimed by the bush. It is now gazetted as part of the *Wallarah North National Park*.

The other mine Archibald had a fifty percent stake in, the *Allies Mine* near Deepwater, still operates today when prices are favourable.

Joseph Aloysius Lynch, Archibald's secretary, whose responsibility was for the engineering side of the business, was assured of on-going employment at the works after the sale. This did not happen despite his repeated appeals to Minister Jensen. He became a travelling salesman, married late in life and had no family. Lynch lived with his sister on Old South Head Road, Bondi Junction, at the time of his death.[9] The painted self-portrait given to him by Archibald has not been traced. The only record of it is a poor reproduction published in a newspaper after Archibald's death.[10]

When he left politics, ex-senator James Long, became publican of the now demolished Powlett Hotel in Wonthaggi, about one hundred kilometres south-east of Melbourne. Later he owned a hotel in Temora, New South Wales. He kept up an interest in horse-

EPILOGUE

racing, owning and training his own racehorse for a time.[11] He died in Melbourne on December 23, 1932, survived by his wife, three daughters and four sons.[12] Leslie Long, the son once apprenticed at the Wireless Works, joined the 4th Light Horse Brigade from August, 1916, until 1919, citing his occupation as a labourer at enlistment.[13] He later fractured his skull in a serious horse-riding accident.

Jens August Jensen, the Minister for Navy lost his job after the Royal Commission. He died in Melbourne in 1936 due to complications from diabetes and bequeathed his entire estate to his cousin and mistress, Maggie Jane Gilbert. In 1937 an unsuccessful challenge was commenced by four of his children from his first marriage.[14]

Fernand Arnoult returned from serving in the Australian Infantry Forces, 1st Battalion Pioneers, where he put his engineering skills to use on the Western Front. He had two children and owned a series of hotels, eventually retiring to Tumut, a short distance from Adelong where Archibald was born. Arnoult donated the land he was gifted in Tasmania where he oversaw the establishment of the King Island Wireless Station, to found what became the Tumut RSL sub-branch.

Albert Cornwell, employed by Archibald to manage the transition of the Wireless Works into munitions manufacture, continued employment at the newly created Naval Wireless Works. He lived at *Archina* with his family. In April, 1919,

> *... the Wireless Works were taken over by the Repatriation Department for use as a trades school for vocationally training returned soldiers, and Mr Cornwell was appointed principal and manager.*[15]

Cornwell remained manager until his premature death on December 7, 1920. He had undergone an operation for appendicitis a week earlier and did not recover.[16] He is buried in an unmarked grave in the Church of England section of Randwick Cemetery after a Masonic funeral service was held in nearby St. Jude's Church. His remains are located in the same cemetery where Archibald was first interred. He left behind a wife and four young children.

By the end of World War I returning soldiers were looking

for work and the *Naval Wireless Works* was quickly converted by the Defence Department into the *Repatriation Electrical and Engineering Trades School*. Ray Allsop returned there as a laboratory assistant after his own war service where he was a wireless operator with the Australian Naval Transport Service. Allsop claims that the first ever wireless-transmitted speech in Australia using a "round glass valve" took place on the Randwick site over a distance of two hundred yards.[17]

Daniel O'Connell, a priest and long-serving director of the Vatican Observatory wrote in a 1952 paper that the Naval Wireless Works at Randwick made a novel kind of seismometer, a device for detecting earthquakes, for Edward Pigot. Pigot was a Jesuit priest and founder of the *Riverview Observatory* in Sydney. The device operated on the principle of electromagnetic induction and was designed by Prince Galitzin in Russia with whom Pigot had been in correspondence. Galitzin intended to have one manufactured in Russia and sent to Edward Pigot at Riverview but revolution, war and the death of Galitzin in 1916 prevented this. Galitzin had earlier sent Pigot his drawings and the devices were made at the wireless workshops at Randwick under Pigot's supervision.[18]

Blanche Amelia Monday lived into old age in Glenbrook at the foothills of the Blue Mountains. She died on August 30, 1950 at eighty-seven years of age.[19] She was married and had one son.

Charles William Fraser Shaw in old age. *Credit: B. Clark*

EPILOGUE

Charles William Fraser Shaw, the younger brother of Archibald, had always been involved in acting and theatrical pursuits. He served as a mature-aged recruit in England during World War I with the rank of Acting Sergeant. He was discharged in the middle of 1917 for 'family reasons'.[20] In his later years he sported a long white beard and used this to advantage, regularly playing Santa Claus for children at one of the large department stores in Sydney city. His life was cut short on July 4, 1941, when he was struck by a train whilst crossing the lines at Mt Druitt railway station. He was seventy years old and had lost his hearing. Remarkably, given all the trouble he had been through with his sister over Archibald's estate, he died intestate. He is buried in Waverley Cemetery next to his wife who predeceased him by six years.

Mary Kennedy, Archibald's sister whom he helped out of poverty, died in 1913. Archibald remained close to her children, particularly his nieces, Amy and Catherine, for whom he paid their school fees for a time. In 1917 Catherine married into the Quigley family at *Woolerbilla*, a house still standing in Higgs Street, Randwick, after working there as a governess for some years. At this house her wedding and reception was held whilst the tower of the Wireless Works could be seen from the front yard just one-and-a-half kilometres to the north. Six years later, in 1923, across the road from where she was married, another aerial tower was set up behind the home of Ray Allsop, one of the Wireless Works' first apprentices. It bordered Byron Street. This was the earliest public broadcast station in Australia, first known as 2SB and later 2BL.

Mary Kennedy's husband, William, who had 'no hope of recovery' in 1905 from a terminal lung condition lived for another twenty-eight years. He survived his wife and Archibald to die in 1933.[21]

Archibald's other niece, Amy Kennedy, a talented musician, married Charles Wollaston in 1918. The marriage did not last. Its breakdown featured a bizarre and extraordinary story widely covered in the press of 1933.[22] This coverage may have been a contributing factor toward her suicide attempt a month later.[23]

Evie Providence Hoad worked with her family at Caves House, a guest-house providing accommodation for visitors to Yarrangobilly

Caves. After Archibald's death she worked at the Government Tourist Bureau in *Challis House* on Moore Street, now Martin Place, Sydney under the director, Edward Palmer. Challis House was also the location of Ernest Fisk's offices when he represented the Marconi Company several years before. Fisk was Archibald's arch-enemy in business. Evie had just taken on a role as manageress at Jenolan Caves House before she was called to given evidence at the Royal Commission. By April, 1919, she contracted the Spanish Flu at Jenolan whilst nursing infected patients in *The Bungalow,* which was Palmer's official residence at the caves. He converted the building into a hospital for fourteen patients. Evie survived the flu epidemic, though not all at Jenolan did.[24]

Evie engaged in a series of affairs following the death of Archibald starting with Edward Palmer.[25] She returned to Sydney and was spotted on the footpath drawing a copy of a newly-arrived Parisian dress on display in the front window of Farmer's large department store on Castlereagh Street. This attracted the attention of the store manager. She sewed-up a replica of the dress based on her drawing and on that basis, was recruited by the store manager as a dress-buyer. She travelled extensively making several trips through Europe, Indochina, Russia, the Pacific Islands, and the Americas throughout her life and when in Sydney lived in a Californian bungalow in Bishop's Avenue, Randwick, driving an American convertible Graham-Paige motor provided by a wealthy lover. The home was purchased in her name and shared with two sisters unrelated to her. She gave birth to a daughter in 1922. Her child was cared for by the two sisters when Evie was away. Occasionally she would return to Yarrangobilly and give popular talks on her travels to the Country Women's Association.[26]

Without a husband, Evie explained her child by way of the following story. She said she hastily married a man by the name of Taylor who was a wealthy plantation owner in Fiji. She had a child with him before he duly fell off a boat, only to be immediately eaten by a shark - *the whole lot of him.*[27] There never was a marriage, nor a shark attack, nor a man called Taylor. She chose the name on the basis that it was the third most common surname, after Smith and Jones, which would make verifying her story somewhat difficult. Henceforth, from the birth of her child she called herself Mrs Eve Providence Taylor.

The location of her home in Bishop's Avenue, Randwick, where she lived the remainder of her life, was such that every time she travelled to the city, or back to Yarrangobilly, she would drive up Frenchman's Road past the site of Archibald's Maritime Wireless Telegraph Company - a poignant reminder of the happiest and saddest times of her life. She never shared anything of these years with her family who, a couple of generations later, knew nothing of her association with Archibald.

Evie found solace in alcohol and died from complications due to alcoholism on July 19, 1962.

I discovered a fascinating coincidence whilst researching this book. One of Evie's great-granddaughters was my student in a school which itself was only a kilometre from the Wireless Works site. Here this great-granddaughter also did something extraordinary with 'wireless'. I had set-up equipment for a pre-arranged amateur radio contact with astronaut John Phillips aboard the International Space Station scheduled for June 2, 2005.[28] It was the first radio contact between NSW school children and the space station.[29] The spacecraft took ten minutes to move from horizon to horizon and there was only time for twelve school children to ask a single question during the pass. As the school had nearly a thousand students, a competition was held and judged by committee to determine who would participate. Evie's great-granddaughter was one of the selected participants. No one was aware of her familial link with Evie whose fiancé did something much more fantastic with wireless just up the road, a century before.

Following Cornwell's death, with much of the Wireless Works machinery and stores now at Garden Island, the workshops were set-up at the end of 1923[30] for another venture: the newly formed *Royal Australian Airforce (RAAF) Experimental Section* which remained on the site for seven years. The experimental facility was the only one of its kind in the British Empire outside of Britain.[31] In 1924 the cloth-winged *Wackett Warbler* aeroplane was designed and built at Randwick. By 1925 a flying boat had also been developed on the site. Both were based on designs by Squadron Leader Lawrence Wackett who, like Archibald Shaw many years before, lived at *Ascot*.

A Wackett Widgeon flying boat developed and built at the Randwick Aero Station, originally the workshops of Maritime Wireless.   *Credit: Sydney Morning Herald, March 18, 1921*

Similarly, other engineers and workers involved in this venture were accommodated in nearby *Archina*.

The novel flying boat, known as a *Wackett Widgeon*, could operate from both land and water. A prototype was transported from Randwick and first took-off from Botany Bay near La Perouse in Sydney. Two more aeroplanes were developed at the Randwick site under Wackett with a staff of about seventy: a two-seater biplane, the *Warrigal I* in 1929, and an improved version, the *Warrigal II* in 1930.[32] During this period, the site was known as the *Randwick Aero Station*[33] or the *Randwick Experimental Station* and served as a training school for Air Force mechanics. At the time of its closure some forty civilian men worked there having trained as aeroplane mechanics.[34]

Engineers at the Randwick workshops were responsible for strengthening the propellers used on Charles Kingsford-Smith's and Charles Ulm's *Southern Cross* aeroplane[35] in preparation for the first attempted flight from Sydney to London. On another flight, the *Southern Cross* would set a world distance record of another sort: it achieved a range of some twelve-thousand eight-hundred miles for short-wave wireless communication.[36] A Wackett designed speedboat was also developed on the site.[37] The story of Lawrence Wackett's life and his contribution to aviation is worthy of a book in itself.

By the end of March, 1930, the RAAF Experimental Section at Randwick closed down on a recommendation from an enquiry held by British Air Marshall Sir John Salmond.[38] Many of the staff, including Wackett, moved from Randwick into a new factory on Cockatoo Island which serviced seaplanes.[39]

By 1931 the carpentry workshop and foundry block had been removed from the Randwick site.[40]

Records on the use of the place following the departure of the RAAF are meagre. In the following decades it was used a suburban military depot. By the 1950s the *Citizens Military Force,* now known as the Army Reserve, used it as a training depot[41] and this use extended through until the 1970s.

In October, 1998, the two houses on the property once used by Maritime Wireless, *Ascot* on Dutruc Street and *Archina* in Avoca Street, were given heritage protection orders and added to the Commonwealth Government's Register of the National Estate, which is,

> *... an inventory of places that have aesthetic, historic, scientific, or social significance or other special value for future generations as well as for the present community.*[42]

During Australia's bicentenary year of 1988 Randwick City Council erected bronze plaques[43] on the front fences of *Archina* and *Ascot* which briefly told something of the story of the site but over the ensuing years, as the buildings changed hands and fences were replaced, the plaques were removed.

By the late 1990s the entire parcel of land where once sat the Wireless Works, including the houses *Ascot* and *Archina,* was sold by the Department of Defence. The land that once housed the tower and workshops of the Maritime Wireless Telegraph Company went in a single parcel to a developer. Some forty-two residences, mostly apartments with some townhouses and a couple of terrace houses, were built on the site and sold individually in 2000.

Two streets are named in memory of Archibald. One *Shaw*

Street is in Currie on King Island leading to the site of the old wireless station. The other is a residential street in Kensington, not far from the Missionaries of the Sacred Heart monastery. The original *Fr Shaw's Road* at Bulga is today called *Gunyah Road,* in memory of 'Gunyah' Green.

♦   ♦   ♦

Author's Note

I never thought it would fall to me to investigate the Archibald Shaw story. It has been my privilege.

I first heard of Shaw from my father as twelve-year-old crossing Avoca Street, Randwick, in the 1970s not far from *Archina* and the Maritime Wireless Works' site. All anyone remembered then was that Shaw started a wireless factory where boys could learn a trade. In my naivety I wanted a job there until I realised it was all too late.

It was a quirk of fate that prevented the loss of invaluable Missionaries of the Sacred Heart archival material and has allowed the reconstruction of this nuanced account. If Shaw was relieved of his vows and fully laicised before death, the MSC would not have retained the volume of information they held on him and the Wireless Works, and much of the story would be irretrievable.

Shaw's correspondence is written quickly. Words are bent to fit the page and he consistently avoids punctuation, perhaps a hangover from his days as a telegraphist. For clarity, the inclusion of punctuation in many quoted passages is mine.

I remain indebted to research conducted by the original Shaw investigator, John McMahon MSC. He began over fifty years ago when contact with some of Shaw's contemporaries was still possible. McMahon arranged for copies of surviving letters to be returned to Australia from the MSC archives in Rome. He died in 1993 with his research incomplete. I have relied significantly on his translation of primary source documents. Those he did not translate I have done myself with the assistance of Baina Masquelier. McMahon wanted to tell the story of Shaw without being an apologist. I have tried to do the same.

I am grateful to the Missionaries of the Sacred Heart for allowing the story to be properly investigated: in particular to Chris McPhee MSC, Provincial, and Steve Dives MSC, Superior at Kensington monastery, who permitted access to their archival material in Australia; to Jim Littleton MSC who read my early drafts and offered historical advice and corrections concerning the society's history in his gentle and unassuming manner; to Roger Purcell MSC, director of the Mission Office and to Pacific Island historian, Peter Hempenstall (University of Newcastle), who both provided invaluable information on the early island missions and the Baining massacre in particular. Special thanks to John Hill, crusader for the underdog and for truth, to Hengki Ponamon MSC, archivist in Rome and to Sabine Heise, archivist in Hiltrup.

Thanks also to historians Rebecca Loder-Neuhold (Austria), Hermann Hiery (Bayreuth University, Germany) and Hilary Howes (ANU, Australia).

In the course this research I've been fortunate to locate descendants of a few characters from the story. It has been an honour to pass on information as it came to light. In some cases they were able to provide background information unavailable from other sources.

Thanks to Brian Kirkby, great-grandson of Edward Kirkby, who readily shared his research into the life of his forebear and offered insight into the political milieu of the era; to Graeme Bartram who generously shed light on the protracted and convoluted patent disputes against Maritime Wireless and drew my attention to some of the lesser known characters in early Australian wireless.

A project of this nature does not write itself and I remain indebted to the following people, in no particular order, for information, contributions, photographs and historical recounts:

Colin Hoad; Michael McDonald; Romina Viglianti & the Romina Riverside Café, Tumut; Carolyn Melbourne, Mukul Sharma & Jenny Whitby (Jenolan Caves); Eve Trefely; Valda & Jim Low; Rhonda Twomey (Tumut Library); Maureen Stathis; Margaret Bentley

AUTHOR'S NOTE

(Adelong Alive Museum and History Centre); Jude Prezens (Physics Department, Melbourne University); Fred Swainston (Wireless Institute of Australia); Peter Wolfenden; Brendan Kleinschafer & Lindsay Fuhrman-Luck (St. Stanislaus' College, Bathurst); Dominic Gleeson MSC (Douglas Park), Michael Fallon MSC (Kensington) & Jim Yeo CP (Marrickville); Larry & Janette Reedman; Lorraine Symons; Arthur Cooper, Judy Yarrington & Judith Jackson (Manning Valley Historical Society); Allan Glassop & Wayne Fitzgerald (Bulga); Luke Agati (King Island) & Frances Burke.

Chapter I: Prologue: Between Two Worlds

1. New Britain Massacre (November 16 1904) in *The Daily Telegraph (Sydney NSW: 1883-1930)*, 8. Accessed April 15 2023 from http://nla.gov.au/nla.news-page25676256
2. Ibid
3. Use of the acronym MSC is derived the French, *Missionnaires du Sacré-Coeur,* or the Latin, *Missionarii Sacratissimi Cordis,* meaning *Missionaries of the Sacred Heart* – initialised to MSH in the early decades of the order in Australia
4. New Britain Massacre (November 16 1904) in *The Daily Telegraph (Sydney NSW: 1883-1930)*, 8. Accessed April 15 2023 from http://nla.gov.au/nla.news-page25676256
5. Some accounts refer to an attack of thousands of natives. Refer *The W.A. Record* Saturday October 15 1904, 12
6. The New Guinea Massacre, Report by Bishop Linckens (September 13 1904) in *The Brisbane Courier (Qld.: 1864-1933)*, 2. Accessed April 18 2023 from http://nla.gov.au/nla.news-page1548248
7. The account of the massacre is based on the following press reports: The New Britain Massacre (September 20 1904) in *Clarence and Richmond Examiner (Grafton NSW: 1889-1915)*, 8. Accessed April 18 2023 from http://nla.gov.au/nla.news-article61410084
The New Guinea Massacre of Catholic Missionaries (October 15 1904) in *The W.A. Record,* 12. Accessed April 18 2023 from http://nla.gov.au/nla.news-page22977324
A Widespread Conspiracy (September 17 1904) in *Northern Star (Lismore, NSW: 1876-1954)*, 5. Accessed April 18, 2023, from http://nla.gov.au/nla.news-article71845314
The New Britain Massacres, (September 13 1904) in *The Maitland Daily Mercury (NSW: 1894-1939)*, 3. Accessed April 18 2023 from http://nla.gov.au/nla.news-page12632895
New Guinea Massacre (November 5 1904) in *The Wingham Chronicle and Manning River Observer (NSW: 1898-1954)*, 6. Accessed April 18 2023 from http://nla.gov.au/nla.news-page16383132
The New Britain Massacre (November 16 1904) in *The Daily Telegraph (Sydney, NSW: 1883-1930)*, 8. Accessed April 18 2023 from http://nla.gov.au/nla.news-page25676256
New Britain Massacre (September 17 1904) in *Moree Gwydir Examiner and General Advertiser (NSW: 1901-1940)*, 2. Accessed April 18 2023 from http://nla.gov.au/nla.news-page12274315
New Britain Massacre (September 20 1904) in *Clarence and Richmond Examiner (Grafton, NSW: 1889-1915)*, 8. Accessed April 18 2023 from http://nla.gov.au/nla.news-page5704732
The New Guinea Massacre, Report by Bishop Linckens (September 13 1904) in *The Brisbane Courier (Qld: 1864-1933)*, 2. Accessed April 18 2023 from http://nla.gov.au/nla.news-page1548248
8. Wireless for Hobart (December 23 1911) in *The Mercury (Hobart: 1860-1954)*, 6. Accessed October 21 2021 from http://nla.gov.au/nla.news-article10124586
9. Arthur C Clarke, *Profiles of the Future: An Inquiry into the Limits of the Possible* (London: Scientific Book Club, 1961), Chapter 2
10. Peter J Hempenstall, *Pacific Islanders under German rule: a study in the meaning of colonial resistance* (Canberra: Australian National University Press, 2016), 122
11. Brian Innes, *Priest & Scientist: Joseph Slattery – Australia's First Radiographer*, (Bathurst, Crawford House Publishing 1996)
12. GEC Review, Volume 7, Number 1, 1991, 50
13. Prebir K Bondyopadhyay, 'Sir J.C. Bose diode detector received Marconi's first

NOTES & REFERENCES

transatlantic wireless signal of December 1901 (The 'Italian Navy Coherer' Scandal Revisited)' *Proceedings of the Institute of Electrical and Electronics Engineers*. 86 (1998): 259

14 https://www.nobelprize.org/uploads/2018/06/marconi-lecture.pdf, 1. Accessed February 25 2023

Chapter II: Boyhood in Adelong

1 Adelong, (July 16 1866) in *The Tumut and Adelong Times (NSW: 1864-1867; 1899-1950)*, 3. Accessed March 28, 2023, from http://nla.gov.au/nla.news-article144778431
2 Publican licenses researched by Geoff Burch held at Adelong and District Historical Society
3 Catherine Shaw probate papers. NSW State Archives. INX-53-29415
4 Adelong Local News, (1875, December 11). *The Gundagai Times and Tumut, Adelong and Murrumbidgee District Advertiser (NSW: 1868 - 1931)*, 2. Accessed March 28, 2023, from http://nla.gov.au/nla.news-article122753527
5 Ibid, October 31, 1868, 3. Accessed March 28, 2023, from http://nla.gov.au/nla.news-article123553448
6 Ibid, June 21, 1873, 3. Accessed March 28, 2023, from http://nla.gov.au/nla.news-page12784935
7 Adelong Police Court, (1875, June 26). *The Gundagai Times and Tumut, Adelong and Murrumbidgee District Advertiser (NSW: 1868-1931)*, 3. Accessed March 28, 2023, from http://nla.gov.au/nla.news-article122756331
8 Manuscript, NSW State Library, Perkins Papers: John Arthur Perkins - 'Monaro District items, 1823-1948', being a chronological collection of references with 'Index 1823-1918', compiled by John Arthur Perkins, ca.1950, Sydney Mail, February 7, 1874
9 Tumut Races, (1873, April 5). *The Gundagai Times and Tumut, Adelong and Murrumbidgee District Advertiser (NSW: 1868-1931)*, 4. Accessed March 28, 2023, from http://nla.gov.au/nla.news-article122751358
10 Adelong News, (1879, December 16). *The Gundagai Times and Tumut, Adelong and Murrumbidgee District Advertiser (NSW: 1868-1931)*, 2. Accessed March 28, 2023, from http://nla.gov.au/nla.news-article127643512
11 Adelong Local News. (1876, June 30). *The Gundagai Times and Tumut, Adelong and Murrumbidgee District Advertiser (NSW: 1868-1931)*, 2. Accessed March 28, 2023, from http://nla.gov.au/nla.news-article122754500
12 Death certificate, NSW BDM, No 6638/1876
13 Adelong Local News. (1876, October 13). *The Gundagai Times and Tumut, Adelong and Murrumbidgee District Advertiser (NSW: 1868-1931)*, 3. Accessed March 28, 2023, from http://nla.gov.au/nla.news-article122752381
14 The Manchester United Independent Order of Oddfellows
15 (1878, November 23). *The Sydney Morning Herald (NSW: 1842-1954)*, 10. Accessed March 28, 2023, from http://nla.gov.au/nla.news-page1433687
16 Australian Town and Country Journal, Tumut & Adelong, Jan 4, 1879
17 A Tour in the Southern Districts, (1878, March 16), *Australian Town and Country Journal (Sydney, NSW: 1870-1919)*, p. 23. Accessed March 28, 2023, from http://nla.gov.au/nla.news-article70615662
18 Australian Town and Country Journal, Tumut & Adelong, Aug 23, 1879
19 Ibid, May 24, 1879
20 Ibid, Mar 16, 1878
21 Advertising (1921, April 1). *South Western Advertiser (Perth, WA: 1910 - 1954)*, 2.

Accessed March 28, 2023, from http://nla.gov.au/nla.news-article148647912
22. Australian Town and Country Journal, December 20, 1879, 37, see also: http://nla.gov.au/nla.news-page5987650
23. Adelong Local News. (1879, January 3). *The Gundagai Times and Tumut, Adelong and Murrumbidgee District Advertiser (NSW: 1868-1931)*, 2. Accessed March 28, 2023, from http://nla.gov.au/nla.news-article127641022
24. Adelong Local News, (1877, April 6), *The Gundagai Times and Tumut, Adelong and Murrumbidgee District Advertiser (NSW: 1868-1931)*, 2. Accessed March 28, 2023, from http://nla.gov.au/nla.news-article122751849
25. Adelong News, (1880, May 14). *The Gundagai Times and Tumut, Adelong and Murrumbidgee District Advertiser (NSW: 1868-1931)*, 2. Accessed March 28, 2023, from http://nla.gov.au/nla.news-article127640889
26. Adelong News, (1880, October 22). *The Gundagai Times and Tumut, Adelong and Murrumbidgee District Advertiser (NSW: 1868-1931)*, 3. Accessed March 28, 2023, from http://nla.gov.au/nla.news-article127639569
27. Adelong, (1880, July 5). *Evening News (Sydney, NSW: 1869-1931)*, 4. Accessed March 28, 2023, from http://nla.gov.au/nla.news-article108735796
28. Inflammation of the stomach according to her death certificate – 6 days duration
29. Death registration, Court House Tumut: 1880, No 274
30. Advertising, (1880, December 3). *Evening News (Sydney, NSW: 1869 - 1931)*, p. 1. Accessed March 28, 2023, from http://nla.gov.au/nla.news-article108747632
31. Adelong Catholic Church records, July 27, 1879, courtesy of research conducted by J F McMahon
32. Adelong News, (1880, October 15). *The Gundagai Times and Tumut, Adelong and Murrumbidgee District Advertiser (NSW: 1868-1931)*, 2. Accessed March 28, 2023, from http://nla.gov.au/nla.news-article127638965
33. Ecclesiastical Jurisdiction, (1881, February 8). *New South Wales Government Gazette (Sydney, NSW: 1832-1900)*, p. 846. Accessed March 28, 2023, from http://nla.gov.au/nla.news-article223689747
34. NSW State Archives, Gold (auriferous) Lease Register 1874-1953, Catherine Shaw, Series 10100, Item 7/3147
35. NSW State Archives, Intestate Estates, Catherine Shaw, INX-53-14747
36. Mary Ann, Catherine's sister and her husband Alfred Carr, were ancestors of ex-NSW Premiere Bob Carr, and Catherine & Mary's half-brother Michael Scanlen married a Sarah Rudd who is related through her grandfather to ex-Australian Prime Minister Kevin Rudd.
37. McMahon, J. F. (1983). Father Archibald Shaw: the wireless priest. [Paper read to the Australian Catholic Historical Society, 2 March 1983]. Journal of the Australian Catholic Historical Society, 7(3), 24–34
38. (1882, September 29). *The Armidale Express and New England General Advertiser (NSW: 1856-1861; 1863-1889; 1891-1954)*, p. 4. Accessed March 28, 2023, from http://nla.gov.au/nla.news-page22104260
39. (1886, September 10). *The Sydney Morning Herald (NSW: 1842-1954)*, 7. Accessed March 28, 2023, from http://nla.gov.au/nla.news-page1400868
40. Adelong, (1899, April 7). *The Tumut and Adelong Times (NSW: 1864-1867; 1899-1950)*, 2. Accessed March 28, 2023, from http://nla.gov.au/nla.news-article133311568
41. Charles enlisted in the Australian Infantry Forces on October 22, 1915. He departed Sydney for overseas duty on August 22, 1916, four days before his brother Archibald died in Melbourne. https://recordsearch.naa.gov.au/SearchNRetrieve/Interface/

NOTES & REFERENCES

ViewImage.aspx?B=8081225 Accessed March 28, 2023
42 Publicans' Licences (1936, February 11). *The Sydney Morning Herald (NSW: 1842 - 1954)*, 8. Accessed March 28, 2023, from http://nla.gov.au/nla.news-article17325569
43 Publican Fined, (1937, April 20). *The Maitland Daily Mercury (NSW: 1894 - 1939)*, 6. Accessed March 28, 2023, from http://nla.gov.au/nla.news-article125469060
44 Charles died in 1941 from injuries received after being struck by a train he apparently was unable to hear, due to deafness, whilst crossing tracks at Mt. Druitt Station, New South Wales.
45 Report of the Royal Commission on Navy and Defence Administration, Melbourne, December 2, 1918, NAA: A6661, 475, 66
46 Interview recorded by the author with Colin Hoad of Tumut, grandson of Walter, 2021
47 Letter to Superior General of the Missionaries of the Sacred Heart, Father Meyer, accounting for mission funds, June 2, 1903. Copy held at MSC archives, Kensington.
48 Adelong News, (1886, March 12). *The Gundagai Times and Tumut, Adelong and Murrumbidgee District Advertiser (NSW: 1868-1931)*, 2. Accessed March 28, 2023, from http://nla.gov.au/nla.news-article128763467

Chapter III: From Messenger Boy to Religious Novice

1 (1886, March 12). *The Gundagai Times and Tumut, Adelong and Murrumbidgee District Advertiser (NSW: 1868-1931)*, 2. Accessed March 28, 2023, from http://nla.gov.au/nla.news-page12722091
2 By coincidence, a *Norman Gilroy,* was also a telegraphist at Adelong Post & Telegraph Office for a short time a decade and half after Shaw. (Adelong & District Historical Society). In 1915, at aged 19 he was a wireless operator on a captured German troop ship, the *Hessen* (renamed *Bulla*), sailing for Egypt and Gallipoli (Aust. Dictionary of Biography. He may have been operating a wireless manufactured at the Shaw Wireless Works. Later Gilroy became a Catholic priest and was installed as Cardinal in Sydney.
3 (1889, June 14). *The Gundagai Times and Tumut, Adelong and Murrumbidgee District Advertiser (NSW: 1868-1931)*, 2. Accessed March 28, 2023, from http://nla.gov.au/nla.news-page12717468
4 NAA: C3629/2, Box 525, 1885659, Appendix G
5 (1890, May 16). *The Gundagai Times and Tumut, Adelong and Murrumbidgee District Advertiser (NSW: 1868-1931)*, 2. Accessed March 28, 2023, from http://nla.gov.au/nla.news-page12717830
6 Christmas, (1891, December 24). *Wagga Wagga Advertiser (NSW: 1875-1910)*, 2. Accessed March 28, 2023, from http://nla.gov.au/nla.news-article101886253
7 NAA: C4076, HN5618
8 Local and General News, (1892, January 30). *Wagga Wagga Express (NSW: 1879 - 1917)*, 5. Accessed March 28, 2023, from http://nla.gov.au/nla.news-article145530924
9 Letter dated June 7, 1995, from Passionist Archivist Jeff Daly to Jim Rowe, editor of *Electronics Australia*
10 Confirmation at St John's Church, (1892, May 20). *The Gundagai Times and Tumut, Adelong and Murrumbidgee District Advertiser (NSW: 1868-1931)*, 2. Accessed March 28, 2023, from http://nla.gov.au/nla.news-article123787427
11 At Mary's Mount, Goulburn, (1892, May 21). *Freeman's Journal (Sydney, NSW: 1850-1932)*, 14. Accessed March 28, 2023, from http://nla.gov.au/nla.news-article111324631
12 Reception at Mary's Mount. (1892, May 18). *Goulburn Herald (NSW: 188 -1907)*, 3. Accessed March 28, 2023, from http://nla.gov.au/nla.news-article103157353
13 Letter to J F McMahon from Passionist Archivist, Fr. Bonaventure, May 25, 1971, MSC

Archives, Kensington
14. The Passionist order continue to live and work in the Marrickville Parish of St Brigid to this day.
15. Reception at Mary's Mount. (1892, May 18). *Goulburn Herald (NSW: 1881-1907)*, 3. Accessed March 28, 2023, from http://nla.gov.au/nla.news-article103157353
16. http://nla.gov.au/nla.news-article237166524 Rev. Father Clement Caine, (1900, April 28). *The Daily Telegraph (Sydney, NSW: 1883-1930)*, 9. Accessed March 28, 2023, from http://nla.gov.au/nla.news-article237166524
17. Government gazette, NSW, Australia, July-August, 1890, 6611
18. Letter dated June 7, 1995, from Passionist Archivist Jeff Daly to Jim Rowe, editor of *Electronics Australia*
19. Ibid
20. Letter of June 22, 1896 from Navarre to Chevalier, MSC Archives, Kensington
21. Notation from Beriena file, MSC Archives Kensington, "arrive Yule Island, Br Placid, Passionist", McMahon, J. F. (1983). Father Archibald Shaw: the wireless priest. [Paper read to the Australian Catholic Historical Society, 2 March 1983]. Journal of the Australian Catholic Historical Society, 7(3), 26
22. Use of the acronym MSC is derived the French, *Missionnaires du Sacré-Coeur,* meaning *Missionaries of the Sacred Heart*. The English acronym MSH was used in Shaw's time.

Chapter IV: Missionary on Yule Island

1. An account given by Fr Armand Pagès at the funeral of Msgr Navarre, "though some of the natives were cannibals, and occasionally would take hold of the calf of a visitor's leg, accompanying the action with a suggestive smack of the lips, there was more danger of a man being killed for his property than for the purpose of a cannibal feast", refer, The Late Archbishop Navarre (1912, January 18). *Townsville Daily Bulletin (Qld.: 1907-1954)*, 5
2. It remained under Dutch control until 1962 & variously known as Irian Barat, then Irian Jaya (1973) and then, somewhat confusingly, as just Papua (since 2002). It is presently under Indonesian control.
3. He was a calculating French nobleman born *Charles du Breie*. He attempted to sell a bucolic vision of a *Nouvelle France* and made grand but unsuccessful attempts to colonise New Ireland & New Britain for the glory of France and of the Catholic Church by establishing a personal empire in the Pacific. He went as far to proclaim himself *King Charles I of New France* attracting investors into his fraudulent scheme with the offer of cheap land, cheap labour and a ready market in Europe for tropical produce. By 1882 he was serving a six-year gaol term for criminal negligence. The earliest presence of the Missionaries of the Sacred Heart in the Pacific, amongst the then Fr. Louis Navarre, came about through their accompaniment of *Nouvelle France* scheme subscribers.
4. Ganter, R. et al, *German Missionaries in Australia – a web-directory of intercultural encounters*, Griffith University. http://missionaries.griffith.edu.au/mission/missionaries-sacred-heart-msc, accessed October, 2021
5. James Griffin 'Verjus, Henri Stanislas (1860-1892)' *Australian Dictionary of Biography*, http://adb.anu.edu.au/biography/verjus-henri-stanislas-4777
6. McMahon, J. F. (1983). Father Archibald Shaw: the wireless priest. [Paper read to the Australian Catholic Historical Society, 2 March 1983]. Journal of the Australian Catholic Historical Society, 7(3), 26
7. Though Australian born, Archibald would have been regarded by the French missionaries as an Englishman because Australia was then a British Colony

NOTES & REFERENCES

8. February 28, 1894 from Yule Island, held at MSC Archives, Kensington
9. April 15, 1894, from Yule Island, held at MSC Archives, Kensington
10. Ibid
11. Tréand to Genocchi, March 9, 1895. Copy in MSC Archives, Kensington. Translation by M Ryan
12. A place where an aspirant to a religious vocation undergoes a period of study, prayer, community living in preparation for a commitment to a religious order made by taking vows
13. Letter of June 22, 1896 from Navarre to Chevalier, MSC Archives, Kensington
14. Ibid
15. Letter of Navarre, November 24, 1896 and letter of Brother Alexis, October 18, 1896, MSC Archives, Kensington
16. Letter of June 22, 1896 from Navarre to Chevalier, MSC Archives, Kensington
17. Ibid
18. Genocchi acted in the role of community superior on Yule. He was living in the MSC house in Port Moresby by at least 1894. Later records show him as superior there, though he may have taken on this role upon arrival. Source: *Australia, City Directories, 1845-1948* [database on-line]. Provo, UT, USA: Ancestry.com Operations, Inc., 2015. Original data: Various publishers. Australian City Directories. Gould Genealogy & History, South Australia, Australia.
19. Monsignor Navarre was blamed by Genocchi, in letters to two other missionaries, for 'making war' against the Governor and the Protestants in British New Guinea. Correspondence from Navarre to Chevalier December 6, 1897. Translated by J F McMahon. See also Leslie Rumble's translation of Ceresi, V., The Life of Father Genocchi MSC, 1934, Tipografia Poliglotta Vaticana: Rome, 271-280
20. Letter of June 22, 1896 from Navarre to Chevalier, MSC Archives, Kensington
21. Ibid
22. Ibid
23. Letter of Fr. Hubert Linckens to the Australian Apostolic Delegate, Archbishop Cerretti, June 9, 1916
24. Obituary (1913, September 18). *Freeman's Journal (Sydney, NSW: 1850 - 1932)*, 16. Accessed September 23, 2021, from http://nla.gov.au/nla.news-article108165881
25. Letter of June 22, 1896 from Navarre to Chevalier, MSC Archives, Kensington

Chapter V: Priest and Procurator

1. Passenger manifest, *Prinz Regent Luitpold*, October, 1897
2. The Australian MSC province was not formally established until 1905
3. R. C. Missionaries (1897, October 19). *Evening News (Sydney, NSW: 1869 - 1931)*, 7. Accessed September 29, 2021, from http://nla.gov.au/nla.news-article108871155. The MSC Monastery at Kensington was opened on December 5, 1897.
4. Gsell identifies himself as a German subject on his 1909 Australian Naturalization Application. See NAA: A1, 1920/21513, 8, though after Alsace was returned to France at the end of World War II, and when he wrote his autobiography, *The Bishop with 150 Wives*, he identified as French.
5. Goodman MSC, A., 'Son Excellence Mgr. Gsell et la mission de Port-Darwin' *Annales de Notre-Dame du Sacré-Coeur*, February 1939, 57-63.
6. Letter from Fr Vandel to Fr Meyer, 1900, translated by J F McMahon. MSC Archives, Kensington
7. Ibid

8. Gsell's age recorded in the passenger manifest of his October, 1897 voyage to Sydney was 27 years. On this evidence he was born in c. 1870. Later references have him born in 1872. An almost identical historical error is found in Archibald Shaw's date of birth, often incorrectly recorded as 1872.
9. See endnote 6.
10. Letter from Fr Vandel to Chevalier, August 30, 1898. MSC Archives, Kensington, translated by J F McMahon
11. Vandel to Meyer, November 2, 1898, MSC Archives, Kensington
12. Francis Xavier Gsell (1872-1960), in Ganter, R., *German Missionaries in Australia - a web-directory of intercultural encounters*, 2009-2018, www.griffith.edu.au/missionaries, accessed September, 2021. See also, Franklin, J., 'Memoirs by Australian Priests, Religious and Ex-Religious' *Journal of the Australian Catholic Historical Society* 33, 2012:142-162
13. McMahon, J. F. (1983). Father Archibald Shaw: the wireless priest. [Paper read to the Australian Catholic Historical Society, 2 March 1983]. Journal of the Australian Catholic Historical Society, 7(3), 26
14. Letter from Vandel to Superior General Meyer, May 16, 1900, copy in MSC Archives, Kensington, translated from French by J F McMahon
15. Consecration to the Sacred Heart (1899, September 16). *Freeman's Journal (Sydney, NSW: 1850 - 1932)*, 18. Accessed October 1, 2021, from http://nla.gov.au/nla.news-article111076215
16. Ibid
17. Letter of Tréand to the MSC General Council, January 24, 1900. MSC Archives, Kensington, translated by J F McMahon
18. Ordinations at Manly (1900, June 9). *Freeman's Journal (Sydney, NSW: 1850-1932)*, 9. Accessed October 5, 2021, from http://nla.gov.au/nla.news-article111313648
19. Letter from Fr Vandel to Fr Meyer, June 16,1900 MSC Archives, Kensington, translation by J F McMahon
20. Church of Our Lady of the Sacred Heart, Randwick, (1900, June 26). *The Sydney Morning Herald (NSW: 1842 - 1954)*, p. 7. Accessed September 29, 2021, from http://nla.gov.au/nla.news-article14320236
21. Published in Analecta ecclesiastica, November 29, 1900, 14
22. The building that the procurator operated from.
23. Notes of J F McMahon, MSC Archives, Kensington
24. Procure file, MSC Archives, Kensington. In 1899, one third of the Randwick Parish income was made available to assist funding the procurate. This only supplemented funds from France and Rome which bore the bulk of the financial responsibility for the missions.
25. De Boismenu visitation report to General Council, 1900, 22. Copy at MSC Archives, Kensington

Chapter VI: Difficult Years

1. MSC Provincial Council minutes, July 31, 1900, MSC Archives, Kensington. Also, *Analecta ecclesiastica,* November 29, 1900, 14. McMahon notes that correspondence between Vandel and Superior General Meyer in November 2, 1899, states Archibald is visiting the monastery at Kensington, implying he could well have been assistant to the procurator from November, 1899.
2. Tréand in writing to the General Council as early as January 24, 1900, notes that Archibald will replace Fr Merg "to advantage"

NOTES & REFERENCES

3. Caruana, A., (2000), Monastery on the Hill, Nelen Yuba Missiological Unit, 57
4. Pro-provincial Council Minutes, May 7, 1901, MSC Archives, Kensington
5. Today the original Federation stone stands under a modern dome commemorating the event.
6. MSC Council notes, May 7, 1901. This minute notes he was put in charge of grounds, which probably relates to MSC properties.
7. MSC General Council minutes, 1901, copy at MSC Archives, Kensington, translated by J F McMahon
8. Report of Meyer during a *visite canonique* to Randwick in 1902, 37. Copied from the Rome Archives in a research report on Shaw by J. Bertolini msc, October, 1977. Held in MSC Archives, Kensington. Translation by M Ryan.
9. McMahon, J. F. (1983). Father Archibald Shaw: the wireless priest. [Paper read to the Australian Catholic Historical Society, 2 March 1983]. Journal of the Australian Catholic Historical Society, 7(3), 27.
10. Letter from Guis to Meyer, October 11, 1909, Copy at MSC Archives, Kensington. Translated by J F McMahon
11. Ibid
12. Letter from Shaw to General Council, September 17, 1913, copy held at MSC Archives, Kensington
13. Letter from Shaw to Meyer, June 1, 1903, copy at MSC Archives, Kensington
14. Letter from Shaw to Meyer, July 1, 1907. Copy at MSC Archives, Kensington
15. Vandel to Meyer, December 28, 1902, copy at MSC Archives, Kensington, translation by M Ryan
16. *Lit*. Thank God
17. Shaw to Meyer, June 2, 1903, copy at MSC Archives, Kensington
18. Some of the main streets in Sydney were covered in tiles of thick wooden blocks before the advent of tar. The blocks provided a relatively smooth surface for horses and horse-drawn vehicles, kept road dust under control and permitted drainage in the wet.
19. Letter from Shaw to Meyer, June 2, 1903, copy at MSC Archives, Kensington
20. Letter from Shaw to Meyer, July 6, 1903, copy at MSC Archives, Kensington
21. This man is probably Brother Fernand Arnoult
22. Letter from Shaw to Meyer, November 1, 1903, copy at MSC Archives, Kensington
23. Letter from Shaw to Meyer, November 1, 1903, copy at MSC Archives, Kensington
24. Shaw also conducted a wedding in New Britain on December 22, 1902
25. Interview with Dr Albert Hahl. (1902, June 2). *The Sydney Morning Herald (NSW: 1842 - 1954)*, 7. Accessed October 13, 2021, from http://nla.gov.au/nla.news-article14475999 and The New Britain Massacres (1902, May 3). *The World's News (Sydney, NSW: 1901 - 1955)*, 5. Accessed October 13, 2021, from http://nla.gov.au/nla.news-article128449334
26. Ibid, 145-146
27. For a detailed account of the circumstances of the murder of Wolff's wife and child, and a concise summary of the causes, refer: Hempenstall, Peter J. (2016). *Pacific Islanders under German rule: a study in the meaning of colonial resistance.* Canberra: Australian National University Press, 143-147, available as a pdf from, https://press-files.anu.edu.au/downloads/press/n1857/pdf/book.pdf Accessed October, 2021

Chapter VII: Inspiration from an Island Massacre

1. In 1905 replacing Arthur Lanctin
2. Letter from Meyer to Tréand, May 4, 1903, MSC Archives, Kensington, translated by J F McMahon

3   Lanctin was Superior General at this time
4   Procurator Minute Book, 654, Copy at MSC Archives, Kensington, translated by J F McMahon
5   Gsell, F. X. (1956), *The Bishop with 150 Wives: fifty years as a missionary,* Angus & Robertson: Sydney
6   Letter from Navarre to Meyer, June 1, 1903, copy at MSC Archives, Kensington, translated by J F McMahon
7   The Recent Massacre Near Yule Island (1876, November 25). *Adelaide Observer (SA: 1843 - 1904),* 18. Accessed October 13, 2021, from http://nla.gov.au/nla.news-article159491778
8   Wireless Telegraphy (1912, February 3). *The W.A. Record (Perth, WA: 1888 - 1922),* 3. Accessed October 13, 2021, from http://nla.gov.au/nla.news-article212515128 and in Wireless for Hobart (1911, December 23). *The Mercury (Hobart, Tas.: 1860 - 1954),* 6. Accessed October 13, 2021, from http://nla.gov.au/nla.news-article10124586
9   Delbos, G., (1985), *The Mustard Seed,* Institute of Papua New Guinea Studies: Port Moresby, republished by MSC Mission Office, 2002, 135-6
10 The Baptism of Blood in Baining, (1929, September 26). *Freeman's Journal (Sydney, NSW: 1850 - 1932),* 11. Accessed October 21, 2021, from http://nla.gov.au/nla.news-page13629553
11 Hempenstall, Peter J. (2016). *Pacific Islanders under German rule: a study in the meaning of colonial resistance.* Canberra: Australian National University Press, 137, available as a pdf from, https://press-files.anu.edu.au/downloads/press/n1857/pdf/book.pdf Accessed October, 2021
12 Ibid, 137
13 Loder-Neuhold, R. 2019. Crocodiles, Masks and Madonnas. Catholic Mission Museums in German-Speaking Europe. Studia Missionalia Svecana 121, 267. Uppsala: Department of Theology. Accessed October 21, 2021 from https://uu.diva-portal.org/smash/get/diva2:1363017/FULLTEXT01.pdf
14 Hempenstall, Peter J. (2016). *Pacific Islanders under German rule: a study in the meaning of colonial resistance.* Canberra: Australian National University Press, 149, available as a pdf from, https://press-files.anu.edu.au/downloads/press/n1857/pdf/book.pdf Accessed October, 2021
15 The murdered missionaries were Fathers Matthew (Matthäus) Rascher & Henri Rutten, Brothers Joseph Bley, Johann Schellekens & Edward Plarschaert, and Sisters Ann (Katherine Utch), Sophia (Emily Schmidt), Agatha (Elizabeth Noth), Agnes (Katherina Holler) & Angela (Wilhemina Balk). All were Missionaries of the Sacred Heart, except for Rutten who was a Trappist monk.
16 Ibid, 147
17 The New Britain Massacre, New Zealand Tablet, volume XXXII, issue 39, September 29, 1904, 3. Accessed October 21, 2021, from https://paperspast.natlib.govt.nz/periodicals/NZT19040929.2.5
18 At the time of the massacres Linckens was visiting a mission saw-mill on the Torio River on the western edge of the Gazelle Peninsula. His account makes interesting reading. See, A Terrible Massacre in German New Guinea, (1904, October 8). *The W.A. Record (Perth, WA: 1888 - 1922),* 6. Accessed October 22, 2021, from http://nla.gov.au/nla.news-article211979540
19 Linckens' widely published accounts were tailored for damage control and served to engender a favourable public perception of foreign mission activity.
20 The New Britain Massacre, New Zealand Tablet, volume XXXII, issue 39, September 29,

NOTES & REFERENCES

1904, 3. Accessed October 21, 2021, from https://paperspast.natlib.govt.nz/periodicals/NZT19040929.2.5

21 Ibid
22 See footnote 7
23 Cause of the Baining Martyrs, in https://www.misacor.org.au/item/962-cause-of-the-baining-martyrs Accessed on October 21, 2021
24 Hempenstall, Peter J. (2016). *Pacific Islanders under German rule: a study in the meaning of colonial resistance.* Canberra: Australian National University Press, 148, available as a pdf from, https://press-files.anu.edu.au/downloads/press/n1857/pdf/book.pdf Accessed October, 2021.
See also, Garrett, John. & World Council of Churches. & University of the South Pacific. Institute of Pacific Studies. (1992). *Footsteps in the sea: Christianity in Oceania to World War II.* Suva, Fiji; Geneva, Switzerland: Institute of Pacific Studies, University of the South Pacific in association with World Council of Churches, 53
25 For an uncoloured account of the Baining massacre, and a concise summary of its causes, refer footnote 12, pp. 147-150
26 Gründer, Horst. 'Die Gründung des Missionshauses Hiltrup aus historischer Sicht.' In Hundert Jahre Missionshaus Hiltrup und Deutsche Provinz der Herz-JesuMissionare. Edited by Fritz Biermann, 32, Münster: Hiltruper Missionare, 1997
27 Rohatynskyj, M. A. (2001). On Knowing the Baining and Other Minor Ethnic Groups of East New Britain, *Social Analysis: The International Journal of Social and Cultural Practice*, 45(2), 26. Accessed, October 21, 2021 from http://www.jstor.org/stable/23170109
28 Ibid, 23–40
29 The New Britain Massacre. (1904, September 20). *The Scone Advocate (NSW: 1887 - 1954)*, 3. Accessed October 22, 2021, from http://nla.gov.au/nla.news-article156332294
30 From the Islands, (1904, November 2). *The Sydney Morning Herald (NSW: 1842 - 1954)*, 12. Accessed October 22, 2021, from http://nla.gov.au/nla.news-article14646022
31 Between 180 and 200 natives were killed in response to the Wolff murders according to this report, Terrible Vengeance. (1902, June 7). *The Telegraph (Brisbane, Qld.: 1872 - 1947)*, 8. Accessed October 22, 2021, from http://nla.gov.au/nla.news-article175170179
32 The Baptism of Blood in Baining, *Freeman's Journal (Sydney, NSW: 1850 - 1932)* 26 September 1929: 11. Web. 22 Oct 2021, http://nla.gov.au/nla.news-page13629553
33 Fr James Power msc, a contemporary of Shaw, recalls that Archibald escaped initially to Nudgee College, Brisbane to avoid the captain's demands for money, acting as Chaplain and giving a retreat there for a short time. Shaw helped Power to enter the MSC seminary. Source: notes of J F McMahon who interviewed Power in 1971, MSC Archives, Kensington.
34 Letter from Shaw to Meyer, March 28, 1905, MSC Archives, Kensington
35 September, 1876, see New Guinea - The Recent Massacre Near Yule Island, (1876, November 14). *The Kiama Independent, and Shoalhaven Advertiser (NSW: 1863 - 1947)*, 2. Accessed October 22, 2021, from http://nla.gov.au/nla.news-article101487859
36 Filling up the ranks, (1904, December 15). *Queensland Times, Ipswich Herald and General Advertiser (Qld.: 1861-1908)*, 7. Accessed October 21, 2021, from http://nla.gov.au/nla.news-article124416341
37 The Papuan Sensation: Father Shaw's Offer, 1911, March 1. *Northern Star (Lismore, NSW : 1876 - 1954)*, 3. Retrieved July 28, 2024, from http://nla.gov.au/nla.news-article72271316

WIRELESS PRIEST

Chapter VIII: Fr Shaw's Road

1. Aboriginal word for *lightning*
2. National Archives of Australia: J3088, QPT301
3. *HMAS Gayundah*, Royal Australian Navy. Accessed October 28, 2021 from https://www.navy.gov.au/hmas-gayundah, also in, with variations, With the Naval Brigade, (1903, April 11). *The Brisbane Courier (Qld.: 1864-1933)*, 6. Accessed October 28, 2021, from http://nla.gov.au/nla.news-article19216493
4. May 20, 1901
5. *Report from HMS Diana on Russian Signals intercepted at Suez,* 28 January 1904, Naval Library, Ministry of Defence, London
6. This was likely one of the plantations gifted to the MSC by the German administration as recompense for the Baining massacre
7. Letter from Shaw to Meyer, September 27, 1904, MSC Archives, Kensington
8. Ibid
9. Letter from Shaw to Meyer, March 30, 1905, MSC Archives, Kensington
10. Ibid
11. Ibid
12. Navarre to Meyer, October 23, 1905, MSC Archives, Kensington, translation by J F McMahon
13. Refer to Arnoult's Attestation Paper for service in World War I, NAA B2455, Arnoult, F. E.
14. Decision of officer Appointed to Hold Enquiry, (1906, January 19). *Government Gazette of the State of New South Wales (Sydney, NSW: 1901 - 2001)*, 486. Accessed October 29, 2021, from http://nla.gov.au/nla.news-article226404936
15. Personal, (1923, September 28). *The Wingham Chronicle and Manning River Observer (NSW: 1898-1954)*, 4. Accessed October 29, 2021, from http://nla.gov.au/nla.news-article166270515
16. Wingham Timber Resources (1912, November 29). *The Farmer and Settler (Sydney, NSW: 1906-1955)*, 2. Accessed October 29, 2021, from http://nla.gov.au/nla.news-article116120173
17. Notes and Comments, (1912, December 4). *The Sydney Morning Herald (NSW : 1842 - 1954)*, p. 17. Accessed May 12, 2023, from http://nla.gov.au/nla.news-article15380372
18. Ibid
19. The location of the road has been established quite accurately by overlaying historical maps which show portion numbers and land-owners with contemporary maps such as those presented in GoogleEarth and can be seen added by hand to historical land registry maps.
20. "Gunyah" Green. (1922, April 14). *The Wingham Chronicle and Manning River Observer (NSW: 1898 - 1954)*, p. 6. Accessed February 10, 2023, from http://nla.gov.au/nla.news-article166223157
21. *Music cabinet made from Australian timbers,* 2021, Museum of Applied Arts and Sciences, accessed 10 February, 2023, https://ma.as/206458
22. Hudson, I., & Henningham, P., (1986), *Gift of God – Friend of Man: A story of the timber industry in New South Wales 1788-1986,* Australian Forest industries, Sydney, 131
23. Australian patent: 1908011239, IP Australia
24. Intellectual Property, Australia, a federal Government agency that administers patents and other intellectual property holding patent records dating back to the years immediately after Federation
25. An Artist in Wood, (1922, April 15). *The Maitland Weekly Mercury (NSW: 1894 - 1931)*, 3. Accessed February 10, 2023, from http://nla.gov.au/nla.news-article136515817

NOTES & REFERENCES

26 Wilfred Spruson was a partner in *Wilfred & Spruson*, *Spruson & Ferguson* and later practiced as *W. J. Spruson*
27 Letter from Dr Gregory Blaxland to Miss Watson, February 10, 1984, Manning District Historical Society
28 Manning Shire Council, (1921, October 16). *The Northern Champion (Taree, NSW: 1913 - 1954)*, 3. Accessed October 29, 2021, from http://nla.gov.au/nla.news-page15610055
29 Mr. Ashford and Bulga. (1918, November 30). *The Northern Champion (Taree, NSW: 1913 - 1954)*, 5. Accessed October 29, 2021, from http://nla.gov.au/nla.news-article157100939
30 (1921, October 16). *The Northern Champion (Taree, NSW: 1913-1954)*, 3. Accessed October 29, 2021, from http://nla.gov.au/nla.news-page15610055
31 Letter from Shaw to Meyer, June 2, 1903, copy at MSC Archives, Kensington
32 Shaw was able to have Arnoult removed and replaced from the mill around the time of the Mawson expedition to Antarctica to manage the wireless station on King Island
33 Letter from Meyer to Tréand, February 7, 1906, MSC Archives, Kensington, translation by J F McMahon
34 Letter from Shaw to Meyer, July 2, 1906, MSC Archives, Kensington
35 Ibid
36 Ibid

Chapter IX: The First Workshop

1 Guis Obituary, (1913, September 18). *Freeman's Journal (Sydney, NSW: 1850 - 1932)*, 16. Accessed November 2, 2021, from http://nla.gov.au/nla.news-article108165881
2 Analecta ecclesiastica, April 16 1907,239
3 Letter from Guis to Meyer, August 26, 1907, Copy at MSC Archives, Kensington. Translated by J F McMahon
4 Waldersee, J., (1995), 'Neither Eagles nor Saints' MSC Missions in Oceania 1881-1975, Chevalier Press: Sydney, 247
5 Letter from Shaw to Meyer, June 18, 1907, copy at MSC Archives, Kensington
6 Recording of Ray Allsop held by the ABC Radio Archives and used in Rapley, Stephen & ABC Radio (Australia). Social History Unit & ABC Radio Tapes (1990). *Bright sparks: Australian radio stories*. ABC Radio Tapes, Sydney, N.S.W
7 Williams, N., Raymond Allsop – WWI wireless operator, engineer, FM pioneer, *When I think Back*, Electronics Australia, Jan, 1990, 52
8 Deputy to the bishop
9 The Late Archdeacon D'Arcy. (1907, May 23). *Freeman's Journal (Sydney, NSW: 1850 - 1932)*, 24. Accessed November 4, 2021, from http://nla.gov.au/nla.news-article111279510
10 Innes, B., (1996), *Priest & Scientist, Joseph Slattery, Australia's First Radiographer*, Crawford House: Bathurst. See also, Wireless Telegraphy. (1904, February 13). *National Advocate (Bathurst, NSW: 1889-1954)*, 2. Accessed November 4, 2021, from http://nla.gov.au/nla.news-article157212826
11 Notes of J F McMahon, MSC Archives, Kensington
12 Innes, B., (1996), *Priest & Scientist, Joseph Slattery, Australia's First Radiographer*, Crawford House: Bathurst. See also, Wireless Telegraphy. (1904, February 13). *National Advocate (Bathurst, NSW: 1889-1954)*, 55
13 Slattery worked and made discoveries independently of Thomas Lyle and Walter Filmer. For the account of the x-ray of Eric Thompson, the boy whose hand was saved, see Country News, (1896, August 1). The Sydney Mail and New South Wales Advertiser

(NSW : 1871 - 1912), p 257. Retrieved July 26, 2024, from http://nla.gov.au/nla.news-article163784815
14. Reville, William. Nicholas Callan: Priest Scientist at Maynooth. The Irish Times, 21 February 2002.
15. Bathurst Free Press and Mining Journal, August 7, 1896, p 2. Accessed July 15, 2024, from http://nla.gov.au/nla.news-article63940904
16. Bathurst, (1900, November 10). *The Catholic Press (Sydney, NSW: 1895 - 1942)*, 21. Accessed November 4, 2021, from http://nla.gov.au/nla.news-article104661528
17. Historic patents register IP Australia. Refer, https://www.ipaustralia.gov.au and for applications before 1900 refer, NAA catalogue.
18. For example: The Block Arcade, State Library of Victoria, the Princess Theatre & Her Majesty's Theatre
19. An ultraviolet light first used to treat bacterial skin infections in 1895 by Niels Finsen
20. Distribution of Prizes, (1880, December 22). *Bendigo Advertiser (Vic.: 1855 - 1918)*, 3. Accessed November 5, 2021, from http://nla.gov.au/nla.news-article88640936
21. Williams, N., *Raymond Allsop – WWI wireless operator, engineer, FM pioneer, When I think Back*, Electronics Australia, Jan, 1990, 52
22. Letter from Shaw to General Council, September 17, 1913, copy at MSC Archives, Kensington
23. Letter from Guis to Visitator Fr Field, May 7, 1911, copy at MSC Archives, Kensington, translation by M Ryan
24. Kirkby had installed the timekeeping clock at nearby Randwick Racecourse and testimony given at the 1918 Royal Commission suggests Shaw was a regular race attendee.
25. May 6, 1911, handwritten account by Shaw, copy at MSC Archives, Kensington
26. Letter from Guis to Visitator Fr Field, May 7, 1911, copy at MSC Archives, Kensington. Translation by M Ryan
27. May 6, 1911, handwritten account by Shaw, copy at MSC Archives, Kensington
28. Letter from Guis to Visitator Fr Field, May 7, 1911, para. 3, copy at MSC Archives, Kensington. Translation by M Ryan
29. Ibid
30. Ibid

Chapter X: Company Business

1. Advertising (1909, June 15). *The Sydney Morning Herald (NSW: 1842-1954)*, 2. Accessed November 8, 2021, from http://nla.gov.au/nla.news-article15065020
2. Advertising (1910, October 5). *The Sydney Morning Herald (NSW: 1842-1954)*, 4. Accessed November 8, 2021, from http://nla.gov.au/nla.news-article15165478
3. April, 1910, is cited by Shaw in a later patent challenge by Balsillie as the date when he seriously started to get involved in wireless. From material preserved in the *Ernest Fisk Papers*, Mitchell Library, Sydney, NSW.
4. May 6, 1911, handwritten account by Shaw, copy at MSC Archives, Kensington
5. Letter from Guis to Meyer, May 7, 1911, copy at MSC Archives, Kensington
6. May 6, 1911, handwritten account by Shaw, copy at MSC Archives, Kensington
7. New Companies, (1910, November 7). *Evening News (Sydney, NSW: 1869 - 1931)*, 4. Accessed November 8, 2021, from http://nla.gov.au/nla.news-page12166553, see also Dun's Gazette Vol 4, No 20, Nov 14, 1910
8. Advertising (1910, November 28). *Construction: Weekly Supplement to Building (Sydney, NSW: 1909 - 1914)*, 6. Accessed November 8, 2021, from http://nla.gov.au/nla.news-

NOTES & REFERENCES

article234762705 and, http://nla.gov.au/bla.news-article234760520
9. Trade and Finance (1910, November 8). *The Daily Telegraph (Sydney, NSW: 1883-1930)*, 6. Accessed November 21, 2021, from http://nla.gov.au/nla.news-article238666805, see also, Dun's Gazette Vol 4, No 20, Nov 14, 1910
10. Patents, (1910, October 4). *The Herald (Melbourne, Vic.: 1861-1954)*, 7. Accessed November 21, 2021, from http://nla.gov.au/nla.news-article241988945
11. Military Wireless, (1910, March 29). *The Sydney Morning Herald (NSW: 1842-1954)*, 8. Accessed November 15, 2021, from http://nla.gov.au/nla.news-article15143353
12. Ibid
13. https://monumentaustralia.org.au/themes/technology/industry/display/21544-first-military-wireless-signal, accessed November 15, 2021
14. Institute of Wireless Telegraphy, (1910, April 23). *The Sydney Morning Herald (NSW: 1842 - 1954)*, 15. Accessed November 15, 2021, from http://nla.gov.au/nla.news-article15133150
15. Cornering the Air? (1910, July 11). *Construction: Weekly Supplement to Building (Sydney, NSW: 1909 - 1914)*, 3. Accessed November 15, 2021, from http://nla.gov.au/nla.news-article234762406
16. Roe, M., 'Taylor, George Augustine (1872–1928)', Australian Dictionary of Biography, National Centre of Biography, Australian National University, https://adb.anu.edu.au/biography/taylor-george-augustine-8756/text15343, published first in hardcopy 1990, accessed online 12 May 2023
17. Institute of Wireless Telegraphy, (1910, March 14). *The Sydney Morning Herald (NSW: 1842 - 1954)*, 4. Accessed November 15, 2021, from http://nla.gov.au/nla.news-article15126489
18. Interstate News. (1910, March 5). *The W.A. Record (Perth, WA: 1888 - 1922)*, 1. Accessed November 15, 2021, from http://nla.gov.au/nla.news-article212337374
19. Residents of such institutions were termed *inmates* during this era.
20. A Personal Servant of Napoleon, (1910, January 26). *The Sydney Mail and New South Wales Advertiser (NSW: 1871-1912)*, p. 36. Accessed November 15, 2021, from http://nla.gov.au/nla.news-article164290176
21. Wireless and Ice, (1911, October 19). *The Daily Telegraph (Sydney, NSW: 1883-1930)*, 11. Accessed November 15, 2021, from http://nla.gov.au/nla.news-article239196345
22. Father Shaw's Wireless Experiments, (1910, July 22). *Southern Cross (Adelaide, SA: 1889-1954)*, 18. Accessed December 9, 2021, from http://nla.gov.au/nla.news-article167020415
23. Wireless Telegraphy Tests, (1910, June 25). *Advocate (Melbourne, Vic.: 1868-1954)*, 28. Accessed November 15, 2021, from http://nla.gov.au/nla.news-article170034846
24. Ibid
25. Moore, P. (2007), *Space: The First 50 Years*, New York: Sterling, p. 178
26. US Emergency Passport Application Register, Ancestry
27. Wireless Interfered With, (1910, July 19). *The Sun (Sydney, NSW: 1910-1954)*, 5 (Final Edition). Accessed November 15, 2021, from http://nla.gov.au/nla.news-article229970306
28. Account by Shaw, May 6, 1911, copy at MSC Archives, Kensington.
29. Letter of Guis to Field, May 7, 1911, copy at MSC Archives, Kensington.
30. Prize of £10,000 (1909, July 31). *Leader (Melbourne, Vic.: 1862-1918, 1935)*, 34. Accessed December 20, 2021, from http://nla.gov.au/nla.news-article197075657
31. Local and General, (1910, July 1). *Molong Argus (NSW: 1896-1921)*, 5. Accessed November 21, 2021, from http://nla.gov.au/nla.news-page10783506

32 Australian Wireless, (1911, February 27). *Barrier Miner (Broken Hill, NSW: 1888-1954)*, 3. Accessed November 15, 2021, from http://nla.gov.au/nla.news-article45152086
33 Ibid
34 Both structures still stand.
35 Personal, (1923, September 28). *The Wingham Chronicle and Manning River Observer (NSW: 1898-1954)*, p. 4. Accessed November 15, 2021, from http://nla.gov.au/nla.news-article166270515
36 Kirkby ran a series of newspaper advertisements selling his Fire Alarm System using the Maritime Wireless Telegraph Company name and address between October 24, 1910 until November 28 1910. For example, refer, Advertising (1910, November 28). *Construction: Weekly Supplement to Building (Sydney, NSW: 1909 - 1914)*, 6. Accessed March 23, 2023, from http://nla.gov.au/nla.news-article234762705
37 Australian Wireless, (1911, February 27). *Barrier Miner (Broken Hill, NSW: 1888 - 1954)*, 3. Accessed November 15, 2021, from http://nla.gov.au/nla.news-article45152086
38 Refer collection held by Powerhouse Museum, Sydney. See, https://collection.maas.museum/object/393805 Accessed March 22, 2023
39 *Men and Matters,* The Bulletin, Vol. 90, No. 4301, May 25, 1968, 52
40 Letter from Shaw to Meyer, October 21, 1913, copy at MSC Archives, Kensington
41 The first international submarine cable was operating between Java and Port Darwin in 1872. By 1902 Canada and Australia were also linked by cable.
42 The last mention of Kirkby working at the Wireless Works is in a report of the PMG Wireless Inspector dated March 17, 1911.
43 *Government Gazette of the State of New South Wales, June 26, 1912, (Sydney, NSW: 1901 - 2001)*, 4076. Accessed December 2, 2021, from http://nla.gov.au/nla.news-page14943535
44 May 6, 1911, handwritten account by Shaw, copy at MSC Archives, Kensington
45 Via personal communication with the author.

Chapter XI: An Extraordinary Year

1 Missing Explorers, (1911, March 11). *Evening News (Sydney, NSW: 1869-1931)*, 3. Accessed November 21, 2021, from http://nla.gov.au/nla.news-article113939085
2 Amos, D. J. (1936). *The Story of the Commonwealth Wireless Service*. Adelaide: E J McAlister, 1
3 Ibid, 3
4 Ibid, 2-9, for a full explanation
5 Ibid, 7
6 Smith, M. S. (1912). Exploration in Papua. *The Geographical Journal*, *39*(4), 313–331. https://doi.org/10.2307/1778660
7 Wireless to Papua (1911, March 16). *The Sydney Morning Herald (NSW: 1842-1954)*, 10. Accessed November 21, 2021, from http://nla.gov.au/nla.news-article15251603
8 Lost Explorers, (1911, February 24). *The Daily Telegraph (Sydney, NSW: 1883-1930)*, 7. Accessed November 21, 2021, from http://nla.gov.au/nla.news-page25724196
9 Ibid
10 Ibid
11 Smith, M. S. (1912). Exploration in Papua. *The Geographical Journal*, *39*(4), 313–331. https://doi.org/10.2307/1778660, Accessed July 13, 2024
12 Still no Tidings, (1911, March 1). *Evening Journal (Adelaide, SA: 1869-1912)*, 2. Accessed November 21, 2021, from http://nla.gov.au/nla.news-article204486828
13 Wireless Contingent Sails, (1911, March 2). *The Daily Telegraph (Sydney, NSW:*

NOTES & REFERENCES

1883-1930), 8. Accessed November 21, 2021, from http://nla.gov.au/nla.news-article238712647

14 Personal (1923, September 28). *The Wingham Chronicle and Manning River Observer (NSW: 1898-1954)*, 4. Accessed November 21, 2021, from http://nla.gov.au/nla.news-article166270515

15 Father Shaw's Expedition Sails, (1911, March 1). *The Sun (Sydney, NSW: 1910-1954)*, 5 (Cricket Edition). Accessed November 21, 2021, from http://nla.gov.au/nla.news-article221575733, and
   Wireless Stations. (1911, March 4). *The Telegraph (Brisbane, Qld.: 1872-1947)*, 6 (Second Edition). Accessed November 21, 2021, from http://nla.gov.au/nla.news-article175255902

16 Lieutenant Taylor's Views, (1911, February 27). *The Daily Telegraph (Sydney, NSW: 1883-1930)*, 7. Accessed November 21, 2021, from http://nla.gov.au/nla.news-article238719806

17 Wireless Contingent Sails, (1911, March 2). *The Daily Telegraph (Sydney, NSW: 1883-1930)*, 8. Accessed November 21, 2021, from http://nla.gov.au/nla.news-article238712647

18 The Papuan Sensation, (1911, March 11). *The Queenslander (Brisbane: 1866-1939)*, 38. Accessed November 21, 2021, from http://nla.gov.au/nla.news-article22290887

19 Father Shaw's Wireless Expedition, (1911, March 1). *Dubbo Dispatch and Wellington Independent (NSW: 1887-1932)*, p. 3. Accessed April 7, 2023, from http://nla.gov.au/nla.news-article228232508

20 They are Lost, (1911, March 17). *The Sun (Sydney, NSW: 1910-1954)*, 8 (LATEST EDITION). Accessed November 24, 2021, from http://nla.gov.au/nla.news-article221582104

21 Papuan Party Safe, (1911, March 24). *The Week (Brisbane: 1876-1934)*, 23. Accessed November 21, 2021, from http://nla.gov.au/nla.news-article185027471

22 Murphy, J., Wireless Inspectors Report, March 17, 1911, 3, Telstra Archive

23 Ibid

24 News in Brief, (1911, April 24). *Daily Advertiser (Wagga Wagga, NSW: 1911-1954)*, 1. Accessed November 24, 2021, from http://nla.gov.au/nla.news-article143073853

25 Letter from Shaw to Field, May 12, 1911, copy at MSC Archives, Kensington

26 Ibid

27 Letter from Field to Shaw, May 12, 1911, copy at MSC Archives, Kensington

28 King Island, (1911, August 5), *Advocate (Melbourne, Vic.: 1868-1954)*, 18. Accessed November 21, 2021, from http://nla.gov.au/nla.news-article170930654

29 A Versatile Priest, (1916, September 2). *The Register (Adelaide, SA: 1901-1929)*, 9. Accessed December 9, 2021, from http://nla.gov.au/nla.news-article59914060

30 Based on evidence provided by Joseph Lynch, Shaw's private secretary and acting secretary of Shaw Engineering, to the Royal Commission on Navy and Defence Administration. Report of the Royal Commission, Melbourne, December 2, 1918, 31, NAA: A3934, SC13/1

31 Letter from Shaw to Meyer, October 21, 1913

32 Dun's Gazette, Vol. 6, No. 15, October 9, 1911, 296

33 Ibid

34 1912 'Wireless Telegraphy', *Gympie Times and Mary River Mining Gazette (Qld.: 1868 - 1919)*, 22 February, 2, viewed 12 Feb 2023, http://nla.gov.au/nla.news-article189213968

35 Making Weapons Innocuous, (1921, November 18). *The Gundagai Times and Tumut, Adelong and Murrumbidgee District Advertiser (NSW: 1868 - 1931)*, 4. Accessed

November 23, 2021, from http://nla.gov.au/nla.news-article123493408
36 Held in the private collection of Basil Low, Department Head, Wireless Works, Randwick, c. 1913

Chapter XII: Adventure on King Island

1 Mawson Expedition, (1911, September 20). *Geelong Advertiser (Vic.: 1859-1929)*, 3. Accessed March 23, 2023, from http://nla.gov.au/nla.news-article150095990
2 Mawson, D., (1915), *The Home of the Blizzard*, London: Heinemann, p 429
3 https://mawsonshuts.antarctica.gov.au/preparation/innovation/signals-from-the-south/ Accessed July 15, 2024
4 Mawson, D., (1915), *The Home of the Blizzard*, London: Heinemann, Appendix VI
5 King Island. (1911, August 5). *Advocate (Melbourne, Vic.: 1868-1954)*, 18. Accessed November 28, 2021, from http://nla.gov.au/nla.news-article170930654
6 Ibid
7 King Island, (1911, August 5). *Advocate (Melbourne, Vic.: 1868-1954)*, 18. Accessed November 28, 2021, from http://nla.gov.au/nla.news-article170930654
8 Everyday Life, (1911, September 23). *Advocate (Melbourne, Vic.: 1868-1954)*, 10. Accessed November 28, 2021, from http://nla.gov.au/nla.news-article170932632
9 Ibid
10 Everyday Life, (1911, September 16). *Advocate (Melbourne, Vic.: 1868-1954)*, 10. Accessed November 28, 2021, from http://nla.gov.au/nla.news-article170932427
11 Wireless in Tasmania (1911, September 12). *The Sydney Morning Herald (NSW: 1842-1954)*, 9. Accessed November 28, 2021, from http://nla.gov.au/nla.news-article15273514
12 King Island News, (1912, January 22). *Examiner (Launceston, Tas.: 1900-1954)*, 6 (Daily). Accessed November 21, 2021, from http://nla.gov.au/nla.news-article50634381
13 Returned Sailors', Soldiers' & Airman's Imperial League of Australia.
14 Leane, Elizabeth, (2019), A Polar Explorer in Insanity's Archives: Transmitting the Story of Antarctic Wireless Operator Sidney Jeffryes, AICCM Bulletin, 40, 1-10. 10.1080/10344233.2019.1672942
15 FitzSimons, P., (2012), *Mawson and the Ice Men of the Heroic Age*. Sydney: Random House, 507
16 National Geographic Society (U.S.), & Shupe, J. F. (1992). *National Geographic atlas of the world*. Washington, D.C: National Geographic Society, and *The Guinness book of world records. (2020-2021)*. Stamford, CT: Guinness Media
17 *Aurora australis*, or the southern lights, are caused by solar particles interacting with strong magnetic field lines near the south pole. The lights are more intense during periods of high solar activity. Despite the expedition being conducted near the solar sunspot minima, aurora was recorded by Mawson throughout the expedition.
18 Riffenburgh, B. (2009). Racing with Death: Douglas Mawson, Antarctic Explorer. London: Bloomsbury Publishing, 158-9
19 An astute reader might reasonably assume Mawson's Telefunken operators could have been under instructions from their supplier, Denison, to ignore communications received by Shaw's station on King Island
20 Wireless Telegraphy, (1911, December 29). *The Week (Brisbane, Qld.: 1876-1934)*, 14. Accessed November 28, 2021, from http://nla.gov.au/nla.news-article185034240
21 Commonwealth Wireless, (1912, March 25). *The Register (Adelaide, SA: 1901-1929)*, 6. Accessed November 28, 2021, from http://nla.gov.au/nla.news-article59059892
22 *"Testimony of Cyril F. Evans"*, Titanic Inquiry Project. Accessed 5 May 2016: *At 11.25 I*

NOTES & REFERENCES

still had the phones on my ears and heard him still working Cape Race, about two or three minutes before the half-hour ship's time, that was, and at 11.35 I put the phones down and took off my clothes and turned in. See, https://www.titanicinquiry.org/USInq/AmInq08EvansCF01.php, Accessed November 28, 2021

23 Amos, D. J. (1936). *The Story of the Commonwealth Wireless Service*. Adelaide: Adelaide: E.J. McAlister, 3
24 Copie de l'act gouvernemental assistant Pere Shaw contre toute perte du fait de possible attaqies contre son systeme, held at MSC Archives, Kensington
25 Mishap at Pennant hills Station, (1912, September 11). *The Age (Melbourne, Vic.: 1854-1954)*, 9. Accessed December 2, 2021, from http://nla.gov.au/nla.news-article196254339
26 Clauson-Thue, W., (1901) *The ABC Universal Commercial Electric Telegraphic Code*, London: Eden Fischer. Various editions of the code book are freely viewable online.
27 Letter from Guis to Meyer, May 14, 1912. Copy at MSC Archives, Kensington. Translation by M Ryan
28 Wireless workers (1912, December 23). *The Sydney Morning Herald (NSW: 1842-1954)*, 5. Accessed November 28, 2021, from http://nla.gov.au/nla.news-article15385389
29 Wireless Men at Dinner, (1912, December 23). *The Daily Telegraph (Sydney, NSW: 1883-1930)*, 14. Accessed December 10, 2021, from http://nla.gov.au/nla.news-article238733028
30 Ibid

Chapter XIII: Prosperous Years

1 Papua, (1914, May 20). *The Daily Telegraph (Sydney, NSW: 1883-1930)*, 11. Accessed December 2, 2021, from http://nla.gov.au/nla.news-article238800074
2 Langmore, D., (1989), *Missionary Lives, Papua, 1874-1914,* Honolulu: University of Hawaii Press, 12
3 National Archives of Australia, NAA: A1 1913/13755
4 National Archives of Australia, NAA: C3131, C1911/2535, 1043437
5 Blue and Blue (1961), Magazine of the Marist brothers high Darlinghurst, Seaborn: Alexandria
6 Not to be confused with a Longford film of the same name made and released in 1923
7 Filmography of Raymond Longford. *Cinema Papers*, no 1, January, 1974, Richmond: Cinema Papers Ltd., 51, see University of Wollongong, Archives Online, https://archivesonline.uow.edu.au/nodes/view/5010#idx31947, accessed December 8, 2021
8 Dun's Gazette, Vol. 10, No. 4, July 28, 1913, Sydney: Dun's Gazette, 1909-1958
9 Letter from Shaw to Meyer & General Councillors, September 17, 1913, Copy at MSC Archives, Kensington
10 Randwick Council Rate Book, 1913, Randwick Library
11 Letter from Shaw to Meyer & General Councillors, September 17, 1913, Copy at MSC Archives, Kensington
12 An expression used by Guis to describe Shaw in a letter to Meyer. In North American Indian culture a manitou is a supernatural being with the ability to control nature.
13 Letter from Shaw to Meyer & General Councillors, September 17, 1913, Copy at MSC Archives, Kensington
14 Perhaps a reference to company shares held in the Bulga Timber Mill venture north west of Wingham, NSW.
15 Letter from Shaw to Meyer & General Councillors, September 17, 1913. Copy at MSC Archives, Kensington

16 Provincial Council minutes, August 24 – September 7, 1913, No. 30. Copy in McMahon notes, Shaw File, MSC Archives, Kensington
17 Letter from Shaw to Meyer & General Councillors, September 17, 1913. Copy at MSC Archives, Kensington
18 Ibid
19 Ibid
20 Letter from Guis to Meyer, May 14, 1912. Copy at MSC Archives, Kensington. Translation by M Ryan
21 Ibid
22 Ibid
23 According to a telegram set by Shaw to Rome in the month following Guis' death, dated October 30, 1913, Copy at MSC Archives, Kensington. The same value is cited in an undated letter from Shaw to Meyer written around the same time.
24 Letter from Shaw to Meyer, October 21, 1913, Copy at MSC Archives, Kensington
25 Letter from Shaw to Meyer, September 16, 1913, Copy at MSC Archives, Kensington
26 Death of Father Guis (1913, September 18). *The Catholic Press (Sydney, NSW: 1895 - 1942)*, 21. Accessed December 9, 2021, from http://nla.gov.au/nla.news-article105155545
27 Letter from Shaw to Meyer & General Councillors, September 17, 1913, Copy at MSC Archives, Kensington
28 Notes of J F McMahon in Shaw File, MSC Archives Kensington
29 Cerretti arrived in Sydney in February, 1915
30 Letter from Linckens to Apostolic Delegate, Archbishop Cerretti, June 9, 1916, Copy held at MSC Archives, Kensington.
31 Letter from Shaw to Meyer, October 21, 1913, Copy at MSC Archives, Kensington
32 NSW BDM, Death Certificate, No 9119/1913
33 Great All-Australian Exhibition, (1913, April 4). *The Sydney Morning Herald (NSW: 1842 - 1954)*, 11. Accessed December 9, 2021, from http://nla.gov.au/nla.news-article15410059
34 Advertising (1913, July 25). *The Sun (Sydney, NSW: 1910-1954)*, p. 3 (FINAL EXTRA). Accessed April 10, 2023, from http://nla.gov.au/nla.news-article229684512
35 Advertising (1913, July 25). *The Sun (Sydney, NSW: 1910-1954)*, p. 3 (Final Extra). Accessed April 10, 2023, from http://nla.gov.au/nla.news-article229684512
36 Electrical Progress, (1913, November 1). *The Herald (Melbourne, Vic.: 1861-1954)*, 16. Accessed December 9, 2021, from http://nla.gov.au/nla.news-article241541573
37 Letter from Shaw to Meyer and General Council, October 21, 1913, Copy at MSC Archives, Kensington
38 Ibid
39 Ibid
40 Loder-Neuhold, R. 2019. Crocodiles, Masks and Madonnas. Catholic Mission Museums in German-Speaking Europe. *Studia Missionalia Svecana* 121, 267. Uppsala: Department of Theology. Accessed October 21, 2021 from https://uu.diva-portal.org/smash/get/diva2:1363017/FULLTEXT01.pdf

Chapter XIV: Hubert Linckens Comes to Town

1 Dun's Gazette, January 19, 1914, 70
2 Fire! (1914, January 22). *Freeman's Journal (Sydney, NSW: 1850-1932)*, 15. Accessed December 20, 2021, from http://nla.gov.au/nla.news-article111291213

NOTES & REFERENCES

3   Sydney, Inward Passenger Lists, June, 1914, Passenger List for the *Zieten*, departing Bremen for Sydney. Ancestry.com. *New South Wales, Australia, Unassisted Immigrant Passenger Lists, 1826-1922* [database on-line]. Provo, UT, USA: Ancestry.com Operations, Inc., 2007 (accessed December, 2021)
4   Shipping, (1914, June 29). *The Daily Telegraph (Sydney, NSW: 1883 - 1930)*, p. 10. Accessed December 20, 2021, from http://nla.gov.au/nla.news-article238811100
5   Caruana, A., (2000), Monastery on the Hill, Sydney: Nelen Yubu Missiological Society, 154
6   Ibid, 116
7   Letter from Power to MSC Sister, October 23, 1960, cited in Caruana, A., (2000), *Monastery on the Hill*, Sydney: Nelen Yubu Missiological Society, 155
8   Caruana, A., (2000), *Monastery on the Hill*, Sydney: Nelen Yubu Missiological Society, 125
9   Ibid, 117
10 Letter from Linckens to Meyer, July 12, 1914. Copy at MSC Archives, Kensington.
11 Undated notes of Archibald Shaw to Meyer, General Archives, III 5B, Copy at MSC Archives, Kensington
12 Letter from Linckens to Bonaventura Cerretti, the Australian Apostolic Delegate, June 9, 1916, copy at MSC Archives, Kensington
13 Declaration signed by Shaw, September 30, 1915, dating from July 1, 1914, witnessed by Linckens and Wemmers. Copy at MSC Archives, Kensington.
14 Letter from Linckens to Bonaventura Cerretti, the Australian Apostolic Delegate, June 9, 1916, copy at MSC Archives, Kensington
15 Letter from Linckens to Apostolic Delegate, Archbishop Cerretti, June 9, 1916, Copy held at MSC Archives, Kensington.
16 Working with Wireless, (1914, August 8). *Evening News (Sydney, NSW: 1869-1931)*, 7. Accessed December 20, 2021, from http://nla.gov.au/nla.news-article115804451
17 Government Gazette Notices (1915, April 1). *Commonwealth of Australia Gazette (National: 1901-1973)*, 613. Accessed December 20, 2021, from http://nla.gov.au/nla.news-article232451460, and
    Government Gazette Notices (1914, August 8). *Commonwealth of Australia Gazette (National: 1901 - 1973)*, 1370. Accessed December 20, 2021, from http://nla.gov.au/nla.news-article232447921, and
    Government Gazette Notices (1914, October 24). *Commonwealth of Australia Gazette (National: 1901 - 1973)*, 2409. Accessed December 20, 2021, from http://nla.gov.au/nla.news-article232448813, and
    NEW SOUTH WALES. (1914, April 4). *Commonwealth of Australia Gazette (National: 1901 - 1973)*, 634. Accessed December 20, 2021, from http://nla.gov.au/nla.news-article232366475
18 According to a co-worker at radio station KGU in Honolulu. See, Jacobs, R., *The First Family of Island Radio*, Honolulu Magazine Holiday Annual, Nov, 1989
19 Mulrony patented the invention in Australia and the US. Australian patent no.: 16,070/15
20 Harnessing the Wind, (1915, June 27). *Sunday Times (Sydney, NSW: 1895-1930)*, 19. Accessed December 20, 2021, from http://nla.gov.au/nla.news-page13273891
21 Australian patent no.: 14,208/14
22 Dun's Gazette, February 26, 1917, 116
23 A New Kind of Motor Car, (1914, October 27). *The Bathurst Times (NSW: 1909 - 1925)*, 2. Accessed December 20, 2021, from http://nla.gov.au/nla.news-article111505318

24 Recounted by a contemporary of Shaw, James Power msc to J. F. McMahon. Refer, McMahon, J. F. (1983). Father Archibald Shaw: the wireless priest. [Paper read to the Australian Catholic Historical Society, 2 March 1983]. Journal of the Australian Catholic Historical Society, 7(3), 29
25 National Archives of Australia, NAA: A2023, A38/3/143
26 Report of the Royal Commission on Navy and Defence Administration, Melbourne, December 2, 1918, v
27 Pixley, N. S, *William Rooke Creswell*, a paper read at the annual meeting of the Royal Historical Society of Queensland, September 27, 1979, 31
28 In May, 1916. Refer, Report of the Royal Commission on Navy and Defence Administration, Melbourne, December 2, 1918, vi
29 Mysterious Engineering Works, (1915, November 27). *The Mirror of Australia (Sydney, NSW: 1915-1917)*, 3. Accessed December 20, 2021, from http://nla.gov.au/nla.news-article104645346
30 National Archives of Australia, NAA: A6661, 475, Minutes of Evidence, Report of the Royal Commission on Navy and Defence Administration, Melbourne, December 2, 1918, 65
31 Ibid, 66
32 Hoad family descendant's remark, via personal communication to the author, on the kind and caring nature of Walter Hoad
33 National Archives of Australia, NAA: A6661, 475, Minutes of Evidence, Report of the Royal Commission on Navy and Defence Administration, Melbourne, December 2, 1918, 66
34 Ibid, 66 - 67
35 National Archives of Australia, NAA: A6661, 475, Minutes of Evidence, Report of the Royal Commission on Navy and Defence Administration, Melbourne, December 2, 1918, 66 - 67
36 Deal in Wireless (1916, July 26). *The Sun (Sydney, NSW: 1910-1954)*, 6. Accessed February 13, 2023, from http://nla.gov.au/nla.news-article223368973
37 Fire! (1914, January 22). *Freeman's Journal (Sydney, NSW: 1850-1932)*, 15. Accessed December 20, 2021, from http://nla.gov.au/nla.news-article111291213

Chapter XV: Crossroads: Meeting Evie

1 *When I Think Back*, Williams, N., Electronics Australia July, 1989, 39
2 Amalgamated Wireless. *The First Direct Wireless Messages from England to Australia*. Sydney, N.S.W.: Amalgamated Wireless (A/sia), 1935
3 Testimony of Albert Cornwell, Royal Commission on Navy and Defence Administration, Minutes of Evidence, December 2, 1918, 7
4 Report of the Royal Commission on Navy and Defence Administration, Melbourne, December 2, 1918, 68
5 Missionary Who Turned Scientist, (1918, December 18). *The Mercury (Hobart, Tas.: 1860 - 1954)*, 7. Accessed January 4, 2023, from http://nla.gov.au/nla.news-article11422635
6 Testimony of Albert Cornwell, Royal Commission on Navy and Defence Administration, Minutes of Evidence, December 2, 1918, 7
7 Shell Found in Garden (1940, December 19). *Kalgoorlie Miner (WA: 1895-1954)*, 7. Accessed January 4, 2023, from http://nla.gov.au/nla.news-article95198191
8 According to Cornwell descendants through personal communication with the author.
9 Shaw Wireless, (1918, December 12). *The Daily Telegraph (Sydney, NSW: 1883-1930)*, 6. Accessed January 4, 2023, from http://nla.gov.au/nla.news-article239573095

NOTES & REFERENCES

10 Testimony of Percy Cotes, Report of the Royal Commission on Navy and Defence Administration, Melbourne, December 2, 1918, 5
11 Letter from Linckens to Meyer, July 23, 1916. Copy at MSC Archives, Kensington, translated by J F McMahon. There was agreement made between Archibald and his creditors that a percentage of their credit would be repaid, not the full sum. A similar agreement must have existed between Archibald and Linckens despite there being no surviving evidence.
12 Report of the Royal Commission on Navy and Defence Administration, Melbourne, December 2, 1918, 65
13 Testimony of Percy Cotes, Report of the Royal Commission on Navy and Defence Administration, Melbourne, December 2, 1918, 5
14 Royal Commission on Navy and Defence Administration 1918, Exhibits 19-37, National Archives of Australia, NAA: CP661/10, NN, 61, also, Report of the Royal Commission on Navy and Defence Administration, Melbourne, December 2, 1918, 7
15 Stock held amounted to several hundred typed pages of items. Refer, NAA: CP661/10, NN
16 Report of the Royal Commission on Navy and Defence Administration, Melbourne, December 2, 1918, viii
17 Ibid, 2
18 National Archives of Australia: NAA: CP661/10, NN, 43
19 It is the author's speculation that this employee was Marion Mulrony based on a letter from Shaw to Cornwell, August 14, 1916. Refer footnote 24
20 Letter from Linckens to Meyer, June 25, 1916. MSC Archives Rome, translated by M Ryan
21 According to descendants of Cornwell via personal communication with the author
22 Testimony of Albert Cornwell, Royal Commission on Navy and Defence Administration, Minutes of Evidence, December 2, 1918, 49
23 US Emergency Passport Applications Register, Ancestry, unreferenced
24 Royal Commission on Navy and Defence Administration 1918. Exhibits 2-16. National Archives of Australia, NAA: CP661/10, NN, 5
25 Personal, (1915, November 23). *The West Australian (Perth, WA: 1879-1954)*, 5. Accessed March 25, 2023, from http://nla.gov.au/nla.news-article26963690
26 Deal in Wireless (1916, July 26). *The Sun (Sydney, NSW: 1910-1954)*, 6. Accessed February 13, 2023, from http://nla.gov.au/nla.news-article223368973
27 Copy made by Linckens dated June 8, 1916. MSC Archives, Kensington
28 Letter from Vandel to Meyer, December 28, 1902, copy at MSC Archives, Kensington, translation by M Ryan
29 Letter from Linckens to Cerretti, June 9, 1916. Copy at MSC Archives, Kensington
30 Letter from Linckens to Cerretti, June 19, 1916. Copy at MSC Archives, Kensington
31 F E Arnoult Military Record, National Archives, NAA: B2455, 15
32 Letter from Linckens to Meyer, July 2, 1916. MSC Archives Rome, translated by M Ryan
33 Ibid
34 Ibid
35 Letter from Linckens to Meyer, July 23, 1916. Copy at MSC Archives, Kensington, translated by J F McMahon
36 Royal Commission on Navy and Defence Administration 1918, Exhibits 2-16, National Archives of Australia, NAA: CP661/10, NN, 9-10
37 Ibid

Chapter XVI: Missing Money & Mysterious Death

1. Death Certificate of Archibald Shaw, d. August 26, 1916, Deaths in the District of Melbourne East, Victoria, No. 243
2. Letter from Guis to Meyer, August 31, 1909. Copy at MSC Archives, Kensington. Translated by M Ryan
3. Death Certificate of Mary Kennedy, NSW BDM, No 9119/1913, d. June 22, 1913 and research notes of J F McMahon
4. Occasional press reports had sometimes referred to Father Shaw as Mister Shaw.
5. Located at 360 Collins Street, Melbourne. The building has now been replaced.
6. Report of the Royal Commission on Navy and Defence Administration, Melbourne, December 2, 1918, NAA: A6661, 475, 84
7. Royal Commission on Navy and Defence Administration, Exhibits 2-16, National Archives of Australia, NAA: CP661/10, NN, 34
8. Ibid, 248, and also, Report of the Royal Commission on Navy and Defence Administration, Melbourne, December 2, 1918, NAA: A6661, 475, 41
9. Report of the Royal Commission on Navy and Defence Administration, Melbourne, December 2, 1918, NAA: A6661, 475, 41
10. Ibid
11. Letter from Linckens to Meyer, September 3, 1916, Copy in MSC Archives, Kensington, translated by J F McMahon
12. Report of the Royal Commission on Navy and Defence Administration, Melbourne, December 2, 1918, NAA: A6661, 475, 84
13. Royal Commission on Navy and Defence Administration, Exhibits 2-16, National Archives of Australia, NAA: CP661/10, NN, 28
14. Report of the Royal Commission on Navy and Defence Administration, Melbourne, December 2, 1918, NAA: A6661, 475, 64
15. Ibid, 56
16. Archibald's patent attorney, Wilfred Spruson, claimed a significant sum from his estate, £681/13/6, probably as payment for defending Shaw against Balsillie's patent action. NSW State Archives, NRS-13660-7-388-Series 4_78020
17. Report of the Royal Commission on Navy and Defence Administration, Melbourne, December 2, 1918, 10
18. Testimony of Long, Report of the Royal Commission on Navy and Defence Administration, Melbourne, December 2, 1918, NAA: A6661, 475, 59
19. Royal Commission on Navy and Defence Administration, Exhibits 19-37, National Archives of Australia, NAA: CP661/10, NN, 114
20. Ibid, 102
21. Report of the Royal Commission on Navy and Defence Administration, Melbourne, December 2, 1918, NAA: A6661, 475, xi
22. Royal Commission on Navy and Defence Administration, Exhibits 2-16, National Archives of Australia, NAA: CP661/10, NN, 29
23. Report of the Royal Commission on Navy and Defence Administration, Melbourne, December 2, 1918, NAA: A6661, 475, 67
24. Ibid, 59
25. August 15, 1918. The works were then known as the Naval Wireless Works and Cornwell continued as manager. For the complete transcript see, Royal Commission on Navy and Defence Administration, Exhibits 19-37, National Archives of Australia, NAA: CP661/10, NN, 74-82
26. Royal Commission on Navy and Defence Administration, Exhibits 19-37, National

NOTES & REFERENCES

Archives of Australia, NAA: CP661/10, NN, 76

27 Report of the Royal Commission on Navy and Defence Administration, Melbourne, December 2, 1918, NAA: A6661, 475, 68
28 Evidence presented to the Commission contained in the missing police report presents a statement from Carter concerning his poor financial circumstances. He states he had pawned his watch in the days immediately following Shaw's death. Refer: Report of the Royal Commission on Navy and Defence Administration, Melbourne, December 2, 1918, NAA: A6661, 475, 68
29 The Late Father Shaw, M.S.H. (1916, September 8). *Southern Cross (Adelaide, SA: 1889-1954)*, 15. Accessed January 13, 2023, from http://nla.gov.au/nla.news-article166422149
30 Letter from Linckens to Meyer, September 3, 1916. Copy at MSC Archives, Kensington. Translated by J F McMahon
31 Report of the Royal Commission on Navy and Defence Administration, Melbourne, December 2, 1918, NAA: A6661, 475, 32
32 Exhibit 15, Royal Commission on Navy and Defence Administration, Exhibits 2-16, National Archives of Australia, NAA: CP661/10, NN, 76
33 Report of the Royal Commission on Navy and Defence Administration, Melbourne, December 2, 1918, NAA: A6661, 475, 66-67
34 Death Certificate, Deaths in the District of Melbourne East, Victoria, No. 243, August 26, 1916, Archibald John Shaw
35 Letter from Linckens to Meyer, August 27, 1916. MSC Archives, Kensington. Translated by J F McMahon
36 O'Haran was no stranger to scandal himself having fought off a case of paternity divorce proceedings brough by cricketer Arthur Coningham in 1900. See, 1901, *The celebrated divorce case, Coningham v. Coningham, O'Haran co-respondent : a full account of the first hearing of the most startling divorce case of the 19th century,* R. Bear, Sydney, accessed 21 July 2024
37 As of 2023 some of the sandstone surround and wrought ironwork still can still be seen around the original plots
38 Randwick (Long Bay) Cemetery, Catholic Row B, grave 76. Refer, Adams, W., (2001), *Randwick General Cemetery: burials from 10 September 1874 to 22 November 1983,* Maroubra, NSW Cape Banks Family History Society
39 Letter from Linckens to Meyer, September 3, 1916. Copy at MSC Archives, Kensington. Translated by J F McMahon
40 Letter from Linckens to Meyer, September 17, 1916. Copy at MSC, Archives, Kensington. Translated by J F McMahon
41 Letter from Linckens to Meyer, January 21, 1917. Copy at MSC Archives, Kensington. Translated by J F McMahon
42 Transcript of a tape recording made in 1980 by Fr. Jack McNamara, from Melbourne, speaking from memory of a conversation with Fr. John Lonergan, administrator of St Patrick's Cathedral, that happened in 1936. MSC Archives, Kensington
43 Local and General, (1919, September 20). *The Bega Budget (NSW: 1905-1920)*, 2. Accessed January 14, 2023, from http://nla.gov.au/nla.news-page11721642
44 Smith, Ferdinand. *Royal Australian Navy Wireless Works Picnic, 1917, Group Portrait Photographed by F. Smith,* 1917.

Chapter XVII: Blackmail, Fraud and a Royal Commission

1 Wireless Plants (1916, July 31). *The Sun (Sydney, NSW: 1910-1954)*, 5. Accessed

February 10, 2023, from http://nla.gov.au/nla.news-page24420097
2. Ibid
3. Letter to Federal Treasurer, August 7, 1916.
4. Wireless Plants (1916, July 31). *The Sun (Sydney, NSW: 1910-1954)*, p. 5. Accessed February 10, 2023, from http://nla.gov.au/nla.news-page24420097
5. *Analecta Societatis Missionariorum, Sacratissimi Cordis Jesu,* Series Tertia, No. 1, 1911, General House: Rome, decree No. 18 (d), 90. This section of the Analecta, published in Latin, identifies four reasons for expulsion or dismissal from priesthood under Canon Law. The part which Linckens refers to as applying to Shaw, Part (d), refers to when vows are not solemn or do not have a solemn effect, including situations where a civil contract of marriage is undertaken whilst under religious vows.
6. Letter from Linckens to Meyer, March 11, 1917. Copy at MSC Archives, Kensington. Translated by J F McMahon
7. Letter from Linckens to Meyer, October 29, 1916. MSC Archives, Rome. Translated by M Ryan
8. Letter from Linckens to Meyer, December 10, 1916. MSC Archives, Rome. Translated by M Ryan
9. Letter from Linckens to Meyer, January 7, 1917. MSC Archives, Rome. Translated by M Ryan
10. Another less likely candidate could be Evie's sister acting on her behalf.
11. Testimony of Albert Cornwell, Royal Commission on Navy and Defence Administration, Minutes of Evidence, December 2, 1918, 49
12. Local priest was centre of radio company scandal, Daily Mirror, Historical Feature, December 1, 1981, 54
13. Andrews, E. M., *Managing the War: the Department of Defence 1914-1919*, Army History Unit, 5, a paper presented at the 1918: Defining Victory conference, National Convention Centre, Canberra, September, 1998
14. No title, (1919, May 7). *The Age (Melbourne, Vic.: 1854-1954)*, 8. Accessed February 16, 2023, from http://nla.gov.au/nla.news-article155210230
15. The First Direct Wireless Messages from the United Kingdom to Australia, Naval Historical Society of Australia, December, 2018. Refer: https://www.navyhistory.org.au/the-first-direct-wireless-messages-from-the-united-kingdom-to-australia/ accessed February 12, 2023
16. Personal correspondence with Melbourne Supreme Court Archivist, February, 2023
17. Report of the Royal Commission on Navy and Defence Administration, Melbourne, December 2, 1918, NAA: A6661, 475, 26
18. Letter from Linckens to Meyer, February 3, 1919. Copy at MSC Archives, Kensington. Translated by J F McMahon
19. This reporting is typical: Navy, (1918, December 12). *The Daily Telegraph (Sydney, NSW: 1883-1930)*, 4. Accessed February 16, 2023, from http://nla.gov.au/nla.news-article239573011
20. Report of the Royal Commission on Navy and Defence Administration, Melbourne, December 2, 1918, NAA: A6661, 475, 65
21. Ibid, 64-66
22. Filmed interview with Colin Hoad by the author, Tumut, January, 2019
23. Royal Commission on Navy and Defence Administration Exhibits 19 – 37, NAA: CP661/10, NN, 8
24. Report of the Royal Commission on Navy and Defence Administration, Melbourne, December 2, 1918, NAA: A6661, 475, v

NOTES & REFERENCES

25 Ibid, xiii
26 Ibid, viii
27 Carroll's testimony was taken on May 14, 1918, several months before the official Commission hearings began in Melbourne on November 12. Refer, Royal Commission on Navy and Defence Administration, Exhibits 19-37, National Archives of Australia, NAA: CP661/10, NN, 99-103
28 Report of the Royal Commission on Navy and Defence Administration, Melbourne, December 2, 1918, NAA: A6661, 475, 84
29 The Daily Telegraph also reports that the stenographer was arranged by the Royal Commission. Refer, Navy (1918, December 12). *The Daily Telegraph (Sydney, NSW: 1883 - 1930)*, 4. Accessed February 16, 2023, from http://nla.gov.au/nla.news-article239573011
30 Cussen went on to become a judge and serve two terms as Chief Justice. Refer, Jenny Cook and B. Keon-Cohen, 'Cussen, Sir Leo Finn Bernard (1859–1933)', Australian Dictionary of Biography, National Centre of Biography, Australian National University, https://adb.anu.edu.au/biography/cussen-sir-leo-finn-bernard-5857/text9959, published first in hardcopy 1981, accessed online 17 February 2023
31 Albert Cornwell to James Long, Royal Commission on Navy and Defence Administration 1918. Exhibits 2-16, Exhibit 13, 3. National Archives of Australia, NAA: CP661/10, NN
32 The Biographical Dictionary of the Australian Senate, Accessed February 10, 2023, https://biography.senate.gov.au/james-joseph-long/
33 Quentin Beresford, 'Jensen, Jens August (1865–1936)', Australian Dictionary of Biography, National Centre of Biography, Australian National University, https://adb.anu.edu.au/biography/jensen-jens-august-6840/text11845, published first in hardcopy 1983, accessed online 10 February 2023
34 Shaw Wireless Purchase, (1919, June 27), *The Age (Melbourne, Vic.: 1854-1954)*, 6. Accessed February 16, 2023, from http://nla.gov.au/nla.news-article155205243
35 Shaw Wireless, (1919, May 9), *The Daily Telegraph (Sydney, NSW: 1883 - 1930)*, 10. Accessed February 16, 2023, from http://nla.gov.au/nla.news-article239594633
36 The Commissioners appointed were William McBeath (Chairman), a national wholesaler and politician who was also principal business adviser to the Department of Defence, James Chalmers, a Sydney Retailer, and Frank Verco, an Adelaide merchant. Refer, Margaret Vines, 'McBeath, Sir William George (1865–1931)', Australian Dictionary of Biography, National Centre of Biography, Australian National University, https://adb.anu.edu.au/biography/mcbeath-sir-william-george-7294/text12651, published first in hardcopy 1986, accessed online 16 February 2023.
37 No title, (1919, May 7). *The Age (Melbourne, Vic.: 1854-1954)*, 8. Accessed February 16, 2023, from http://nla.gov.au/nla.news-article155210230
38 Transcript of a tape recording made in 1980 by Fr. Jack McNamara, from Melbourne, speaking to Fr. Tom Linane of events that happened in 1936. MSC Archives, Kensington
39 Ibid
40 Quentin Beresford, 'Jensen, Jens August (1865–1936)', Australian Dictionary of Biography, National Centre of Biography, Australian National University, https://adb.anu.edu.au/biography/jensen-jens-august-6840/text11845, published first in hardcopy 1983, accessed online 11 February 2023
41 Transcript of a tape recording made in 1980 by Fr. Jack McNamara, from Melbourne, speaking to Fr. Tom Linane of events that happened in 1936. MSC Archives, Kensington
42 Report of the Royal Commission on Navy and Defence Administration, Melbourne, December 2, 1918, NAA: A6661, 475, xix and xv

43 Father Shaw Dead, (1916, August 27), *Sunday Times (Sydney, NSW: 1895-1930)*, 2. Accessed February 13, 2023, from http://nla.gov.au/nla.news-article121350417
44 In 1928 Amalgamated Wireless purchased twenty-six stations, including the land title, from the Government for £39,574. Refer, Sale of Wireless Stations to Amalgamated Wireless (Australasia) Limited, (1928, November 8). *Commonwealth of Australia Gazette (National: 1901 - 1973)*, 3084. Accessed February 13, 2023, from http://nla.gov.au/nla.news-article232533110

Chapter XVIII: Settling Matters

1 Letter from Linckens to Meyer, October 29, 1916. Copy at MSC Archives, Kensington. Translated by J F McMahon
2 NSW State Archives, NRS-13660-7-388-Series 4_78020
3 Letter from Linckens to Meyer, July 23, 1916. Copy at MSC Archives, Kensington, translated by J F McMahon
4 Letter from Linckens to Meyer, December 5, 1917. MSC Archives, Rome. Translated by J F McMahon
5 According to the affidavit supplied to the Equity Court by Blanche Monday on December 4, 1916, there were about 160 creditors owed by Shaw's estate. See, NSW State Archives, NRS-13660-7-388-Series 4_78020
6 Letter from Linckens to Meyer, July 22, 1918. MSC Archives, Rome. Translated by M Ryan
7 See appendix 3: NSW State Archives NRS-13660-7-388-Series 4_78020
8 Wireless Wizardry, (1913, December 28), *Sunday Times (Sydney, NSW : 1895-1930)*, p. 3 (SUNDAY TIMES GLOBE PICTORIAL). Accessed June 2, 2023, from http://nla.gov.au/nla.news-page13507888
9 Late Rev. A. J. Shaw, (1916, August 30), *The Sydney Morning Herald (NSW : 1842-1954)*, p. 9. Accessed June 2, 2023, from http://nla.gov.au/nla.news-article15689303
10 Miners Stay Below in Grim Fight for Rights, (1937, February 27). *The Labor Daily (Sydney, NSW: 1924-1938)*, p. 7. Accessed March 25, 2023, from http://nla.gov.au/nla.news-article237441300
11 See appendix 2: Royal Commission on Navy and Defence Administration 1918. Exhibit #5.
12 Royal Commission on Navy and Defence Administration, Exhibits 19-37, National Archives of Australia, NAA: CP661/10, NN, 102
13 Royal Commission on Navy and Defence Administration 1918. Exhibits 2-16, Exhibit 13, 4. National Archives of Australia, NAA: CP661/10, NN
14 See appendix 3: NSW State Archives NRS-13660-7-388-Series 4_78020
15 http://nla.gov.au/nla.news-page1258127 and http://nla.gov.au/nla.news-article180511757
16 Letter from Linckens to Meyer, December 5, 1917. MSC Archives, Rome. Translated by J F McMahon
17 Letter from Linckens to Meyer, March 11, 1917. MSC Archives, Rome. Translated by M Ryan
18 Report of the Royal Commission on Navy and Defence Administration, Melbourne, December 2, 1918, NAA: A6661, 475, 9
19 Based addresses provided in contemporary electoral rolls
20 *New South Wales Government Gazette (Sydney, NSW: 1832 - 1900)*, (1887, November 4). 7453. Accessed February 23, 2023, from http://nla.gov.au/nla.news-page14455900 and Patents, (1914, September 8). *The Herald (Melbourne, Vic.: 1861 - 1954)*, 3. Accessed February 23, 2023, from http://nla.gov.au/nla.news-article242301911 and

NOTES & REFERENCES

Australian Patent: 1918008907, application No. 8907/18, IPAustralia

21 The Nomination for the Southern Gold-Fields (1874, December 29). *The Sydney Morning Herald (NSW: 1842-1954)*, 3. Accessed February 23, 2023, from http://nla.gov.au/nla.news-article13342112

22 The Milburn Creek (N.S.W.) Mystery, (1881, November 4). *The Express and Telegraph (Adelaide, SA: 1867-1922)*, 3, (Third Edition). Accessed February 23, 2023, from http://nla.gov.au/nla.news-article208196506, and, Scandal in N.S.W., (1881, November 14). *Gippsland Times (Vic.: 1861-1954)*, 4, (Morning). Accessed February 23, 2023, from http://nla.gov.au/nla.news-article61918457

23 A Molybdenite Mine, (1918, December 2). *Glen Innes Examiner (NSW : 1908-1954)*, p 3. Accessed June 2, 2023, from http://nla.gov.au/nla.news-article180511757

24 Letter from Linckens to Meyer, July 8, 1918. MSC Archives, Rome. Translated by M Ryan

25 The Late Rev. A. J. Shaw, M.S.H., (1916, August 31). *Freeman's Journal (Sydney, NSW: 1850-1932)*, 24. Accessed February 16, 2023, from http://nla.gov.au/nla.news-article115592185

26 Topics of the Time, (1916, September 2). *The Wingham Chronicle and Manning River Observer (NSW: 1898-1954)*, 4. Accessed February 16, 2023, from http://nla.gov.au/nla.news-article166785979

27 Adelong, (1866, July 16). *The Tumut and Adelong Times (NSW : 1864-1867; 1899-1950)*, p. 3. Accessed June 2, 2023, from http://nla.gov.au/nla.news-article144778431

28 Meyer to Linckens, November 21, 1918. MSC Archives, Rome. Translated by J F McMahon

29 Caruana, A., (2000), *Monastery on the Hill*, Nelen Yuba Missiological Unit, 155, footnote 172

30 Ibid, 155

31 Ibid, 155-5

32 NSW State Archives, NRS-13660-7-388-Series 4_78020

33 Letter from Vandel to Meyer, December 28, 1902, copy at MSC Archives, Kensington. Translated by M Ryan

Chapter IXX: Epilogue

1 Innes, B. 1996, *Priest & Scientist: Joseph Slattery – Australia's First Radiographer*, Crawford House Publishing: Bathurst

2 John P. Wilkinson, 'Slattery, Joseph Patrick (1866–1931)', Australian Dictionary of Biography, National Centre of Biography, Australian National University, https://adb.anu.edu.au/biography/slattery-joseph-patrick-8453/text14863, published first in hardcopy 1988, accessed online 22 February 2023.

3 Jacobs, R., *The First Family of Island Radio*, Honolulu Magazine Holiday Annual, Nov, 1989

4 Buckingham, D., *Hawaii's War Correspondents*. See, https://www.hawaiireporter.com/hawaiis-women-war-correspondents-2/ Accessed April 6, 2023

5 The original building housing the Honolulu Advertiser and Mulroney's KGU transmitter and tower still stands at 605 Kapiolani Boulevard, Honolulu.

6 Loder-Neuhold, R., (2019), Crocodiles, Masks and Madonnas. Catholic Mission Museums in German-Speaking Europe. Studia Missionalia Svecana 121, 267. Uppsala: Department of Theology. Accessed October 21, 2021 from https://uu.diva-portal.org/smash/get/diva2:1363017/FULLTEXT01.pdf

7 https://gkakabin.wordpress.com/2017/10/23/the-baining-massacre-a-story-by-levi-tomitikot-r-i-p/ Accessed March 25, 2023

8 "Stay-in" in Mine, (1937, February 27), *The Argus (Melbourne, Vic.: 1848 - 1957)*, 15. Accessed February 21, 2023, from http://nla.gov.au/nla.news-article11973935
9 Death Certificate, NSW BDM, No 3392/1970, NAA: NRS-13660-60-27, Series 4_697973
10 Death of Father Shaw, (1916, August 28), *The Daily Telegraph (Sydney, NSW: 1883-1930)*, p. 7. Accessed April 10, 2023, from http://nla.gov.au/nla.news-article239207343
11 Accrington's Brilliant Win (1920, November 17). *Referee (Sydney, NSW: 1886-1939)*, 5. Accessed February 21, 2023, from http://nla.gov.au/nla.news-article121165059
12 *The Biographical Dictionary of the Australian Senate, vol. 1, 1901-1929*, Melbourne University Press, Carlton South, Vic., 2000, pp. 245-248
13 National Archives of Australia. NAA: MT1486/1, 9739974, Leslie Harold Long
14 Judge Upholds Jensen Will, (1937, October 8), *The Daily Telegraph (Sydney, NSW: 1931 - 1954)*, 8. Accessed February 21, 2023, from http://nla.gov.au/nla.news-article247227518
15 Mr A. E. Cornwell, (1920, December 14), *The Sydney Morning Herald (NSW: 1842 - 1954)*, 5. Accessed February 21, 2023, from http://nla.gov.au/nla.news-article16879717
16 Death of Mr A. E. Cornwell, (1920, December 10). *Lithgow Mercury (NSW: 1898-1954)*, 4. Accessed February 21, 2023, from http://nla.gov.au/nla.news-article218453945
17 Wireless Weekly, *How a Radio Engineer is Made*, June 17, 1927
18 O'Connell, D. J. K. (1952). Father Edward Francis Pigot, S J: Part II. *Studies: An Irish Quarterly Review*, 41(163/164), 326, http://www.jstor.org/stable/30099948, Accessed February 23, 2023
19 Obituary (1950, September 7). *Nepean Times (Penrith, NSW: 1882-1962)*, p. 5. Accessed February 21, 2023, from http://nla.gov.au/nla.news-article117917472
20 National Archives of Australia, NAA: B2355, Shaw, Charles William Fraser, 13
21 Waverley Cemetery records grave W-18-RC-SL-4312. Also refer letter from Shaw to Meyer, September 27, 1904, MSC Archives, Kensington
22 Donned False Whiskers and Plowed Paul Pry! (1933, April 9). *Truth (Sydney, NSW: 1894-1954)*, 17. Accessed February 21, 2023, from http://nla.gov.au/nla.news-article169308045
23 Said to be Victim of a Drug, (1933, May 27), *The Labor Daily (Sydney, NSW: 1924 - 1938)*, 7. Accessed February 21, 2023, from http://nla.gov.au/nla.news-article236576570
24 Jenolan Caves Outbreak, (1919, April 25). *Lithgow Mercury (NSW: 1898-1954)*, 4. Accessed February 22, 2023, from http://nla.gov.au/nla.news-article218610866
25 According to Colin Hoad, Evie's nephew.
26 Yarrangobilly C.W.A., (1947, November 4), *The Tumut and Adelong Times (NSW: 1864-1867; 1899-1950)*, p. 1. Accessed February 22, 2023, from http://nla.gov.au/nla.news-article139317508
27 Recounted by Colin Hoad who as a child spent time with his cousin, Evie's daughter.
28 Phillips, A., & Ashley, M. (2005). Cloud Imaging from Meteorological Satellites and its Application to Robotic Observing. *Publications of the Astronomical Society of Australia*, 22(4), 306-310. doi:10.1071/AS05024, 309
29 Sydney Morning Herald, February 14, 2004
30 Construction of Aeroplanes, (1923, December 15). *The Daily Telegraph (Sydney, NSW: 1883-1930)*, 7. Accessed February 22, 2023, from http://nla.gov.au/nla.news-article245988268
31 Aircraft Manufacture (1936, February 17), *Advocate (Burnie, Tas.: 1890-1954)*, 7, (Daily). Accessed February 22, 2023, from http://nla.gov.au/nla.news-article91789923
32 Meggs, Keith Raymond, (2009), Australian-built Aircraft and the Industry Volume 1. Seymour, Victoria: Finger-Four Publishing, 294-301

NOTES & REFERENCES

33 Randwick Aero Station (1929, September 25), *The Labor Daily (Sydney, NSW: 1924-1938)*, 7. Accessed February 22, 2023, from http://nla.gov.au/nla.news-article239772734
34 Retrenchment, (1929, July 5), *The Sydney Morning Herald (NSW: 1842-1954)*, 13. Accessed February 22, 2023, from http://nla.gov.au/nla.news-article16546058
35 Armouring Propellers, (1929, March 18), *The Sun (Sydney, NSW: 1910-1954)*, 9, (Final Extra). Accessed February 22, 2023, from http://nla.gov.au/nla.news-article222698222
36 Smith, Robert L., (1928), The Fourth Propeller, A New Industry, *San Francisco Business*, Vol. XVII, No. 11, July 1928, 14-15, 35, Accessed February 22, 2023, from https://archive.org/details/sanfranciscobusi1728sanf/page/n41/mode/2up?view=theater
37 Commercial War in the Air? (1935, September 7), *The Telegraph (Brisbane, Qld.: 1872-1947)*, p. 15 (Latest Final). Accessed February 22, 2023, from http://nla.gov.au/nla.news-article181218310
38 Air Force (1928, October 8), *The Sydney Morning Herald (NSW: 1842-1954)*, p. 11. Accessed February 22, 2023, from http://nla.gov.au/nla.news-article16499793 and Civilians Will Leave, (1929, June 25), *The Daily Telegraph (Sydney, NSW: 1883-1930)*, p. 3. Accessed February 22, 2023, from http://nla.gov.au/nla.news-article245640298
39 Air Station Abolished, (1930, April 3), *Chronicle (Adelaide, SA: 1895-1954)*, p. 33. Accessed February 22, 2023, from http://nla.gov.au/nla.news-article90056171
40 Department of Works and Railways, (1931, February 26), *Commonwealth of Australia Gazette (National: 1901-1973)*, p. 226. Accessed February 22, 2023, from http://nla.gov.au/nla.news-article232190473
41 Department of the Army, (1954, June 3). *Commonwealth of Australia Gazette (National: 1901-1973)*, 1615. Accessed February 22, 2023, from http://nla.gov.au/nla.news-article232904703
42 "COMMONWEALTH OF AUSTRALIA, Australian Heritage Commission Act 1975 NOTICE OF INTENTION TO ENTER PLACES IN THE REGISTER OF THE NATIONAL ESTATE" *Commonwealth of Australia Gazette. Periodic (National: 1977-2011)* 27 October 1998: 6. Web. 22 Feb 2023, http://nla.gov.au/nla.news-article238039548
43 Refer, https://www.randwick.nsw.gov.au/about-council/history/historic-places/plaques, Accessed February 23, 2023

WIRELESS PRIEST

INDEX

2BL. *See* 2SB (2BL)
2SB (2BL) 163, 255

Adelong 18, 23, 24, 25, 26, 27, 28, 29, 30, 31, 33, 180, 243, 244, 253, 262
Adelong Hotel 25
Al-Jazari 11
Amalgamated Wireless Company 175, 186, 222, 223, 226, 227, 250
amateur radio 257
America 15, 16, 181, 198, 210, 230, 231, 241, 245, 246
Analecta ecclesiastica 186
Antarctica 138, 139
antenna tower 115, 116, 153, 161, 178, 235, 236, 255
Apostolic Delegate. *See* Cerretti, Archbishop Bonaventura
Archina 153, 161, 162, 188, 192, 194, 196, 253, 258, 259, 261
Arnoult, Fernand 47, 116, 162, 198, 202, 253, 263
Ascot 103, 106, 153, 161, 162, 164, 176, 192, 214, 217, 218, 235, 241, 246, 258, 259
Atlantic Ocean 56
Avoca Street 153, 188, 196, 239, 259, 261
AWA Ltd 186, 222, 226, 227, 236, 250, 251. *See* Amalgamated Wireless

Baining 1, 3, 7, 10, 69, 71, 72, 166, 240, 251, 262, 273, 274
Baker, E. A. 242, 243
Balsillie, John G. 159, 182, 195, 196, 209
bankruptcy 239
Bathurst 13, 14, 48, 249, 263
beam antenna 13, 186, 250
Berti, Gaspara 11
Boer War 56
Braun, Karl 14
Bulga Saw Mill Co. 154, 198
Bursar, *See* Econum

Caine, Clement 34, 50
Callan, Nicholas 12, 13
Carnegie, Andrew 15
Carr, Mary-Ann 26
Carroll, August 210, 215, 232, 240
Causon, John 26
Cerretti, Archbishop Bonaventura 161, 195, 197, 199, 217, 223
Chevalier, Jules 35, 38, 48, 55
Circular Quay 127, 171, 220
Clarke, Sir Rupert 150, 190, 191, 206, 214
Clarkson, Rear Admiral 192
coal mine, North Wallarah 239, 240, 241, 252
Coastal Wireless Service 150, 159, 175, 182, 195, 236, 247
Commonwealth Bay 138, 139
continuous wave 175
Coolidge, William 13
Cornwell, Albert 187, 188, 189, 194, 195, 198, 200, 208, 209, 211, 212, 215, 220, 225, 232, 233, 240, 242, 253, 257
Couppé, Louis 64, 66, 67, 218
Court of Marine Enquiry 228
Cresswell, Commander Frank 179, 191, 200, 210, 230, 232
Creswell, Capt. William 179, 230
Crookes, William 11, 12
Curran, Milne 244
Cussen, Leo 233

Davy, Humphry 11
de Boismenu, Alain 54
debt 57, 58, 83, 92, 105, 154, 155, 174, 176, 177, 190, 199, 206, 217, 239, 246
Deepwater, NSW 241, 242, 243, 252
Denison, Hugh 138, 139, 222, 225, 226, 251
diode valve 186
dispensation & laicisation 39, 184
Douglas Park 220, 252, 263
Dutruc Street 18, 106, 153, 176, 181, 214, 259

Econum 60
Edison, Thomas Alva 9, 15, 16
electric car 200
embezzlement 174, 224
Eveline, Fr 68
extortion 15, 223, 225

Faraday, Michael 12
Fisk, Ernest 186, 227, 236, 251, 256
Fleming, John 10, 11
Ford, Henry 15
fraud 226, 227

Galilei, Galileo 11
Garden Island 235, 257
Gayundah 179
Gazelle Peninsula 6, 9, 72, 251, 273
Geissler, Heinrich 11
General Electric Co. 210, 232, 240, 241, 246
Genocchi, Jean 39
Göbel, Heinrich 11
Goulburn 32, 33
Green, George William 'Gunyah' 243
Gsell, Francis Xavier 47, 48, 49, 59, 60, 70, 71, 93
Guis, Joseph 94, 103, 105, 153, 157, 160, 161, 162, 164, 202, 217, 246

Hahl, Albert 3, 272
Hempenstall, Peter 262
Henry, Joseph 12
Hertz, Heinrich 180
Hertzian Waves 14
Hiltrup 55, 92, 166, 251
Hoad
  Evie 27, 180, 181, 182, 184, 187, 190, 194, 198, 203, 210, 211, 215, 216, 217, 224, 225, 228, 229, 230, 231, 232, 241, 245, 246, 248, 255, 256, 257, 293
  Walter & Olieve 27, 180
horses 209
Hospital, Miss Garlick's 160, 213, 214
Howell-Price, Lieutenant David 226

ignition coil 12
induction coil 12, 14

Jenolan Caves 230, 256, 262
Jensen, Minister Jens 189, 191, 192, 195, 210, 212, 222, 223, 226, 227, 232, 233, 234, 235, 243, 252, 253
judicial enquiry 234, 246

Kaiser Wilhelm Land 37, 48, 53
Kelso 14
Kennedy, Amy 162, 163, 245, 255
Kennedy, Catherine 163
Kennedy, William 26, 229, 245
Kensington monastery 48, 58, 262
KGU Honolulu 178, 250, 284, 292
King Island 138, 189, 204, 253, 263
Kirkby, Edward Hope 14, 103, 105, 106, 156, 216, 217, 235, 246, 262

Lanctin, Arthur 58, 59, 70
Linckens, Hubert 72, 84, 92, 154, 161, 165, 166, 171, 172, 173, 174, 175, 176, 177, 182, 184, 186, 188, 189, 190, 192, 193, 194, 195, 196, 197, 198, 199, 200, 201, 207, 213, 214, 215, 217, 218, 223, 224, 225, 228, 229, 238, 239, 241, 242, 243, 244, 245, 246, 251
Linsday, James 11
liquid cells 13
Little Sisters of the Poor 157
Lodygin, Alexander 11
London Bank 190, 204, 205, 207, 211, 226
London Missionary Society 37
Lonergan, John 214, 218, 219
Long Bay Cemetery. *See* Randwick Cemetery
Long, Senator James 160, 189, 190, 191, 194, 195, 208, 209, 210, 211, 212, 217, 218, 232, 233, 234, 252, 253
Lynch, Joseph 210, 213, 214, 232, 252

Marconi, Guglielmo 14, 56, 156, 159, 175, 182, 186, 194, 256

INDEX

Maritime Wireless Telegraph Co. 115, 116, 155, 159, 160, 163, 177, 180, 184, 186, 187, 189, 191, 194, 197, 204, 205, 206, 207, 211, 217, 220, 222, 235, 236, 241, 243, 245, 251, 257, 259, 261, 262
Marquis de Rays 37
Mary's Mount, Goulburn 32, 33
Mataram 127
Mawson, Douglas 138, 139
Maynooth 12
McMahon, J. F. 26, 49, 57, 219, 261
McNamara, Jack 234
Merg, Emile 49, 51, 54, 55, 63, 68
Meyer, Eugène 50, 53, 57, 58, 59, 61, 62, 63, 66, 70, 71, 92, 94, 156, 160, 164, 165, 175, 192, 193, 195, 199, 203, 207, 213, 215, 223, 224, 229, 238, 239, 242, 244
Milburn Creek Affair 243
Missionaries of the Sacred Heart (MSC) 3, 6, 7, 17, 35, 47, 55, 94, 116, 194, 220, 241, 245, 246, 251, 261, 265, 268, 269, 273
missionary diseases 51, 202
molybdenite 241, 242
Moran, Cardinal Patrick 13, 50, 216
Morse code 15, 29, 30, 56, 114
Morse, Samuel 15
Mulrony, Marion 108, 112, 126, 134, 149, 177, 178, 186, 195, 200, 249, 250
munitions manufacture 187, 188, 189, 190, 253

Naval Wireless Works 220, 253, 254
Navarre, Louis-André 35, 37, 38, 39, 48, 60, 93
New Britain 9, 10, 37, 47, 53, 61, 63, 64, 65, 66, 68, 69, 70, 71, 72, 84, 92, 166, 176
New Guinea 35, 36, 37, 38, 39, 47, 48, 53, 59, 61, 64, 66, 70, 84, 93, 115, 116, 128, 129, 150, 165, 176
New Ireland 37, 240
Nobel Prize (1909) 14

Nouyoux, Edward 164, 216

O'Haran, Denis 153, 216
ordination 34, 38, 47, 50, 94, 184, 220, 247

Pagès, Armand 161
painting 38, 57, 58
Palmer, Edward 256
Parer's Hotel 204
Passionists 33, 34, 50, 247
patents 15, 174, 178, 179, 182, 191, 195, 205, 242, 276
Pearl Harbour 250
Pearl, schooner 240
photographs 159, 194, 225, 262
Pigot, Edward 254
Pius XI, Pope 14
Placid, Brother 34, 35, 38, 48, 49, 50, 54, 57, 247
Port Moresby 37, 129, 130
Postmaster-General 179, 187
poverty, vow of 15, 17, 27, 197, 255
Probate 238
procurator 47, 49, 51, 53, 54, 55, 56, 57, 62, 70, 71, 72, 83, 92, 93, 94, 153, 157, 160, 161, 244, 246
prostitutes 212

Randwick 18, 48, 53, 92, 161, 177, 187, 196, 198, 202, 216, 223, 235
Randwick Cemetery 160, 217, 253
Randwick church, Our Lady of the Sacred Heart 50, 55, 116
Randwick Experimental Station 258
Randwick presbytery 83, 92
Randwick site 179, 258
Rascher, Matthäus 2, 3, 4, 5, 6, 166, 251, 273
Raves, Ewald 180
recapitalisation 150, 157
Riverview Observatory 254
Robber Barons 15
Rockefeller, John D. 15
Röntgen, Wilhelm 11

Ross, Herbert 191, 192
Ruhmkorff coil 12
Russo-Japanese war 83

Scanlen, Patrick 26
Shaw
  Blanche Amelia 10, 25, 207, 214, 239,
    241, 243, 244, 245, 254
  Catherine 23, 24, 25, 26, 163, 180, 240,
    245, 255
  Charles William Fraser 26, 27, 207, 216,
    239, 245, 254
  Elizabeth (Bessie) 25, 26, 27
  Mary Frances 25, 26, 163, 203, 245, 255
Sin Poo, Charley 25
Slattery, Joseph 13, 14, 249
Sleight, Gordon 216
Smith, Miles Staniforth 129, 256, 258
Southern Cross 258
Spruson, Wilfred 242
Starke, Hayden 229, 230
St. Paul mission 1, 2, 5, 9
St. Stanislaus College 13, 249, 263
Sturgeon, William 12
submarine, remote controlled 178
Swan, Joseph 10, 11

Taylor, George 127, 256, 257
Telefunken 138, 156, 159, 175, 182, 186
telegram, anonymous 173
Telegraph Office 29, 30, 31, 32, 33, 247
theft 193, 194, 195, 198, 199, 213, 246
The Sun, newspaper 138, 222
Thompson, Ruby 162, 198
Thomson, John Joseph 11
Thursday Island 48, 59, 71, 129
Tolai 72, 251
Tomari 1, 2, 3, 4, 5, 6, 8, 166, 251
Torricelli, Evangelista 11
Tréand, Peter 39, 47, 48, 49, 58, 60, 70,
    92, 116, 161, 162, 217
Tumut 18, 24, 25, 26, 180, 253, 262

vacuum pump 11
valves, thermionic 12

Vandel, Jean-Marie 48, 49, 50, 62, 63, 197,
    247
Vanderbilt, Cornelius 15
Varzin War 69
Victoria Police 212, 219
von Guerick, Otto 11

Wackett, Lawrence 257, 258, 259
Wagga Wagga 31, 32, 33
Wemmers, Jozef 175, 218, 244
wet-cell. *See* liquid cells
Whiting and Aitken 206, 214
Wilkinson, Reg 108, 110, 111, 240
windmill generator 178
Wireless Institute of Australia 262
wireless station 198, 204, 253, 260
Wolff massacre 68

x-rays 11, 12, 13, 14, 163, 178, 249

Yarrangobilly Caves 27, 180, 255, 256, 257
Yule Island 35, 36, 37, 38, 39, 49, 53, 59,
    60, 61, 64, 70, 71, 72

www.ingramcontent.com/pod-product-compliance
Lightning Source LLC
Chambersburg PA
CBHW041723070526
44585CB00006B/129